Machines of Youth

Machines of Youth

America's Car Obsession

GARY S. CROSS

The University of Chicago Press
Chicago and London

The University of Chicago Press, Chicago 60637
The University of Chicago Press, Ltd., London
© 2018 by The University of Chicago
Published 2018
Printed in the United States of America

27 26 25 24 23 22 21 20 19 18   1 2 3 4 5

ISBN-13: 978-0-226-34164-4 (cloth)
ISBN-13: 978-0-226-55113-5 (paper)
ISBN-13: 978-0-226-34178-1 (e-book)
DOI: https://doi.org/10.7208/chicago/9780226341781.001.0001

Library of Congress Cataloging-in-Publication Data

Names: Cross, Gary S., author.
Title: Machines of youth : America's car obsession / Gary S. Cross.
Description: Chicago : The University of Chicago Press, 2018. | Includes
    bibliographical references and index.
Identifiers: LCCN 2017049913 | ISBN 9780226341644 (cloth : alk. paper) | ISBN
    9780226551135 (pbk : alk. paper) | ISBN 9780226341781 (e-book)
Subjects: LCSH: Teenage automobile drivers—United States. | Automobiles—Social
    aspects—United States.
Classification: LCC HE5620.J8 C76 2018 | DDC 306.4/6—dc23
LC record available at https://lccn.loc.gov/2017049913

⊖ This paper meets the requirements of ANSI/NISO Z39.48-1992 (Permanence of
Paper).

Contents

First in America: Coming of Age in Automobiles

In modern America, growing up has meant getting the driver's license, buying, driving, and maybe crashing the first car; the ritual of being picked up for the date and "making out" in the front or back seat; even the pleasures of repairing, customizing, or racing that car. Like so many others, I remember vividly getting my "learner's permit" at fifteen and a half; having to endure my mother's anger when I nervously turned into cross traffic, thinking somehow that I had the right of way; nearly flunking my driver's license test when I knocked down a pole in the parallel-parking portion of the exam, but later enjoying the thrill of driving just a little fast up and down a two-lane country road with "Hey Jude" playing loudly on the radio; and, yes, the embarrassment of rejection when I clumsily took a "back road" with my date to the prom, not too subtly trying to con her into "parking" with me.

The automobile and the teen come together in the transition from the dependency of childhood to the responsibilities, freedoms, and frustrations of adulthood. The car has shaped generations of American teens. So important is this car ride into adulthood that the automobile culture has become a stand-in, a shortcut, in what millions of Americans remember about their coming of age. Around the automobile is often built a romantic nostalgia for youth, especially for men, and even more for white working-class men—a first love of a machine and a first love in it.

This was nearly unique to the United States, a place where by 1930 personal vehicles were mass-produced and quickly passed on to a used-car market, cheap enough for even sixteen-year-olds to buy. Elsewhere, teens walked or took buses or trains. Even in industrial Europe, the lives of youth were confined to family neighborhoods and mass-transit routes. During the Thirties, by contrast, older American teens, except in large cities, were beginning to have access to cars, even if many of those vehicles were beat-up jalopies. Even those down the income scale, especially the white working-class male youth, could own one of these powerful machines.

For those who grew up with automobiles, this appears natural, even matter-of-fact. But it was hardly so before about 1930, and it appears no longer to be so true at the beginning of the twenty-first century. In the early decades of the twentieth century, the car was an expensive toy of the rich, and youth was a time of subjection. The idea that teens—especially those from families of farmers, factory workers, and shopkeepers—would have access to, much less possess, these novel, expensive, and powerful machines seemed absurd. No one then considered the possibility that some of these youths would actually transform the look, use, and meaning of the automobile.

In fact, the origins and significance of teen car culture are shrouded in mystery, with practically no mention of them in any of the standard histories of the automobile. And early witnesses almost entirely ignore the subject. Likewise, studies of an emerging teen peer society in and around high schools mention the automobile mostly in passing. Yet the dramatic increase in the number of American teens attending high school from the 1930s created a youth-dominated consumer culture, the center of which was the used automobile. The car and the modern teen experience emerged together; their stories were linked by the confluence of economic and social forces that were particularly American.

The First Cars in the United States

An invention imported from Germany in 1886, the internal-combustion motor vehicle was a plaything of the rich for more than a decade after the Duryea brothers first manufactured it in the United States in 1893. An oft-quoted 1906 comment of the future president, Woodrow Wilson, sums up a common opinion about the car in these early years: "Nothing has spread socialistic feeling in this country more than the use of automobiles. To the countryman they are a picture of arrogance of wealth with all its independence and carelessness."[1] Car prices averaged at $1,784 in 1905, while annual wages averaged about $500. And this mean price included unreliable surrey-type cars (tiller-steered, motor-under-the-seat horseless carriages) as well as more luxurious models costing $4,000 or more. Until the late teens, virtually all cars were purchased with cash. And no doubt Wilson was right that farmers and small-town dwellers were upset when their horses and buggies encountered the new high-end touring cars with protruding front engines that gave the vehicles an aggressive, even sexually alluring appearance. Most of those cars

FIGURE 1.1. An early (1904) example of the motorized carriage of a well-to-do family, a vehicle well beyond the dreams of the common American, much less the youth. Library of Congress, LC-USZ 262 38171262 2950.

came from the posh parts of town and belonged to well-to-do profession-als, merchants, and industrialists who sometimes displayed their wealth and power by parading their fleets of automobiles. Often these "swells" sped along roads designed for horses and wagons, seeming to threaten the lives and limbs of those deprived of the power of internal combustion.[2] And elites in those early years were anxious that the car remain a thing for the privileged; they resented additional traffic and doubted that the hoi polloi had the finances to afford these machines or the temperament to drive them safely.[3] No one anticipated ordinary teens at the wheel.

In the opening years of the twentieth century,Europeans especially identi-fied the automobile with the rich. The car offered the elite machine-driven speed and personal power that contrasted with the lot of those people still stuck in the ancient biological world of the horse and the newer world of the annoyingly crowded and track-dependent railroad. The car symbolized the social superiority of the urban bourgeoisie, and this remained true in Europe in the first half of the twentieth century as the rich pushed for car-friendly roads, often to the disadvantage of those on foot or in horse-drawn wagons. As late as 1962, only 27.3 percent of West German households owned a car.[4]

But the United States took a different course that ultimately made the car a vehicle of mass/individual mobility. It also became a critical prop in the rites of passage to adulthood. After 1905, Henry Ford, among others, sought to expand the market for cars. In the American context, this was almost inevitable. Demand for luxury cars was limited, and competition for selling these vehicles was stiff. More important, given the relatively high disposable household income of average Americans, manufacturers had an incentive to reach out to a broad middle class of consumers. By 1905 this market had already been explored by producers of low-quality, often outdated vehicles (for example, a high-wheeled surrey-type car sold through Sears's catalogs). But these cars were underpowered (some with inefficient chain drives); they lacked suspension and pneumatic tires, and relied on wooden parts that seldom lasted more than a couple of years.

Henry Ford is usually credited with introducing a new type of vehicle: a cheap but sturdy and reliable car in the Model N in 1906 (a fifteen-horsepower runabout) and then the Model T (1908–27), complete with lightweight vanadium steel construction, a forward four-cylinder engine rated at twenty horsepower, a drive shaft, a planetary two-speed transmission, pneumatic tires, a flywheel magneto for electricity, and even acetylene headlamps. It was also very simple. The Model T lacked water, fuel, and oil pumps and a gas gauge; and of course it required manual crank starting and a mastery of tricky controls, which included a "spark advance" lever for starting and an accelerator lever, both of which were mounted on the steering wheel, and three floor pedals: one for first and second gear, a second for reverse, and a third for braking. Its top speed was forty-five miles per hour.[5]

The initial cost of $950 was still out of reach of many farmers and middle-class townspeople. Nevertheless, by 1916 the Model T comprised half of the American car market, largely because of Ford's progressive decrease in the price: $360 that year. By 1927 the cheapest version of the Model T cost merely $290. The secret to this drop in nominal and real price was, of course, the assembly line, fully operative by early 1914 at Ford's Highland Park plant. This innovation eliminated customized and nodal production methods, but was too costly and complex for even the British to implement fully until 1934, at Morris Motors. Lower prices also met a growing middle class. Between 1925 and 1929, average wages were about 60 percent higher in the United States than in Britain, and roughly two and a half times the purchasing power of French workers. The Model T became the car of the "great multitude," in Ford's words, even with only intermittent advertising and without car-company financing.[6]

Not only did the Model T democratize automobility, but in America it was surprisingly easy to drive motor vehicles legally. Despite the power and thus

FIGURE 1.2. Ford's Model T (1908), the classic bare-bones vehicle that often became the first car of many Americans. Later, when used and cheap, it could be customized and souped up by American youth. Library of Congress, LC-USZ-262-2.

danger of even the earliest cars in the hands of unskilled operators, driver's licenses at first required no testing. In 1904, Milwaukee authorities demanded only that drivers have the use of both arms (and, curiously, that they be eighteen years old). As cars became faster and more plentiful, auto clubs favored stricter rules on licensing to keep incompetent drivers off the road. Still, driving tests came only about 1906, years after being adopted in Europe. As late as 1909 only twelve states required licenses, and there was no regulation in South Dakota until 1954.[7] The car became a symbol of democracy and freedom accessible to many, ultimately even to inexperienced youth.

Car ownership increased dramatically from 1910, shortly after Wilson's unprophetic warning. The ratio of cars to population dropped from 1 to 201 in 1910 to 1 to 5.4 in 1930. Much of this change occurred outside cities as the car's utility became evident and prices decreased. While in 1910 only 17 percent of American farm families owned cars, by 1930, 53 percent of rural households possessed a motor vehicle (half of the 23 million registered that year).[8]

Americans stood out. In 1929 there was one car for every 5.4 Americans, but only one car for every 43 Britons and one for every 335 Italians. In fact, the United States was responsible for 81.6 percent of global production of vehicles in 1927.[9] This American output led to a vast used-car market in the 1930s, despite the Depression, which in turn made the car available to those down the income scale, even teens without rich parents.

Horseless Carriages, Horses, and American Youth

It was not just the quantity of cheap vehicles that paved the way to the kids' car. It was what the automobile meant. The car in America was not a mechanical extension of the luxurious carriage, as it was in Europe, but rather, the successor to the common horse that millions of Americans had long owned and to which they were often introduced at a young age. While in 1904 the Vanderbilts paraded their luxury touring cars at their summer mansions in Newport, just as they had previously shown off their elaborate carriages, a decade later cars were carrying farmers and tradespersons on daily chores, much as country horses had once done. In fact, in 1900 Americans transferred attitudes about their horses to their cars. As historian Steve Gelber notes, the first cars had "horselike willfulness and unreliability," with the need to hand-crank the "temperamental" engine to start it, and the frequency of breakdowns. Moreover, the car, like the horse before it, became an object of personal pride as well as of necessity, especially in the countryside where isolated farms prevailed.[10]

As often noted, by the 1930s, with few and diminished public transportation alternatives for many Americans, the car was a psychological as well as an economic necessity. As the horse had done, the automobile also provided owners with the quintessential display of status and marker of personal economic progress. Prestige and identity came with General Motors's full line of cars that offered a rising scale of vehicles, from the Chevrolet to the Cadillac. Almost everyone could tell the difference between them. The auto promised both mass access and class distinction that simultaneously democratized American life and reinforced a status system.[11]

By 1930, while almost everyone could read the code of car consumption, it was a game played mostly by men. This, too, reinforced the link with the horse. As Gerber notes, in the nineteenth century "men wanted their horse to project a public image of themselves as powerful, knowledgeable and shrewd." And, as in Thorstein Veblen's observation about conspicuous consumption: "A fine horse, like a fine wife, was a public representation of male wealth and power." Still more, the possession and control of cars, like that of horses, gave the man physical dominance. Accordingly, Paul Nystrom wrote in 1919, there was "the pleasure of knowing that the machine beneath him will respond to his touch. There is a sort of enchantment in being able to control so easily a thing so powerful."[12] Men even adapted traditions of horse-trading to the buying and selling of cars, by bargaining and rejecting the fixed-price model of most corporate consumer goods.[13] All this became part of the teen car culture.

Horse culture abided in the car age in still other ways. Despite the technological advance of the internal-combustion engine, the car was often linked to nostalgic dreams of pioneer-era individualism, especially the cowboy on his horse. It was an alternative to the crowd experience and clock- and timetable-watching of train passengers. The auto offered the man freedom of choice and an opportunity "to extend one's control over his physical and social environment," notes the historian James Flink. Especially in an era of corporate conformity and the dehumanized assembly line, the car in the parking lot was a gift of freedom after work.[14] Sitting behind the wheel and a powerful engine gave the same feeling as sitting atop a horse, reins in hand, but with a lot more "horses" in control. As the historian Cotten Seiler observes, the car culture was a throwback to the individualism of the nineteenth century, restoring men's "formerly and naturally authoritative, robust, creative, and mobile traits." Men compensated for a loss of artisan, agricultural, and business skill in an age of salaried employment when they mastered knowledge about and upkeep of their cars. A man at the wheel was the opposite of "the stereotypical . . . subservience of women and slaves."[15]

Women (and nonwhite men) challenged all this when they drove cars. But men, and especially males down the power and income scale, tried to hold on to their sense of superiority by making fun of women drivers, despite significant female mastery of early automobiles and their operation. Working-class men, especially, preserved a measure of dignity behind the wheel and under the hood.[16] The car's delivery of power on command was merely the prelude to the ultimate enhancement of the self: the freedom of the "open road," freedom from the constraints of family, neighborhood, work, and even one's own cares.[17]

Yet those feelings (both on the horse and in the car) often were illusory or temporary, especially for the increasingly dependent and insecure worker, clerk, or salesman. Peter Ling defines "motoring as a therapy which adjusted individuals to the strains of modern life while tying the people concerned more tightly to the existing order." This went beyond economics. The ecstasies of motorized power and freedom were countered by the fact that cars crashed (and horses less often did). The need for constraint challenged the promise of speed. As noted by Seiler, automobility offered the semblance of freedom and choice, but only within a tight regime of rules and regulations designed to minimize crashes: the "driving subject moves along grooves created, surveyed, and administered" by a complex apparatus of regulation. Little in daily life is so constrained by laws and so subject to police surveillance and prohibition as is driving a car. American "citizenship," says Seiler, meant both personal liberty and public regulation. And this right of citizenship was defined by the drivers' license.[18]

FIGURE 1.3. This young blade terrorized all on the road in his sports car (1904). Cover of *Scientific American*, Library of Congress, LC-DIG ppm scg-42527.

Vehicular mobility required, in effect, a new social contract: conformity to the detailed rules of the road in exchange for free movement on that road. Of course, these rules continuously ran against the power of the automobile (as in speeding), and many drivers found it difficult to adhere to this set of laws. The demands of responsible freedom often clashed with the aspirations of youth to unimpeded liberty. Though seldom acknowledged by car historians, this conflict between that social contract and youthful impulse put the teen driver at the center of the question of who could drive and thereby become a modern citizen.

The right to drive a car was inevitably defined by age, as was the right to vote. This was because the driver's license, like the voter's registration, was a marker of socially defined maturity. The driver "earned" the right to the freedom of the road precisely because he or she followed the rules and coolly manipulated so much power in the often tight conditions of motoring.[19] Adults inevitably believed, often with reason, that those not yet adult were still too emotionally immature to embrace these subtle behavioral traits.

Yet Americans were curiously tolerant of very young people driving. While the quintessential marker of maturity—the right to vote—was confined to those over twenty-one years of age (until 1971, when it was lowered to eighteen), driver's licenses could often be obtained at a younger age. While the more urban Eastern states of Pennsylvania and New York in 1909 and 1910 imposed restrictions on licensing drivers under eighteen, other, less populated states, especially in the Midwest and West, demanded less stringent rules: four states granted licenses at age fifteen, and two did so at fourteen, including California in a 1923 law. The age of sixteen became a national standard from about 1950. This curious permissiveness is nearly unique to the United States (elsewhere, especially in Europe, licensure usually required eighteen years of age).[20]

There was plenty of alarm about young Americans behind the wheel. As early as 1927, a New York State Crime Commission complained: "Rural children are allowed junior licenses for restricted use, but they have gone beyond the limits of the privilege. . . . A good many of the boys as young as 16 either have automobiles of their own or are allowed the privilege of taking out their parents' car whenever they wish and take girls regularly to country dances." But such statements only affirmed the amazing access of teens to cars. In 1949 Maureen Daly, in her compilation of attitudes of American teens, noted the obvious: "Sixteen, when a driver's license can be taken out in most states, is a far more important milestone in the life of a typical American male than twenty-one, when he reaches his majority and can vote. . . . Not that more than a handful of boys waits till they are sixteen to learn to drive, whatever the law may say. The majority start around twelve or thirteen, and many as young as ten."[21]

Part of this indulgence can be explained by the special relationship between youth and mobility, especially on the American frontier and in rural areas. This recalls once again the cultural linkage between the car and the horse. American youths working on farms and in trades had long been assigned jobs that required hauling goods or tilling fields at the reins of a horse. Moreover, with mechanization in the early twentieth century, children as young as ten on farms were expected to operate agricultural machinery, including tractors and trucks—often a necessity because of the expense or shortage of farm hands. Very simply, in these settings, letting teens drive often was advantageous to adults.

Where elsewhere the car remained a machine of the elite, in the United States it could and often had to be operated by a child. This historical link between youth in the saddle and behind the wheel put automobility at the center of the maturation process, especially for males. Yet this indulgence of the youthful driver can be fully understood only by looking at changes in the American teen experience at a time when the automobile was emerging as the centerpiece of American consumer society. As we shall see, youth embraced the individualist ideology of an emerging adult car culture. But even more, exposure to the car as young Americans were "coming of age" shaped their lives and values in ways not experienced by previous generations or elsewhere.

New Ways of Growing Up in Early Twentieth-Century America

Since colonial times, outsiders have remarked on the comparative freedom of American youth. The absence of a strong apprenticeship system liberated young Americans from the tight adult supervision at work that was common in that European tradition. Land for Western expansion also explains the early departure of farmers' children from family homesteads and, with it, independent youth. Beginning in the early nineteenth century, Americans valued novelty and youth over tradition and the aged. All this was certainly compounded by growing affluence, which gave even youths who were nominally under the control of their parents surprising access of their own earnings. Immigrant families, in which the pooling of the wages of all members of the household had once been a common practice, now found that teens and youth increasingly kept at least part of their own earnings.[22]

Generational autonomy and new wealth came together to create a consumer culture in which youth carved out an important niche. Historians have noted a rise in the disposable income of older teens and youth in the United

States during World War II, when afterschool jobs were plentiful. This left teens with cash for dates, clothes, and even cars.[23] Still, this phenomenon was hardly new to the 1940s. Even in the Depression, young people had spending money that created mass markets for candy, toys, clothes, comic books, and child-oriented movies (e.g., for Saturday matinees). The ultimate purchase, especially for rural and small-town teens, was the cheap—often very cheap—used car and salvageable junked vehicles and parts.[24]

There were many reasons to make this purchase. The automobile was a superb tool for youth to escape adult tutelage. Moreover, American youths had long tended to identify with the latest technology. They had been early adopters of phonographs, cameras, and radio in the first three decades of the century. Boys especially, growing up in the 1910s and '20s, identified with storybook heroes like Tom Swift, a small-town boy with a knack for motorized inventions (motorcycles, motorboats, airships, and of course cars) that took him on adventures far from home. Even the fictional teenage girl detective Nancy Drew, in a book series that began in 1930, chased criminals in her red roadster.[25] Inevitably, early-twentieth-century youth abandoned past obsessions with the horse and the steam train for motorized vehicles. Boys played with toy cars as soon as the real thing appeared, giving up their horse and carriage miniatures, which soon shifted into their sisters' play worlds.[26] A piece in the popular magazine *Look* in 1959 states what teen males had thought long before: "Bikes are for boys, cars are for men." At sixteen, the boy craved and often got "'jet' power under his right foot," and in the driver's seat he was "closeted in a private, mobile space in which he may begin the ritual of courtship."[27]

The peculiarity of the American coming of age in the twentieth century went further. It was shaped by the unique role of the public high school, the setting where many American youths were introduced to cars. While in the nineteenth century high school was the domain of a small group of relatively privileged youths, by 1940 this institution had become a common experience of American teens.[28] The proportion of American youth attending high school rose 650 percent in the first three decades of the twentieth century, reaching about half.[29] In the 1930s the proportion of enrolled fourteen- to seventeen-year-olds climbed to three-fourths.[30] Though many dropped out before graduating, high school shaped the coming of age of a majority of American youths.

The educational impact of secondary schooling, of course, has been stressed by historians. And a middle-class bias of educators in favor of college preparatory courses long prevailed. But the high school was also a setting where peer groups, rather than adults, shaped attitudes and desires that extended well beyond the classroom. In the 1880s there emerged a rather distinctive American culture of extracurricular activity which, even after the high school was "democratized" in the twentieth century, retained the middle-class bias of the high school's origins. These afterschool programs consisted of organized sports, music, theater, and so on, rather than manual skill hobbies.[31]

To be sure, some high schools introduced auto shop classes in the 1920s, partially at the behest of interested students and as a way of encouraging mechanically inclined students not to drop out.[32] Still, the persistent middle-class tilt of most high schools meant the marginalization of newly enrolled working-class students. All this would later shape the teen car culture, effectively dividing it by social class.[33] Though the high school was supposed to be a "classless" realm apart from the workplace and market, it was in reality the place and time in which the young learned their place in the class structure. This was seen in student parking lots, where the year and make of teens' cars defined their owners as much as did the cut and quality of the high schoolers' clothes.

As we shall see, this helped to produce two automobile subcultures. A group of mostly working-class youth, marginal to high-school academic and peer culture, often embraced the skills and values of craft achievement in customizing and racing old cars (which I will feature), while a more middle-class group borrowed cars from parents or owned newer vehicles for displays of social status and social engagement. High school led to a distinct, often rebellious world of working-class hot rods (later also Latino low riders) and a middle-class car culture integrated into the world of parties and school dances.[34]

The high-school peer culture was the setting not only for class and race) identity but for the learning of gender roles, especially through the dating system. The historian Beth Bailey defined dating as a form of courtship conducted "in public places removed, by distance and by anonymity, from the sheltering and controlling contexts of home and local community." Dating began years before the mass car culture and certainly before teen access to cars, especially in the urban working class. Still, in the early twentieth century the automobile accelerated the decline of the parent-controlled system of the male "calling" on the female at home. The car both facilitated the escape from home and neighborhood and promoted a special form of privacy—in the enclosed vehicle, usually under cover of night. The motor vehicle, owned and driven by the male, further reduced female control over her own relations with the boy or man.[35] The car came to shape the American teen experience just as youths were beginning to enter high-school peer cultures and learn the sexual cultures of dating. This marriage of teen time and vehicular mobility shaped generations of American youth, introducing the young to class, consumption, gender, and sexuality at a most impressionable age and life stage.

Kids and Cars Create a Culture

Perhaps not surprisingly, teens adapted to cars in ways very similar to those of adults: as expressions of individuality, status, and competence. Getting the driver's license gradually became a rite of passage into adulthood, not a privilege or just a practical necessity, as in farm families. Teens adopted the behaviors of early drivers in the car parades and competitions of the rich; and even the reckless intrusion of elite youth into the countryside in the 1900s was imitated in the kids' antics in the '30s and '40s.[36]

Yet teen car culture was different from that of adults. It reflected the distinctive characteristics of the American way of growing up in an age when gender roles and sexuality emerged in a peer society largely free of adult control. Robert and Helen Lynd famously claimed in 1929 that teens in the midsized town of Muncie, Indiana, went out in family cars without parents 40 percent of the time. Even if the Lynds may have exaggerated its influence, the car tended to break up family relationships by creating opportunities for youths to gather away from home at roadhouses and lovers' lanes.[37] The auto broadened the horizons of small-town and rural youth, fostering a wanderlust that created tensions within families and probably contributed to young adult migration from farms and villages to larger towns and cities. And it added new elements to emerging dating rituals, affecting gender roles and sexual behavior in new ways.

Although there were middle-class forms of youth car culture as well as distinct female linkages to automobility, I will stress a large and distinctive stream of youth automobility: that of the white, working-class, and largely male hot-rodder. For these youths, the customized car represented dignity as well as mobility. In the high-school setting, where the disadvantaged working class were tracked to "remedial" courses and snubbed in extracurricular clubs, the hot rod offered a counterculture for the mechanicallyskilled male "underachiever." It led also to the impulse to test those skills in street racing, an activity long identified with the "greaser." With the car, the working-class male retained a pride in craft skill that otherwise was in decline in twentieth-century America. But there were ethnic variations, especially in the development of Latino/a styles of customization and display with the low rider. As I will note, African Americans joined the movement, but in smaller proportions, due to poverty and big-city upbringings in which cars were less important. Although a nationwide phenomenon by the 1950s, the teen car culture was shaped by teen exposure to used cars in Southern California as early as 1930.

By the 1950s, that teen hot-rod culture both clashed with and adapted to the adult world. The teen at the wheel forced educators, legislators, and law enforcement to confront but also to accommodate the auto-adolescent. Moral panic over teen lawlessness occurred again and again when kids raced on public streets, paraded in defiantly customized cars, and experimented with sex while parked on "lovers' lanes." Police cracked down on lawbreakers, harassed kids in cars, and demanded adherence to newly established rules of the road. Yet high-school authorities accepted student car parking lots and offered driver training courses and auto repair classes. Adults also sponsored teen car clubs. In turn, teens both defied adult laws and adapted to adult standards, often seeking the approbation of their elders.

The teen car culture was a striking contradiction in an adult world. It was often the last gasp of adult-youth bonding in an embrace of machinery and individual achievement; and yet it was also often a break from intergenerational ties, as youths used the car to form distinctive teen identities. The car arose at a time when old skills and technologies were in sharp decline, making a rising working class vulnerable and making the social and economic value of older workers less valuable. The humiliation of being tracked into low-prestige classes and being snubbed by children of the affluent and educated was still another affront to the dignity of white working-class youths. But the motor vehicle offered a temporary respite, insofar as automotive expertise restored and preserved their dignity, at least within their own communities. That skill became associated with the upcoming generation's newfound competence, creativity, and independence. The auto offered a new venue of craft pride for the white working-class teen that sometimes, but not always, was shared by son and father.

This golden age of American teen car culture spans the decades from the 1930s through the 1980s. By the close of the twentieth century, however, the automobile was no longer a gateway to adulthood in America. The authorities also became less tolerant of teen car play by the 1980s, leading to a decline of car-focused socializing, especially in the eclipse of weekend cruising along the main streets of many American towns and suburbs. New licensing restrictions discouraged sixteen-year-year olds from pursuing that old rite of passage. Moreover, automobility had become simply too costly for the average teen. Digital engine technology and new auto body construction had deskilled the teenage tinkerer and customizer. Especially for the descendants of the white male working-class hot-rodder, a measure of dignity was lost. No longer was the lad good with wrenches valued. And with this, the idea of teenage technical and manual competency declined, partially replaced by skill and adaptability to digital technology. This change was reflected in the decline of the working-class car culture and of the cross-generational male bonding that it brought.

At the same time, youth found new forms of liberation—virtual as opposed to physical, in the case of the smartphone. And with both parents away from home at work, the "privacy" of the back seat of the car was no longer necessary. Yet this nearly unique blend of teen peer and car culture has shaped generations of Americans, defining the passage to adulthood and creating for many, in later years, a nostalgia for a lost youth of cars.

This is a story in which some youths had privileged voices—especially those who were white and male, for whom the car was especially important—a working class seeking dignity in a world increasingly dominated by white-collar professionals. The automobile created a distinct peer community that, in spite of its inherent ephemerality, shaped attitudes, memories, and economic prospects later in the lives of its members. It is hard not to be critical of this youth culture: it was sexist and sometimes racist, and often was a dead end for its devotees. Yet I want to tell this story with an eye to fairness, letting the participants share their memories where possible.[38] This encounter with the car shaped the transition to adulthood for nearly a century.

Customizing and Souping-Up in the 1930s and '40s

The car was no toy, despite how adults played with and in it. From 1900 it was a powerful machine that set its owner apart from others. It was a successor to the horse, a powerful animal that for six thousand years had pulled and carried people and their possessions across often great distances, liberating the fortunate individual from trudging along a few feet a second. Through much of history, the poor had walked; thus the sixteenth-century English proverb "If wishes were horses, beggars would ride." Like the horse, the car enhanced status and dignity by empowering personal movement. Even more than that of the horse, the car's muscle was readily and dangerously at hand; a small amount of individual human effort produced power that could easily get out of hand. Such a machine could not be understood or mastered by mere children. In a vast country still dominated by enterprising farmers, craftspeople, and merchants, where mobility and individual self-mastery were both valued and required for success, driving and maintaining the car became the rite of passage into adulthood—a privileged personal place of power.

But the automobile was much more than a motorized steed. It was the quintessential expression of cutting-edge technology of a very particular type. Unlike the steam engine, dynamo, and other machines owned and run by corporations, the car was still a technology that could be understood, operated, and even improved upon by the average individual, especially when that vehicle was mass-produced and bare-bones, as was the Model T. As much as harnessing mobile power defined the child's transition to the adult world, so did mastery over the innards of the car, at least for many, especially white working-class boys. Young Americans, often from rural backgrounds, had for a long time cut their teeth on tinkering with farm machines, leading to patents and improvements in harvesting, woodworking, and many other gadgets in the nineteenth century. Even more, the automobile offered innovative youth an opportunity for personal expression and achievement. The car fit perfectly in a transition from an era of individualistic invention to one of scientific corporate technology, shaping several generations of American youth. Automotive tinkering was the swan song of that unique culture of mechanical self-expression, even as the auto and its parts were provided by the corporation. The motor vehicle introduced youth both to a national car consumer culture and to the personal experience of control and achievement.

The automobile created special if ultimately limited ways for white working-class boys to acquire and display distinctly modern mechanical skills not only in driving, but in repairing, restoring, and retrofitting used cars. This offered opportunities for cross-generational bonding (when fathers and sons shared mechanical interests), but also enabled youths to become vanguards of mechanical progress, leaving their dads and granddads behind. The car reinforced the gender divide by putting young males in control of the wheel. Female teens also drove, and early in the twentieth century the car became a mark of liberation for many women,[1] but more common was the identification of the machine and automobility with the male. This culture of customizing and souping-up had its roots quite naturally in the world of young adult men that was gradually passed down to teens. The transition may have been inevitable, but it required crossing a number of bridges.

How Kids Got behind the Wheel

Despite the name *auto*mobile, many early witnesses expected the car to be a vehicle of family togetherness. Robert and Helen Lynd, in their perhaps too often quoted book *Middletown*, noted how in the early 1920s one of the presumed benefits of car ownership was the opportunity for dads to take their families out on country drives, the family-sized compartments of a car (unlike the all too public bus or train) being ideal for domestic bonding. Yet by the end of the 1920s, the Lynds noted, the car was scattering family members as older children got in the driver's seat and went separate ways. This trend can be exaggerated. Adults controlled the family car. Certainly, multicar households were rare; in a 1932 survey, only 6 percent of families owned more than one car.[2] But the tension between the car as site of familial unity and youth's attempt to "hijack" it for independence was apparent from the start.

The cause of this generational conflict was simply the high cost of the car. Still, the turnover on automobiles was surprisingly high. There was surprising little "loyalty" to any particular vehicle, whatever its symbolic or practical meaning. And ultimately this led to the huge used-car market, opening up opportunities for teens to get behind the wheels of their own cars even if they were only jalopies. Even at the depths of the Depression in 1932, 46 percent of cars were no more than three years old and only 5.2 percent were as old as seven years.[3] While cars seldom went long before major repairs, another factor explains much of the turnover: by the 1920s the car had become, like other consumer "durables" in America, a fashion-and-status-driven ephemeral possession. The dynamics of "planned obsolescence," so obvious in the annual model changes of the 1950s that induced car owners to trade in and trade up frequently, were already well underway in the 1920s. General Motors chief Alfred P. Sloan upgraded his entry-level Chevrolet in 1925 to counter the now obsolete Model T of Ford. GM established a "line" of car models, rising in price and prestige from Chevrolet to Pontiac, Oldsmobile, Buick, and, at the top of the heap, Cadillac—all to encourage consumers to move "up" the line as quickly as possible. Two years later, Ford also realized the need for change, and took the almost twenty-year-old Model T out of production. The tall and boxy cars of the teens and early '20s gave way to the long and low look of Harley Earl's GM cars by 1927, and in 1928 Henry Ford replaced the "T" with the sportier Model A, with a modern transmission and other new parts. In the hope of bringing consumers back into the market at the depth of the Depression, Ford went much further with his 1932 V8 model, replacing the four-cylinder Fords that had long prevailed with a much more powerful eight-cylinder engine.[4] Changing car fashion and enhanced power fed into turnover, and filled used-car lots with vehicles, some in the price range of teens.

During the Depression, when new-car sales dropped precipitously, "consumer engineers" sought ways of bringing drivers to dealerships. Slanted windshields and radiators made the old perpendicular ones look "antiquated," noted Charles Parlin and Fred Bremier in a 1932 study of the economics of the retail car industry. They predicted that more sales would come with technological innovations like the synchromesh transmission and "automatic clutch." They also expected that sons and daughters would soon want to drive their own vehicles to school or college, and to visit "extensively scattered friends."[5] Such words were wishful thinking in 1932 at the depth of the Depression, and at best they applied only to the shrunken cadre of the affluent. But they reflected an American quest for novelty, power, and autonomy that reemerged at the earliest moment of economic recovery. Again, all this encouraged the notion that teens should have their own used cars, or at least access to their family vehicles.

Despite the hard times, few gave up their cars. While at the onset of the Depression auto purchases declined from 4,587,400 in 1929 to 1,135,491 in 1932, five years later sales had rebounded to 3,915,889. By the end of the Depression, in 1941, the number of cars on American roads had risen to 29,524,101.[6] Part of this was due to the reduced mean price per car sold, which dropped from $1,007 in 1925 to $778 in 1940, even as the mean horsepower per car rose from thirty-two to eighty-five. Engineering and stylistic novelties helped revive car sales, and in the long run the multivehicle family became the norm, even giving many sixteen-year-olds their own cars. In many places, you were a nobody without wheels.[7]

But these figures also point to the centrality of the *used* car. In 1919, car dealers sold one used car for every new one, but by 1940 that ratio was two to one.[8] The backlog of used cars (many from the era of the Model T) made auto ownership possible even for the jobless. Buying the discarded vehicle had long been the strategy of the less affluent. As the National Automobile Chamber of Commerce noted in 1924, "The growth in the motor vehicle market depends on the ability of the lower income brackets to purchase *used cars*, not necessarily new ones."[9] Think of the Joad family in Steinbeck's *Grapes of Wrath* crossing the dust bowl to California looking for farm work. They made the trip in a beat-up Model T. If this penniless family could afford a car, as many such families obviously could in reality, so could many a teen from even a family of modest income, especially if the car came from a junkyard.

But why were used cars so cheap? It had a lot to do with the strategy of automobile manufacturers and dealers in their quest for selling expensive new cars. One of the curious facts of the retail automobile industry is that new cars lose value immediately after being driven off the lot. This has long been the case. In fact, as early as 1906, cars as little as a year old could be bought for half the price of a new model. By 1953 a used 1946 two-door Ford retailed at about $250, while new four-door Ford cost $1,995. This made used but still quality cars, rather than value-priced utility new cars, the vehicle of choice for many lower-income buyers.[10]

GM and the others had little incentive to produce a cheap competitor to the Model T in the 1920s or, later, to market a utility vehicle like a Volkswagen Beetle from the 1950s. Instead, manufacturers held new car prices high, and retailers used advertising to promote exciting new features and styles to sell them at a premium. In turn, consumers were willing to pay these prices in part because they expected to sell their old cars as "trade-ins," reducing the cost of their next new cars. As Parlin and Bremier complained, this situation gave the new car buyer a price advantage over dealers in the trade. Dealers had to sell their allotments of new cars before they became outdated and before they had to be discounted (selling them at full price in the spring rather than at a discount in the summer, for example). A buyer could often delay a purchase if the trade-in price on their old car was unsatisfactory. This obliged dealers to buy used cars that sometimes were hard to resell: often they had a surplus that had to be sold before winter to avoid depreciation and storage costs. All this made the trade-in business unprofitable for dealers and a bargain for consumers.[11] Thus, high prices for new cars meant low prices for used ones, and with this came the rise of the cheap junker, the entry vehicle for the teen car owner.

Just as the hand-me-down car was a product of the dynamics of the new car market, so the teen car culture was an offshoot of the adult car culture. Youth especially embraced the early American impulse to make the car an instrument of speed and to improve on its looks through customizing and tinkering. As Jack DeWitt, poet and old car expert, notes, "Speed is the great elixir in American life from the beginning when colonial planters raced horses for a harvest combining skill and daring, preparation and risk-taking. From the beginning through generations of hot rodders, Americans create[d] a culture centered on home-built, handmade works of automotive art that ran fast, looked beautiful and sounded like a Futurist symphony."[12]

The quest for velocity and appearance was deep-set in the American psyche; it entailed the search for a personal thrill, but also the longing to be appreciated. Yet both were realized through another appeal: the do-it-yourself (DIY) culture that engendered feelings of self-satisfaction and autonomy in reaction to the frustrations of automatic machines and technological systems. Ironically, the Model T became a quintessential symbol of self-sufficiency to many owners, and yet that car existed because of the vast complex of managers, mines, and mills of Ford's carmaking empire in the 1910s and 1920s. Corporate capitalism made possible tinkerer individualism. And this, too, passed from adult to youth.

Origins of Speedsters and Customizers

Before discussing the teen hot-rodder, we need to acknowledge that speed and customization trickled down from the rich. This aggressive individualism of the car culture had elite roots before World War I, when young (but not usually teen) rich raced their modern cars down country lanes, scaring the farmer and his beasts. Having a fast car was what distinguished the son of the successful businessman from the farmer with his reliable Model T that scooted around at twenty-five miles per hour. It is hardly surprising that a quest for speed was emulated by the less wealthy tinkerer, who upgraded his cheap and slow vehicle with additional power. Frank Hoffman, a pioneer racer, recalled challenging the wealthy and their chauffeurs to a speed duel with his "hopped up" Model A Ford in the early '30s: "These old guys who were wealthy could have a faster car, but not when you'd ding your car up."[13] Similarly, the ostentatiously rich turned their motorized carriages into fashion statements, commissioning Le Baron or Coach Craft to personalize stock luxury cars (e.g., Pierce-Arrows, Packards, or Duisenbergs). The flamboyant actors of the silent era in Hollywood had their chariots dolled up with flipper hubcaps, paddled convertible tops, and fake pipes—features that, again, trickled down to the masses when working-class Ford owners from Los Angeles copied the affectations. This is the world from which emerged Harley Earl, who was a customizer for the stars before moving to Detroit in 1926 to set up GM's Color and Style Division to popularize his vision. He transformed the boxy vehicle of the '20s into low and oblong beauties like his famous 1927 Cadillac LaSalle. Featured in popular magazines, elite stylistic ideas were seen, admired, and copied in relatively cheap, often DIY modifications by the ordinary Joe.[14]

Both racing and customization required a culture of amateur auto mechanics. This was built on the male amateur tinkerer and inventor that dated back to the nineteenth century in the United States. Kathleen Franz notes in her history of "tinkering" with cars that from the first decade of the twentieth century, Americans embraced the automobile as a way of escaping urban space. The car meant self-sufficiency, freeing time, and conquering public space. Tinkering with cars was part of that same impulse, enhancing independence through improved automobility. Early car owners wanted knowledge of and control over their vehicles. These machines were "personal technologies," much like the phonographs, radios, and other new devices introduced to the modern consumer that often were also objects of tinkering.

This passion was shared by teenage boys as well as their elders. That mechanical culture expanded with the appearance of popular magazines like *Popular Mechanics* and *Popular Science* as well as specialized magazines like *Fordowner*, each in its own way flattering readers with assurances that they could understand, repair, and improve their mass-produced machines. And, at least until the 1920s and '30s, female tinkerers were sometimes included. The amateur inventor, notes Franz, fostered the common belief that Americans with "little or no technical training could imitate the lives and hopefully share in the fame of famous inventors such as Henry Ford or Thomas Edison."[15]

Early American cars, especially the ubiquitous Model T, encouraged this confidence, for they were simple and easy to repair, soup up, and customize. Until the 1930s, in fact, especially the low-end car models were bare bones, often without the "accessories" we expect today on the most stripped-down vehicles, thus inviting owners to add on the aftermarket headlights, trunks, oil gauges, speedometers, and camp and tourist gear that many manufacturers advertised in tinkerer magazines. Amateur inventors flooded the US Patent Office and mailrooms of the car companies with drawings for inventions to improve the look, performance, or convenience of store-bought cars. As Franz notes, by 1930 manufacturers began to include many of these accessories on even the basic models. But the impulse to tinker hardly disappeared with those changes.[16]

Some American teens followed their elders in the highly individualized art of tinkering with cars from the late 1920s on. In fact, personal mechanics gained new life especially after 1930, when used Fords and Model Ts, but later Model As and Bs, became the building blocks of young, often working-class American tinkerers who focused less on the comfort, convenience, and looks desired by adult tinkerers than on speed and racing. The key was to get more air and fuel into the cylinders, which, when ignited with an electric spark, drove the pistons down, sending power ultimately to the wheels. This became possible by improving or adding carburetors, which delivered air and fuel, and, of course, additional cylinders, as in switching from a four- to an eight-cylinder engine in the V8. Installing stronger and lighter pistons and connecting rods—linking the pistons to the crankshaft to convert reciprocating to rotary motion—also gave a car more power. Enhancing the evacuation of exhaust with improved manifolds and headers contributed to the engine's efficiency, as did superior camshafts, which regulated the valves, and other modifications to increase the density of the air–fuel mixture that was ignited in the cylinders.

A big improvement came from replacing a camshaft assembly below the pistons with an overhead valve (OHV) unit. The Model T was especially easy to modify, due to its simple construction and plentiful parts. Even more, it was easy to improve on. The car lacked pumps to circulate coolant, oil, and gas, which were moved respectively by heat, crankshaft scoops, and gravity. The transmission was a primitive two-speed design, and its usually imbalanced cast-iron pistons and weak connecting rods made for maximum speeds of perhaps forty-five miles per hour. Hot rodders could do much to enhance the speed of their Model Ts by equipping them with aftermarket crankshafts and lightweight aluminum pistons and rods. Some tinkerers also added larger carburetors and later even installed overhead valves. The result was often a 100-percent increase in horsepower. And, of course, Model Ts were stripped of fenders and standard seats (sometimes replaced with low-profile "seats" made from oil barrels, to reduce the vehicle's weight for greater speed). Modifications continued, reducing the T to little more than a body frame (known from the 1950s as a "T bucket"). Similar speed equipment was available for the T's successor, the Ford Model A (1928–31). Through these changes, the owner could increase the horsepower of a standard Model A from 40 to 80 or even

FIGURE 2.1. A 1930s "speed shop" on San Fernando Road in the Los Angeles area, where some of the first "hot rods" were customized. *Hot Rod Magazine*, May 1948. Used with permission of *Hot Rod Magazine*, © 2017. All rights reserved.

120, raising the top speed from fifty-five to ninety and well over one hundred miles per hour with the replacement of the four-cylinder engine with Ford's V8. Owners employed even simpler modifications like stripping off fenders, and hoods and replacing tread tires with bald ones, and dropping the front axle. These modified cars became the first hot rods (the name was viewed as derogatory at first and was not used by hot rodders until after World War II).[17]

Ford flathead V8s (with valves in the engine block, introduced in 1932) inspired several generations of youthful tinkerers, many of whom trained in high school auto shops and worked in small garages. These 1930s Fords came in many forms, but most popular with youth were the roadsters (two-seaters with convertible tops) and coupes (two-doors with or without backseats and with solid roofs). Ford's flathead put out only sixty horsepower and could reach a top speed of about seventy-five miles per hour, but it had a lot of potential. The early rodders fabricated their own multicarb manifolds to increase airflow in the pistons, constructed their own exhaust systems, bored the cylinders, replaced stock pistons with larger ones, milled camshafts for more efficiency, and upgraded transmissions. The result could be as much as a fourfold increase in horsepower.[18]

Small-scale aftermarket manufacturers provided many of these parts, which were often installed in cars at locally owned "speed shops" run by skilled mechanics. To many drivers, including many dads, all this was a mystery, just as was the new technology of the radio in the 1910s and 1920s. Yet these modifications were entirely doable by the clever teen in the 1930s and 40s. The supply of cheap used cars, even in the Depression, gave young American men access to automobility as seen nowhere else at the time. And their goal—unlike that of the older, often more middle-class tinkerers of the 1920s—became less to accessorize a vehicle with conveniencer than to make the thing go faster. The tinkerer became the hot rodder.

Stories of Pioneer Rodders

While hardly representative of the experience of many youths, the biographies of early Southern Californian hot rodders suggests something of the process by which teens and kids came to join the tinkerer's car culture in the 1930s and 1940s. These men were mostly from small towns, rather than cities, and were introduced to cars usually by an older male member of the family. They purchased very inexpensive cars (usually Model Ts and later Fords), which at first were often not operable. Some of the oldest members of this group were teens in the 1920s when they learned of the possibilities of souping up Model Ts. Typical was the youth of Ed Winfield (1901–82), a legendary speed-shop figure from Glendale, California, who rebuilt Ts in his teens, learning the skill from a mechanic while working as a delivery boy at a local YMCA. He revved up the engines to go one hundred miles per hour in local races on the relatively quiet streets of suburban Los Angeles in the early 1920s, quitting competition in 1925 after marrying, but thereafter teaching new generations to customize old cars in speed shops in California, and later in Las Vegas.[19]

Others were introduced to speed tinkering in the 1930s. Chuck Red Abbott, also hailing from Glendale, learned at the age of fourteen about souped up Ts from a neighbor in 1935. Abbott and his brother bought a junked T and a battery for a dollar each(!) and, with friends, pushed the car home. With the help of a *Dyke's Automotive Encyclopedia* borrowed from the local public library, Abbott and his pals drilled holes in the rods (to reduce weight) and installed performance pistons, taking a year to make the clunker not only run, but race at 101 miles per hour. Abbott moved on to Ford Model As and Bs, getting a lot of speeding tickets along the way, much to the consternation of his father. Stan Betz learned his craft from an uncle, beginning at age ten. For fifty dollars he bought a 1929 Model A Roadster, to which he then added a 1932 V8 flathead engine, and was racing it by the end of the 1930s. Another high school student, Bob Stelling, was a regular at the races at the Muroc Dry Lake north of Los Angeles, and earned money for his hobby by swapping stock four-cylinder engines for V8s in a number of Model As. Stelling also engaged in street races in the San Fernando Valley on Sunday mornings. In the mid-1930s, claimed Dick Ford from Pomona, it was easy to challenge rivals to car races, covering the half-mile between stop signs on a nearby street. Ford

FIGURE 2.2. A stripped-down hot rod priced to sell to a teen, parked in front of Hollywood High School (1937). Photograph by Herman Schultheis. Los Angeles Public Library, used with permission.

recalled with glee how he was able to dispense with mufflers and headlights without any encounters with the law.[20]

Slightly younger was Joe Bailon, born in 1923, who took to the "artistic" side of car craft instead of speed. The miniature car had long been a child's plaything, so it isn't surprising that he was whittling toy autos from wood at six years of age. Bailon's older brothers owned a Dodge truck, and when Joe was fifteen one of them bought him a Model A for ten dollars, which he primed and painted in a local body shop using a brush. Later, just before World War II, he bought a 1934 Ford coupe for sixty-five dollars; the first of a series of used Fords that he modified and sold. After the war, Bailon made a career of customizing cars.[21]

Far better known from this group of customizers that matured in the early '40s are the brothers George and Sam Barris. Born in 1925 and growing up near Sacramento, at age ten George assembled model toys. Early in high school, he and Sam were given a 1925 Buick in exchange for restaurant work. They jazzed it up with hubcaps—pots and pans—bought at the local Woolworth's, then sold it to buy a 1930 Model A to which they added six antennas, though it had no radio. George quickly moved on from such juvenile "customizing," however. He hung out at Brown's Body Shop in Sacramento, where he learned from Harry Westergard how to make body panels. Joining this training with classes in technical drawing at their high school, in 1941 he and Sam organized the Kustoms Car Club. Sam (1924–64) entered the Merchant Marine in 1942 and was stationed in Los Angeles. George joined him when he graduated from high school the next year. In Los Angeles George learned the ways of the nascent hot rod movement, especially at the Clock and Piccadilly drive-ins on Sepulveda Avenue in Culver City. He joined the racing crowd, but his real interest was in design. He customized a 1936 Ford, impressing the girls with his handleless doors that opened electrically. By 1944 he had his own body shop, and his brother joined him there when he returned after the war. So successful were George and Sam that by 1949 they owned several shops, in and near Bell, California. George continued to race, but by the age of twenty-three he was already a famed customizer, later building novelty cars for movies and the eccentric rich and becoming perhaps the most famous craft car designer in the country, a career that ended only in 2015 when he died at eighty-nine. George was introduced to the wider public by journalist Tom Wolfe, along with another famous customizer, Ed "Big Daddy" Roth.[22]

A German immigrant born in 1932 who grew up in the Los Angeles suburb of Bell, Ed Roth was always artistically inclined. He claimed that he drew pictures of American and Nazi planes in school instead of paying attention in class, but his creativity was focused early on cars. With the approval of his father, he was already driving at the age of fourteen, which was legal in California at the time. In 1946 he bought a pricey 1934 Ford sedan for $350 and drove his "first man squeeze," his girlfriend Sally, to school. This must have impressed his schoolmates, even though, Roth noted, "all the guys at Bell High had rods." The popular cars of his school were "fat fendered" 1939 to 1940 Fords, though some students had 1935 Plymouths, which Roth remembered as uncool. While his classmates raced at night, Roth focused on drawing attention to himself with his customizations. He bought, customized, and then sold cars not only for the money but for the thrill of moving on to the next car. For example, in 1948 he purchased a 1939 Chevy coupe with purple hubcaps; but it was slow, and he soon replaced it with a 1932 Ford three-window coupe, ideal for introducing a newer engine and running gear. All this was expensive, but Roth worked at a number of jobs to pay for his hobby, obtaining little financial help from his struggling but tolerant dad.[23]

Like most young men of the postwar era, Roth went into the military—in his case, the US Air Force, where he found time to refine his artistic skill by making signs and painting other servicemen's duffel bags while stationed in North Africa. After that, he opened a customizing shop in Bell. Later, in the late 1950s and early 1960s, Roth became famous as a maker of wacky cars and even outrageous model toys for boys, with names like "Mother's Worry."

Though his talents brought him rare fame, Roth, like so many other ordinary hot-rodders, grew up in a youth car culture, learning from older tinkerers. School for him was unimportant.[24]

Not all of this first generation of hot-rodders were Californians. Bill Waddell (1928–89) was from Michigan. His father had been a car racer from the age of eighteen, but he died in a crash when Bill was a baby. Bill, however, was always close to customized racing. When only fourteen he rebuilt his mother's car; and, while attending a technical high school in Flint, Waddell worked at A.C. Spark Plug Company. With a friend he rebuilt a Model A coupe that he had bought for thirty-five dollars. Following high school, he was drafted into the US Army, and while stationed in Southern California he used his time meeting and learning from the guys at the speed shops that had sprung up there since the war. Returning to Flint in 1948, he joined the Genesee Gear Grinders, a club of about fifteen mostly teen members. After marrying young in 1949, Bill worked at and later bought a local speed shop, where he customized racers. The shop became a site for training younger racing and customizing enthusiasts. Though his wife, Barb, urged him to quit, he raced on and off until 1986, and died in 1989.[25]

Speed and Custom: Racing and Display

The teen motorists chronicled above came of age when American youths could first operate and even own automobiles and, with unique mechanical skills, modify and improve them. Viewed from a global perspective, this is astonishing. These teens did not come from privileged families, nor did they have access to or advanced training in sophisticated technology. The unique character of the American car market and homegrown traditions of mechanic crafts made these stories possible. These pioneer teen tinkerers hardly represented all youth experience with cars in this period: some of those who were not tinkerers were affluent teens who borrowed their dads' Buicks; others received new cars from indulgent parents; and many more, especially those growing up in cities or in poverty, had little access to cars. They, by contrast, were boys who became men by building their identities around racing and customizing. Though a minority of youths, in many places these hot rod pioneers, with their quest for speed and for display, shaped the coming of age of several generations of American teens.

For the maturing youth, the motor vehicle offered the allure of danger and escape from confinement at home and work. This quest for power was most clearly expressed in the impulse to race and to do so on public roads. For a youth, the car also meant competition: showing that one's vehicle, with

FIGURE 2.3. Though rare, this picture (1941) of African American teens from Palocet, South Carolina, with their old Model T suggests the range and availability cars to youth at this time. Library of Congress USF 33–02 0807-M1.

all its clever modifications, was faster than the next person's car. In order to compete, cars and their owners had to meet and form rivalries, and thereafter they had to race.

This inevitably led to confrontations with the police. The veteran professional racer Elton Snapp recalls how, in the late 1930s, high-school boys who belonged to the Los Angeles–based Road Runners raced other clubs after their meetings. Lookouts spotted police and flashed spotlights to warn the racers, who would "scatter like quail" when squad cars arrived. The few racers whom the police caught were fined for missing hand brakes, and for other minor code infractions. Few were caught for racing.[26]

Traffic in Los Angeles was still light at that time, especially on what were then outlying suburban roads, but in March 1939 the Traffic Advisory Board of Los Angeles condemned racing on public highways. This was in response to citizen complaints of youths racing on country roads at midnight. These racers frustrated the police, who found them hard to catch: According to the *Los Angeles Times*, "offenders made their escape across vacant lots of plowed fields in their cars." Teen car clubs required initiates to drive at eighty miles per hour in a twenty-five-miles-per-hour zone. The 100 MPH club reportedly required its new members to race at that speed on public roads. Presumably, a typical game involved twelve to fifteen cars playing "follow the leader" at high speeds. Police reported in April 1940 of "suicide clubs" of young racers who, after midnight, raced on Riverside Drive in Los Angeles, with lookouts posted at either end of the course to warn of cars and cops. When the police chased the racers off one road, the racers reconvened on another. In June 1940, new groups of racers were reported on Wilshire and Venice Boulevards. Some of them competed at high speeds, three or four cars abreast. A race in Compton drew as many as 1,500 spectators. In the summer of 1940 a judge suspended the licenses of fourteen youths, aged seventeen to twenty, and warned of jail time for repeaters.[27]

All this was the culmination of a decade-long antagonism between police and racers in Los Angeles. Inevitably some people, usually older racing enthusiasts, sought an alternative to the street and to these confrontations. They looked for surfaces better adapted to speed than ordinary roadways; even more, they sought sites far from the commercial and residential tracks regulated by the authorities. There were, of course, race ovals that accommodated the competitive speed spirit. But a particularly noteworthy venue for racing were the dry lakes northeast of Los Angeles. Though speed enthusiasts had been racing on these densely packed surfaces as early as 1923, when the American Automobile Association (AAA) held speed trials on Muroc Lake, it was only in March 1931 that a formal race, sponsored by Gilmore Oil, took place there.[28]

By 1937 the Sidewinders of Glendale and the Throttlers of Hollywood led a coalition of seven car clubs to form the Southern California Timing Association (SCTA), comprised of about four hundred members, to race on the dry lakes. The SCTA fostered the thrill of acceleration on the fast surface of a dry lake, but also imposed strict rules. Originally they raced side-by-side in several classes (stock versus modified roadsters, for example). The side-by-side race was abandoned in 1939 for the time trial that became the basis of drag racing: a quarter-mile acceleration from a standing position with flags at both ends of the course and a stopwatch timer. After the war, a second timing association, Russetta, was formed to accommodate sedans and coupes as well as roadsters. Racing at Muroc was suspended in 1938 when the US Army, which owned the land, demanded that the property be vacated for military service as an aircraft practice bombing site. Racing moved to the smaller Rosamond Dry Lake. Dry lake racing was abandoned altogether in 1942 and resumed only briefly after the war.[29]

Though some racers at Muroc were as old as forty, many were high-school and college students. But unlike much street racing, these gatherings consisted not of kids testing each other's emerging manhood but of seasoned and relatively sober competitors and their emulating and admiring youthful followers.

The SCTA was keen on respectability, careful to prevent accidents that would damage the group's reputation, and it warned racers to avoid speeding off the course: "Do not get tough with the patrols for they can get tough with you."[30] Characteristically, the SCTA even set up monitors to discourage eager participants from engaging in road racing away from the official drag strip.[31] Still, given the great distance to the isolated dry lakes, as well as the fact that many hot rodders were unorganized and frankly unwilling to submit to their elders' authority, spontaneous street racing continued. The point of the hot rod was, after all, to break the boundaries with personal power. As a result, there was tension between adult and teen hot rodders that continued after the war (see chapter 3).

The first owner-modified cars were built for speed. They were all engine, with as little as possible in body and passenger interior. This explains the preference among hot rodders for the roadster coupe (a roofless single-seat vehicle) rather than the two bench seats of the enclosed sedan. Given the insistence that these were not family cars, two-door rather than four-door models were de rigueur. Who needed easy access to any back seat?

Yet, as we have seen from the stories of George Barris and Ed Roth, not all teen car enthusiasts by the end of the 1930s were racers. A fully developed customizing culture had emerged that influenced teens as much as did the SCTA. Car historians usually date its birth to the work of Harry Westergard in the late 1930s on 1936 Ford Cabriolets (cloth-topped convertibles) in his shop in Sacramento. Westergard chopped his cars (reducing the body's height by cutting out parts of the roof pillars) and sectioned them (removing an entire section from the body, making it more squat). He replaced stock with costly Packard grills. He also receded door handles into the body, a process called "frenching" that was later applied also to taillights, license plates, radio antennas, and headlights. These techniques shaped a tradition of customizers—notably George Barris, who settled in Los Angeles. Barris and others—like Gill Gaylord of Lynwood, California, who influenced Roth—also lowered the car body by cutting springs. They also channeled (lowering the body into the frame rails to make the car sit closer to the ground) and raked it (lowering the front end or raising the back). Customizers also installed glasspack mufflers for a rumble sound and rounded the corners of doors, hoods, and trunks. In many ways, all this work was just accentuating a trend in auto styling that had been evident in the efforts of Harley Earl and others in the 1920s to give the car a long and low appearance. By eliminating trim and other protrusions and reshaping the body, customizers gave the car a sculpted, unitary look.[32] Other stylistic modifications followed: lacquered paint (the standard of the day) and other kinds of custom painting ("candy apple," scallops, fades, lacing, cobwebbing, and fish scales) were also common treatments. Pinstriping also was made famous by Roth, Dean Jeffries, and others.[33]

Of course an industry emerged to provide exotic parts and installation as well as professional customization. In the 1930s, some small companies became famous for their carburetors, overhead valves, and headers or for their engine work (Chappel's Speed Shop in Los Angeles and Bell Auto Supply in the northern suburbs). Later there were the custom shops of George Barris and Ed Roth.[34]

This could get expensive. While in the late 1930s an ambitious would-be racer could buy a 1929 Model A Roadster for $50, to make the vehicle "special" he had to add a race-quality Model B engine ($23), camshaft ($15), carburetor-manifold assembly ($40), oversized rear tires ($40), custom valves ($25), and other speed equipment that hit the sum of $385 at a time when a mechanic earned about $25 a week. An early-1930s Ford Roadster could be "put together" for $75 in 1940, but with inflation and the increasing popularity of the sport, a 1932 Ford could cost $900 by 1948. Inevitably, most hot-rodders, especially the youngest ones, could not afford professional work and specialized parts. They did their own modifications, using junkyard parts and often cutting corners, with results that hardly would pass modern annual inspections.[35] Car customization encompassed a broad range from pricey professional modification to cheap and shoddy DIY.

This was a culture of craft that produced the ecstasy of speed and competition as well as display and artistry. Though a distinctly male tradition, hot rod customization followed trends common in fashion—following a design theme sometimes to an extreme, often later pulling back, and occasionally making a big break, all to display the imagination, individuality, and artistry of the customizer in competition with others. But customization also depended on a "new world of expanding consumerism precariously casted as female," as Ruth Oldenzeil notes. Automobile aesthetics was an arena where male youths could abandon a habitual manly disdain for women's fashion and consumption. In outfitting cars, young men could immerse themselves in the esoterica of automobile types, capacities, and styles, and even more in that of highly specialized consumer goods—like Winfield carburetors, advertised in magazines as accessories that alone could make a good hot rod into a great one. While males fancied themselves to be "active producers" and women "passive consumers of technology,"[36] men and boys in fact were strongly tied to a consumer culture as complex and hypnotic as any of their sisters' longing for cosmetics, clothes, and celebrities. And these young males were willing to work and sacrifice for these purchases.

Even so, guys didn't see dolling up their cars to be like dressing up fashion dolls. For them, car stuff was only part of an often highly individualistic effort that had nothing in common with presumed feminine conformity and frivolity. Male hot-rodders did not think they were consumers of commodities produced by impersonal and manipulative corporate businesses, even though they most definitely depended on the technological systems of Ford and the retail network of aftermarket parts makers. They saw themselves as creating power and the cool. Yet the teen's car in these early years integrated him into the modern adult cycle of wage work and shopping, and of sacrificing time to pay for membership in a community of consumers where, if he was lucky, he found a niche. Even though he was part of an often conformist consumer culture, with his hot rod the teen won a measure of respect and an escape from a workaday life.

Even more to the point, the crafted car represented a challenge to the established order, especially adult male responsibility. The chopped, channeled, and raked rod was the material expression of rebellion and even a mockery of respectability. It was the opposite of the family sedan with dad at the wheel, his wife seated next to him, and the kids and the dog in the back. Customizers took delight in painting dour black or dark blue family cars with wild colors, and turning their conventional, utilitarian appearance into a look of defiance. The hot rod, be it for racing or display, stood out in traffic, telling the world (even if also alerting wary police) that a youth with skill, daring, and an attitude was on the street. The tension between personal expressiveness and defiance on one side and commercialism and conformity on the other permeated decades of customizing culture, and became especially intense in the generation after World War II (see chapter 5).

The sites of this car culture were seldom institutional. As we shall discuss later, the hot rodder's peer group often came from high school, and the auto shop at school may have been a space where some skills were acquired and relationships established. Nevertheless, teens often learned their hot rodding technique and lore in garages and speed shops. These were owned and operated by adults, sometimes by parental figures, but not institutions like schools or adult organizations. Yet, as we will also discuss more fully later, early hot rodders also formed car clubs of teen and youth peers, where adult authority was often absent. In the Los Angeles area during the 1930s, among the larger and longer lasting clubs were the Rod Tattlers (of North Hollywood), the 90 MPH Club (of Hollywood), and the Knight Riders (of Fullerton).[37]

Perhaps as important were the informal conversations heard and contacts found at drive-in fastfood restaurants, where the young, without much adult intervention, learned to prepare for the challenge of competition and display. Drive-in restaurants first appeared in 1923, and became very popular in car

FIGURE 2.4. The camaraderie of teen boys working on their hot rod (1957). Photograph by Jim Hansen. *Look* Magazine Photograph Collection, Library of Congress, Prints & Photographs Division, reproduction number LC- 57–7575-E, frame 14. Permission: Greg Hansen.

towns like Los Angeles during the 1930s and 1940s. These casual food stands were inevitably the hangouts of teens and youths, offering freedom from parents, teachers, bosses, and family as well as serving as venues for romance and male competition. Recall the impact of the Clock and Piccadilly drive-ins on George Barris and Ed Roth. It was only in the 1960s that many of these teenage hangouts were replaced by squeaky-clean McDonald's restaurants that dispensed with the female carhops of the earlier drive-ins that had attracted crowds of boys. Young hot rodders may have learned some of their skills and attitudes in adult-controlled spaces (high-school auto shops, or garages and speed shops), but at least as influential were the peer groups they met at the drive-ins or at the street races. The gang of motorized teens was an abiding challenge to the adult order.

By the 1930s the car had become much more than a substitute for the horse, train, and feet. With its unique capacity for automobility in an extraordinarily powerful mechanized form, it had become the veritable embodiment of power and self-expression for many American youths. This was especially true for rural, largely white working-class boys for whom older forms of individual projection and display were in decline with the rise of corporate capitalism. The car's central meaning in redefining and perpetuating attitudes about male power, and in compensating the working class for economic insecurity and humiliation, have often been noted. But, as we have seen in this chapter, the auto has also redefined the rites of passage from childhood to adulthood, precisely because of how it has embodied power and self-expression.

These two impulses came together in male teens from wage-earning families. Inevitably, perhaps, the auto became the conduit for a unique form of defiance of bourgeois and adult norms through the act of street racing. On the public road, meanwhile, the hot-rodders realized the power of the car in a setting in which elites and elders demanded restraint in the use of that power. Only with much effort was this impulse to race on the street domesticated in contained off-street drag racing. Those same teen males also embraced the individuality of personal display in accessorizing mass-produced vehicles, and did so in an equally rebellious fashion. The channeled, chopped, and raked rod challenged the meaning of this most ubiquitous consumer good, the family car. These young men defied the stylistic standards of the auto industry, setting themselves on a collision course with the respectable adult world—a crash, as the next chapter will show, that many sought to avoid in the years after World War II.

Hot Rod Wars: Youth, Their Elders, and Defining Maturity on the Road

California's car counterculture of the 1930s consisted of older racers and customizers passing on manual skills to young ones. But even before the war, tensions across the generations appeared that broke out into sharp divisions after the veterans returned in 1945. The hot rod became not only an expression of masculine working-class ingenuity and a marker of boys entering the world of men, but an expression of the tensions between youth and adults over what defined masculine maturity.

World War II accelerated this division by creating a more distinct teenage group of hot rodders when their elders were sent off to war. Ultimately, this was part of a gap between youth and adults as teens in high school formed their own separate consumer culture identified by age. In 1942 the racing clubs in the SCTA broke up as their older members dispersed to the war's many fronts while sixteen-year-olds remained at home. Without the influence of older mechanics and drivers, often fathers, some teens took to street racing with abandon. Widely reported in the press and doubtlessly exaggerated, teens gathered at drive-ins and arranged races on the streets, terrorizing or at least threatening the tranquility of respectable drivers and their families. After the war, these dangerous races were widely publicized and exploited in teen novels like Henry Felsen's *Hot Rod* (1950) and films like *Rebel without a Cause* (1955), *Hot Rod Rumble* (1957), and *Dragstrip Riot* (1958). The hot rod movement expanded well beyond California, introducing some youths to an adult-defying culture of competitive street racing. The unrestrained duels of speed and shortcut car modification, sometimes in violation of sober standards of safety, also offered youths a rebellious risk-taking model of "growing up," a way of passing from the passivity and innocence of boyhood into a grown-up world of unrestrained power, competition, and display. Moral panics over dragsters led numerous state and local authorities to ban gatherings of hot rods and street races, and to require all vehicles to have fenders and other equipment that racers deemed unnecessary impediments.

At the same time, some returning veterans, as well as educational and law-enforcement officials, desired or were willing to make hot rods and drag racing "respectable," but in so doing challenged both teen delinquency around cars and the resulting moral panic. Local officials promoted special off-street sites for drag races, thus offering an alternative to the reckless speed contests; and many hot rod clubs cooperated with the police and sought to eliminate any signs of criminality from their ranks and activities. High-school officials also tried to instill in their charges the virtues of "sportsmanlike" driving, recognizing the psychological attractions of automobility for teens but offering an alternative model of "growing up" to youths tempted by the hot-rod image of "being a man." All this had roots in California, especially in the southern part of the state; but it had expression across the country.

Returning Vets Cut Loose

At war's end in 1945, thousands of young veterans returned to civilian life after many months of living cheek-by-jowl with fellow soldiers on ships and in tents, and traveling en masse in trucks and planes with little money in their pockets. Most were eager to pick up where they left off— at the controls of their own vehicle and able to go when and where they wanted. A few, who had had the opportunity to hone their skills in the services' motor pools and ship and airplane maintenance shops, returned with enhanced ability to rebuild and customize old cars. Especially after the excitement of battle or the suffocating rigors of military discipline, the thrill and personal power exhibited in the competitive auto race was a temptation. A style with origins in the military, the leather jacket with jeans and T-shirt with cigarette pack rolled into the sleeve, was adopted by hot rodders and passed down to a group of admiring, mostly white, working-class teens. This became the uniform of the "greaser" of the late 1940s and 1950s.[1] Widely publicized expressions of this rebellious streak were motorcycle gangs like the Boozefighters, who terrorized the small Southern California town of Hollister in 1947, fictionalized in *The Wild One* (1953). More famous still were the Hells Angels, originally a motorcycle gang of displaced and action-hungry veterans led by Arvid Olsen, a member of a famed corps of pilots called the Flying Tigers during World War II. But the hot rod movement was the main expression of the restlessness of these young vets who were not yet settled in jobs and marriage.[2]

Not surprisingly, some vets from Southern California who had been hot rodders before the war returned to this first love, purchasing cheap 1930s Ford roadsters. These lightweight and roofless vehicles were often stripped of fenders; many had easy-to-modify stock flathead eight-cylinder engines. Gradually, the raw simplicity of these early hot rods was challenged when General Motors introduced high-compression overhead-valve (OHV) engines in the 1948 Cadillac, a change that became universal by 1955. Still, for years the art of finding junked jalopies, installing special camshafts, and even replacing flatheads with OHV engines remained a mark of manliness and often popular respect.[3] An extensive culture of arcane distinctions and specialized language emerged. One scholar found 250 terms in a study of hot-rodders in the Pasadena area in the early 1950s—"pop the clutch," "haul ass," and "souped up," for example—many still in common use. Other terms were more obscure and remained part of an insider's argot: like "pot" for carburetor, "rail job" for a hot rod without a body, and "A-bomb" for a Model A with speed equipment.[4]

Differences between hot rodders quickly emerged, as they seem to do in all hobby cultures. Some hot rodders modified coupes and sedans, though they were family cars, partly to avoid unpleasant contact with police who "profiled" the roofless roadsters as typical of troublemakers. Especially in the northern and eastern United States, where weather made the roadsters unusable much of the year, these closed cars were preferred.[5]

The sharpest difference among hot rodders was between the racers and the customizers. In Southern California, vets who were devoted to building for speed and competition returned for several years to the dry lakes until the surfaces became too soft. The elite of devoted racers shifted to the Bonneville Salt Flats in 1948, and to local drag-racing courses in Pasadena and elsewhere. The customizers were centered in and near the Los Angeles suburb of Lynwood, led by the likes of Barris and later Roth. They focused on chopping and channeling cars from the 1930s, and later shifted to the so-called "lead sleds," often based on the 1949 Mercury.[6]

Whether they raced, customized, or restored, young vets gathered at drive-ins, garages, speed shops, or even gas stations. Don Montgomery, author of a number of illustrated hot-rod memoirs and story collections, learned from vets the art of the hot rod at the age of fifteen in jalopy hangouts around Pasadena. By 1948 he had joined the Glendale Coupe and Roadster Club—like so many other such groups, a loose association of mostly sixteen- to twenty-four-year olds. The drive-ins played host, he remembers, to a "traveling circus of 'show boats' flaunting their polished custom cars," and they served as meeting places to plan local races, often from stoplight to stoplight along arterials such as San Fernando Road.[7]

In these settings teens, sometimes alienated from high school, met older hot rodders who were still unmarried, and from whom they learned the lingo, craft, and rituals of rod culture. Some met at the dry lakes, just as others had done before the war, where older men, some of whom had raced there from their early thirties, interacted with sixteen- to eighteen-year-olds, and often even younger enthusiasts. In many cases, older fellows sold their dated rods to the kids who were eager to get a start. Though it was organized into clubs, some of which were affiliated with the SCTA, the culture was still far from being regulated. Ken Jones, a high-schooler and hot-rodder from the late 1940s, recalled how his enthusiasm was frowned on at his suburban Los Angeles school: "We never looked for trouble but there were some pretty rough gangs" with cars. "These bad groups kind of worked their way . . . into ours." These "rough gangs," showed up, for example, at the dry lake races, where they would strip the cars of competitor gangs or groups, even taking the windshields.[8]

This mixture of age and motivation confused outsiders and caused image problems for the "serious" customizer and racer, especially when the hot rod was identified with "irresponsible youth."Despite evidence of interaction between vets and teens after 1945, the division between the "serious" vet and the "irresponsible youth" was an inevitable result of the war.

Teens and Moral Panics

The declaration of war on December 7, 1941, set in course one of the most dramatic mobilizations of young people in history, certainly in the United States, as some 17,867,000 men were called into military service. One of the small, but for our story significant, effects of this was the disappearance of the older members of the car-racing culture from the drive-ins and tracks of the United States, especially Southern California. The activities of the SCTA were suspended, and youths deprived of the sometimes more mature influence of the older members were cut loose to race. "Are These Our Children?" in *Look* (1943) warned of thousands of unsupervised teen boys "stumbling into delinquency" and "stealing cars, seducing girls." Youths presumably were easily lured into gangs because "home now is a lonely place." Rather than massive repression, however, the writer advised more recreational facilities and group activities, like the Scouts. Despite this positive advice, the story led to two war-time films exploiting the dangers of unsupervised youth in 1944, Monogram's *Where Are Your Children?* and RKO's *Youth Run Wild.*[9]

But a bigger problem was older teens with access to internal combustion and wheels. Adult authorities were convinced that boys were able to possess these dangerous machines because they often had money in their pockets in the wartime economy of full employment. In turn, the argument went, teen boys took to racing because they lacked the steadying hand of fathers or older brothers. A *Los Angeles Times* article from 1943 suggests the looming moral panic: Truant teens were free to steal accessories from parked cars (their "midnight auto supply"), a temptation made all the more likely if a teen or his older brother owned a hot rod. One common solution of local authorities from 1943 was to enforce curfew laws, barring youth under eighteen from the streets after 10 p.m.[10] But sixteen-year-olds still remained on those streets ready to race: "Wild eyed kids in hopped-up jalopies" roared "up and down the streets . . . at dizzy breakneck speeds," as *Colliers* reported as early as 1941. Cops only added to the problem when they chased the kids fleeing in their cars. Throughout the war, these teens met at drive-ins and conspired to find alternatives to rationed gas, using alcohol and cleaning solvent to fuel their cars and their need to race.[11] This response was part of a broader moral panic after the war in response to the widespread perception that young people were out of control and were threatening the moral order, especially through their exposure to violent and sexually suggestive comic books.[12]

Sporadic reports during the war gave way to more extensive coverage between 1945 and 1950, especially in the Los Angeles area. On July 9, 1945, police seized twenty "hopped up cars" and their mostly underage drivers near Long Beach. Law enforcement officials believed that these teens were preparing to race, and charged them with "unlawful assembly," though within hours they were returned to their parents.[13] Ed Roth described a seemingly typical scene shortly after the war's end, around Bell, another Los Angeles suburb: Teens and youths eager to race met at the Clock and Hula Hut drive-ins to "choose off" competitors to meet for quarter-mile races, which would be run quietly so that several races could be completed "before the heat came down Slauson Avenue with their sirens and lights blastin' away." The police mostly ticketed drivers for muffler and fender violations. Roth claims that one fellow, who was good with both cars and girls, claimed that he had hung his two hundred tickets to a wall as a trophy. (Later he owned an upholstery business.)[14]

The *Saturday Evening Post* added to the panic with a September 1946 feature, identifying the newfangled hot rod as "a car that some speed-crazy school boy has rebuilt," and noting that some such cars could outrun the police when they were equipped with "big car power plants." In February 1947, cops at Laguna Beach told a reporter that hot-rodders were "multiplying like rabbits," and Culver City authorities feared that their main drag was turning into a speedway. The next year, youths blockaded a strip of road in the San Fernando Valley to race four abreast at 105 miles per hour. In response, police arrested thirty-five, many of whom spent five days in jail and had their licenses suspended for thirty days.[15]

The press reported on the games played by speeding racers. These included "chicken," in which two daring youths would race toward each other at sixty to eighty miles per hour, with the first to swerve to the other lane becoming the "chicken"—which, according to a *Life* article of 1949, was "a fate sometimes considered worse than living to an old age." "Rotation" involved a driver, going at fifty or sixty miles per hour, opening his door and walking along the running board to the backseat at the same time as "a friend in the front took control of the wheel while another in the back seat rotated to the front."

These exhibitions of daring and danger were by no means restricted to the West Coast. The press reported that youths around Dallas played a game called "pedestrian polo," in which the hot-rodder tried to "just brush, but not hit" a pedestrian—or, as an alternative, to just graze the fender of a parked car. Another variant was "fenders," in which three or four drivers would race abreast, "creasing each other's fenders.[16] This image of speed-crazed hot-rodders was also fed by B-movie makers in the late 1940s, especially in *The Devil on Wheels* (1947) and *Hot Rod* (1950). *Variety* reported that the *Devil on Wheels* made "audiences conscious of the peril of . . . hopped-up autos." Still, the exploitation of the nihilistic hot-rodder developed fully only after 1955, following the appearance of *Rebel without a Cause* and its famous scene of teen drivers playing "chicken," racing toward a cliff daring each other not to turn away.[17]

Southern California police used various tricks to catch speeders, including trapping racers between barricades at either end of a known road-racing route. Culver City police claimed to have nabbed three hundred youths that way. Sometimes police raids were made on a grand scale. In February 1947, an army of fifty motorcycle cops attacked a gathering of about one hundred hot rods in Van Nuys. This led to a chase down Mission and Sepulveda Boulevards, where the police nabbed the kids blocking the road with barricades: thirty were ticketed, and four jailed.[18] In March 1947, Los Angeles Chief of Police William Parker launched a campaign against the "speed shift boys" by equipping the LAPD with a fleet of one hundred motorcycles. At the same time, a local judge warned that racers would be jailed for lacking legally required equipment like wipers and fenders.[19]

Public outrage reached a peak by the end of 1949 as the hot rod phenomenon had spread far and wide. Lou Holland, president of the AAA, demanded a national police response to the hot rodders, claiming that clubs had proliferated "in virtually every state during the past year" and that underage drinking and driving had become special problems. Holland noted that the vehicular death rate of fifteen- to twenty-four-year-olds was up 86 percent from 1929.

The *Los Angeles Times* reported that 558 California teens had been killed in cars in 1949, as compared to 630 in the previous three years.[20]

California remained the epicenter of youth speeders, but the AAA was partially right that the craze had passed well beyond the West Coast. Midwest towns like Council Bluffs, Iowa, called for a ban on hot rod races. Even a Greenville, Mississippi, newspaper reported in 1950 that teens driving their parents' cars had raced two abreast to the cheers of friends despite not having licenses. Local authorities scolded parents for lack of supervision, warning that future such occurrences would lead to confiscations of their vehicles. In an effort to compete with the souped-up rods, the Detroit Police Department joined the LAPD by ordering one hundred squad cars capable of reaching speeds of 110 miles per hour to outgun the rodders.[21] By 1949 the craze had reached as far as suburban New York City, as police in Westchester and Long Island set traps to catch teenage street racers.[22] The moral panic over hot-rod racing may have peaked by the early 1950s, but it reappeared sporadically thereafter. For example, the *Saturday Evening Post* in 1956 featured "52 Miles of Terror," a story of street racing, with the provocative claim: "They were looking for excitement, and if they hurt someone, so what?"[23]

While existing laws against speeding, "unlawful assembly," and illegal and inadequate auto equipment were often sufficient to control the hopped-up car culture, pressure to step up the attack led to a number of new regulations after 1945. Most notably in California, a state statute in 1947 required all cars to be equipped with stock mufflers. Two years later, California explicitly banned street racing and outlawed the posting of street barriers by racers. Since 1946, the Greater Los Angeles chapter of the National Safety Council had advocated raising the drivers' licensing age from fourteen to sixteen, a goal achieved in 1948 by California state statute.[24] In 1951 New York took a different approach, requiring liability insurance on any car belonging to anyone under twenty-one before it could be registered.[25]

In 1953 the National Automobile Dealers' Association (representing thirty-five thousand local car merchants) vowed that it would refuse to sell or service "souped-up" cars. Dealers were asked to inquire into their customers' intentions, and to promise not to sell youths high-powered engines.[26] That same year, a judge in Tampa, Florida, made news by punishing three eighteen-year-olds for burglary of car parts. He forbade them from owning hot rods for five years, on the assumption that such cars were expensive and thus encouraged stealing![27]

Yet, despite all these efforts at crackdown, the reaction of adults and authorities was often not nearly as severe as the press and legal response of the postwar period might suggest. Even in 1947, when teens were caught racing

FIGURE 3.1. As an alternative to jail, a teen traffic violator is obliged by Los Angeles police to place a sign on his windshield branding him as a highway danger (July 23, 1947). *Herald Examiner* Collection, Los Angeles Public Library. Used with permission.

on a public street in Los Angeles at 100 miles per hour, the penalty was merely a thirty-day license suspension. Often the police were content to drive the jalopies off the road. By 1948, restrictions on windshield size and headlight height and the requirement of fenders were enforced at "red light stops."[28] In July 1947, a group of thirty-one hot-rodders from Los Angeles, all between fifteen and eighteen years of age, were cited for "illegal assembly"—but, instead of lowering the boom, the police set up a committee to find an alternative to street racing. While 119 youths were rounded up by forty cops in a raid for racing or "encouraging" racing, their jail sentences were suspended and, again, their licenses were revoked for only thirty days. The judge noted, "I know your natural desires"; but he advised the youthful offenders to get off the streets and go to drag strips "to show your skill, prowess and stamina."[29]

This story of "understanding" courts was repeated in Chicago and elsewhere. In 1955, youths blocked off streets along Cicero Avenue in Chicago for a race of fifty hot rods. Still, police claimed that they understood the kids' desire to "test" their cars. In 1960, police in Chicago arrested fifty-nine youths for racing two abreast, but insisted merely that their parents come to the jail to post a twenty-five-dollar bond.[30]

This treatment of really dangerous lawbreakers, who sometimes raced on public streets at one hundred miles per hour, defies simple explanation. But the willingness of authorities to "understand" the teens' desires and, even more, to appeal to their parents to take charge suggests a common belief that hot-rodding was different from the juvenile delinquency of poor ethnic and minority gangs in the inner cities. Street racing clearly attracted white working-class and even middle-class teens, as dramatized in James Dean's role in *Rebel without a Cause* as a troubled hot-rodding son of respectable parents. In none of the incidents reviewed here were the motorized rebels identified as nonwhite. This may explain why hot-rodding was labeled a "family" or psychological problem, something that could be solved by redirecting "enthusiasm" or turning supervision back on the white parent whom many in authority believed had the right, duty, and often ability to supervise their offspring.

In 1956 the *Chicago Tribune* featured a speech by Max Hayman at the convention of the American Psychoanalytical Association in which he claimed, in classic Freudian style, that hot-rodding was a reversion to the baby's love of being "rocked, tossed, dawdled, or swung." When "over-permissiveness meets prohibition" (presumably when parents indulged their offspring with cars, but then placed all sorts of rules on their use), teens responded with the desire for "speedy gratification before the denial catches up" with them.[31] The moral panic over the young hotfoot on the accelerator was moderated by an "understanding" of white boys coming of age with fast cars. The response of police and judges would have been much different if the offenders had been black or Latino—as witnessed by the police involvement in the Zoot Suit Riots of 1943 in Los Angeles, in which Latino youths were attacked by whites.

Even those who condemned the reckless racers sometimes conceded the skill and effort required to take a beat-up, fifteen-year-old car and turn it into a power machine. A *Saturday Evening Post* feature in November 1950 characterized the hot-rodder's garage as a "clinic" in which car surgeons worked miracles. An *Amarillo Daily News* reporter made the point: "A boy can do a lot worse things than drive an old car that sounds like a B-29." The theme was dressed up by a psychologist who claimed that the hot-rodder's "activities are channeled into constructive pursuits."[32] There seemed to be room for adapting to the hot rod—if it could be cooled down.

Cooling the Hot Rod

There remained a deep contradiction between the obvious immaturity of the teen and the power of the modern motor car, especially when it was hopped up as a "hot" roadster or even a sedan. And the returning World War II veter-

ans who wanted to resume what had become essentially a hobby had a press-
ing interest in separating themselves from that immaturity, which many of
them had only recently outgrown. In the decade after the war, leaders of this
generation of vets presented a model of adulthood that separated the display
of manhood in a fast customized car from the defiance and risk-taking of boys
wanting to be men.

The vets' alternative had roots in prewar hot-rod organizations, especially
in California's SCTA and the local car clubs that were reconstituted in 1946.
With its three hundred members in small hot-rod clubs, the SCTA promoted
the relatively safe ritual of the timed quarter-mile drag race of individual vehicles at off-the-highway drag strips. In January 1948 the SCTA also sponsored
a show at the Los Angeles Armory featuring eighty premium hot rods and
equipment suppliers along with police safety demonstrations. Later that year,
SCTA members met with the National Safety Council in front of a local judge
to pledge support for safe driving. Timing association clubs promised to ban
any member from racing who had been convicted of a moving vehicle violation. The next year, a second hot-rod exhibition was held in Los Angeles by the
SCTA (claiming 58,000 visitors). Many attendees were teens who gawked at
the "chromed hop-ups, a far cry from the common variety roaming the highways and byways" of Southern California at that time. The SCTA offered these
youths an alternative to the merely stripped-down roadsters than many teens
thought were "hot rods."[33] And this appeal to legitimacy was not restricted to
Southern California. Beginning in 1949, a roadster show was regularly held
in Oakland, California.[34]

Perhaps most notable in this quest for respectability was the publication of
Hot Rod Magazine by Robert Petersen in 1948, and the appearance in 1951 of
the National Hot Rod Association, led by the magazine's editor, Wally Parks, a
racer from the old dry lakes days. Petersen (1926–2007), a laid-off movie pub-
licist for Metro-Goldwyn-Mayer, promoted the 1948 Armory hot rod show,
and shortly after decided to publish *Hot Rod Magazine*. Peddled at first by
hawkers at drive-ins and drag races, the magazine reached a circulation of fifty
thousand in 1949, and by 1950 it was distributed nationally. Though his father
was a mechanic, Petersen was primarily a businessman. He went on to become
a very successful publisher of a wide range of car magazines for various markets. While legitimizing the hot rod, Petersen and his magazines attempted
to reach every corner of American auto enthusiasm; articles on "aftermarket"
accessories were sometimes accompanied by advertising from the companies
that made them.[35] Petersen helped to commercialize and professionalize the
hot rod hobby.[36] *Hot Rod Magazine* promoted special-purpose "drag strips"
of asphalt with timing traps for single-car speed tests as a sane alternative to

FIGURE 3.2. A drag race on the Pomona Drag Strip (November 1955). Photograph by Earl Theisen. *Look* Magazine Photograph Collection, Library of Congress, Prints & Photographs Division, reproduction number e.g., LC-L9–60–8812, frame 8. Used with permission of Roxann Livingston.

paired competitive street racing. Like many other magazines and clubs, *Hot Rod Magazine* nevertheless retained an aura of rebellion, mocking the flash and expense of standard production cars of the 1950s and glorifying the hard work, skill, and individuality of customizers. Fords and Mercurys from the 1930s and '40s remained the favored dragster vehicles throughout the 1950s, mocking a generation of rapidly changing, long, low, and finned family cars from Detroit.[37]

Petersen and Parks, however, had ambitions beyond a profitable, heavily illustrated magazine. They played an important role in separating the image of the responsible hot rodder at the drag strip from that of the irresponsible youth with his jalopy, racing on the street. In the spring of 1951, Parks undertook the task of organizing the presumed three hundred thousand rodders in

America into the National Hot Rod Association (NHRA) for "safety, sportsmanship and fellowship" and to counteract the negative image of the "speed-happy jalopy drivers." In its first year, the NHRA attracted about twenty-five thousand members from numerous small and local clubs. By 1952, NHRA staff asked leaders of old clubs with provocative names (and often deeds) like Hell Drivers, Killers, Fender Rippers, and Sideswipers to adopt more respectable monikers like Piston Pushers and Gents' Club. Under the banner of safety and respectability, Parks and other NHRA officials toured the country, organizing affiliates as far East as New England and Miami, assuring worried local officials that NHRA members were law-abiding citizens. In 1954 Parks launched the "Drag Safari" to promote drag racing (as opposed to street racing), leading to the US Nationals for drag racing in 1955 in Kansas City, Kansas. By 1957 the NHRA claimed 57,000 members, many of whom were teens. Some were organized by high-school auto shop teachers and met at school facilities or local garages; some even had police advisors.[38]

Yet Petersen and his magazine strongly opposed the moral panic against the hot rod. In an April 1947 interview with the *Los Angeles Times*, Petersen rejected restrictive legislation because it would "never stop boys from racing." In opposition to the Los Angeles Safety Council and the Auto Club of Southern California, both of which opposed hot-rodding in any form, Petersen insisted that if boys were not given access to racetracks, "they'll find a place somewhere." In November 1951 his magazine challenged statutes that required fenders on street cars, claiming that, while hot-rodders should obey the law, they were a persecuted group.[39]

This, of course, did not mean unqualified support for teen rodders. In fact, Petersen and the NHRA tried to separate in public opinion the "irresponsible bunch of careless jerks" with their "shot rods" from the "thousands of upstanding young people in the U.S. who don't deserve to be classified as 'delinquents' because of their natural interest in mechanical tinkering."[40] An editorial in *Hot Rod* added that while the "shot rod" is merely an old car that some teens bought and "in a short time" modifies slightly to give "a hot rod appearance," the "real hot rod is a car that is lending itself to experimental development for the betterment of safety, operation, and performance." Few real hot-rodders would ever use these finely crafted and expensive machines as "battering rams" in reckless racing games.[41] Such distinctions were essential to counter the blanket condemnation of the rodder in 1949 by T. W. Ryan of the New York Division of Safety, who declared that "possession of the 'hot-rod' car is presumptive evidence of an intent to speed."[42]

Significantly, Petersen and Parks convinced some police. In 1950 the California Highway Patrol helped organize the Highway Patrol Reserve Corps,

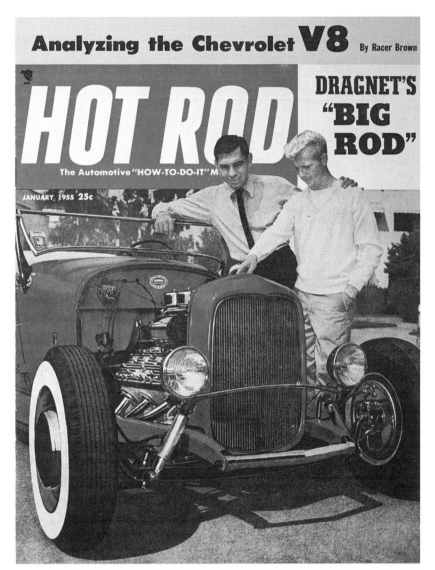

FIGURE 3.3. Jack Webb, famed lead in *Dragnet*, a true-to-life police procedural series on television and radio in the 1950s, poses with a teen, apparently embracing the image of the "good" teen hot-rodder. This picture appeared on the cover of *Hot Rod* magazine shortly after the airing of a *Dragnet* episode featuring the contrast between lawless and law-abiding youth. *Hot Rod*, January 1955. Used with permission of *Hot Rod*, © 2017. All rights reserved.

hot-rod clubbers trained to aid after traffic accidents by rerouting traffic.[43] The Highway Patrol issued a press release in March 1952 that distinguished between the shot-rodders, with their dangerous jalopies, and the hot-rodders, with their "imaginative engineering" and "many hours of work and expenditure of hundreds of dollars." Money and labor redeemed the rebel. Even LAPD chief William Parker, long an opponent of street racing, wrote an article in 1953 entitled "Living at Peace with the Hot Rodder." Jack Webb, Parker's friend and the famed producer and star of *Dragnet*, a gritty police procedural TV show, embraced this view. In one notable episode, "The Big Rod," aired in December 1954, Webb contrasted a law-abiding, self-regulating hot rod club with an isolated shot-rodder who ran down a helpless lady.[44] This distinction was repeatedly embraced by local newspapers throughout the country in the early 1950s.[45]

What strikes me about this movement is how its official face never featured youth as such. In *Hot Rod Magazine*, for example, the "look" was never that of a teen, even though many rodders were under twenty, and almost all started well before that age. The visual message seemed to be that hot-rodding was not a hobby that the young were supposed to grow out of. Instead, they were to grow into manhood with their rods and remain enthusiasts as adults. This conformed to the self-image of the older hot-rodder, as well as the financial interests of the magazine. The ages and occupations of dragsters were scarcely ever mentioned in *Hot Rod* or its competitors. Yet it was no accident that *Hot Rod Magazine* readily presented its Public Service Award in 1952 to a thirty-two-year old businessman, as if to affirm that hot-rodding was not just for boys, or just for the working class. And the magazine pictured youths and their elders together, never gangs of teens. *Hot Rod Magazine* reported that in the summer of 1953 the Kiwanis club in West Toledo, Ohio, invited hot rod clubs to a drag race where fathers and sons were asked to sign a "safety agreement" abjuring street racing. All this contributed to the cooling of the hot rod.[46]

The NHRA and its allies went beyond defending the hot-rodder's image and movement. These groups attempted to shape the behavior of teen hot-rodders. They helped to produce a series of short propaganda films, not just to denounce shot rods and warn of the dangers of speeding, but to promote a positive image of the "good" teen hot-rodder.[47] Most notable was *Cool Hot Rod* (1953), sponsored by *Hot Rod Magazine* and Southern California hot rod clubs, which was widely shown to teen groups.[48] *Cool Hot Rod* features a teen hot-rodder new at the local high school, intent on showing the "sleepy Joes" there his daring style of driving. Instead of becoming the leader of the pack and passing on dangerous tricks from his old club, he runs into members of a different sort of club, the Knights, organized by a local speed-shop owner whose son, a war veteran, has recently been killed trying to beat a train to a crossing. In the hope that other youths will not make the same mistake as his son, he works with the local police to recruit young hot-rodders to the Knights, setting up strict rules for membership that exclude teens with moving violations and unsafe cars. The new kid is stopped for reckless driving; and instead of getting a fine or jail, he is sentenced by a school court to traffic school. Of course, the former shot-rodder discovers that the Knights aren't behind the times; he is, with his show-off ways. The Knights are not just goody two-shoes; they have great rods and even beat an auto design engineer in an off-street race. The new kid eventually is allowed into the Knights, realizing that "a reckless kid in an old junker is not a hot-rodder at all. He's a square."[49] The unreservedly didactic narrative of *Cool Hot Rod* offered a new image of hot-rodders organized in adult-sponsored clubs, who helped old ladies with flat tires and only raced on drag strips financed by local businesses. Similar movies followed.[50]

Many teen hot-rod clubs embraced this message, at least officially. The Dolphins car club of Long Beach willingly accepted police affiliation and the sponsorship of the local chamber of commerce in 1947. Police were also assigned to the Headhunters of Hayward, California, and a Highway Patrol officer gave lectures at club meetings.[51]

These efforts to isolate the "shot-rodder" and to enlist the police in a defanged hot-rod culture were not isolated to Southern California. In 1950 the Roadster Racing Association of Madison, Wisconsin, won positive newspaper coverage with the claim that their members were young, but also often "'family men' who did not rip off fenders and roofs" as some high-school kids did; instead, they installed rollover bars on their cars for safety, raced only on the track, and built masterpieces "from the ground up."[52] The Lions Clubs and other civic organizations built drag strips in Sioux Falls, South Dakota, and in Long Island, New York, in the early 1950s.[53] A major theme was to win teens over to the idea that "safety is socially acceptable" in driving. In an effort to enlist youth to the cause, the American Motorist Insurance Company of Chicago asked teens for ideas. Among them was the suggestion that girls pledge not to ride with speed-crazy boys, and the slogan "It's better to be a live chicken than a dead duck." In suburban Chicago high schools, students set up their own "courts" to rid campuses of reckless drivers.[54]

Hot Rod Clubs and the Cal-Rods

Probably more effective than any of these sometimes ham-handed efforts of adults to shape teen car culture were the student-run hot rod clubs. Following a long tradition of the school extracurriculum in sports, music, and hobbies,

the hot rod clubs were organized with the "cooperation" of adult clubs, police, and sometimes school officials. In 1949 teachers and administrators in
Oakland, California, started car clubs in four of the six public high schools,
but students set their rules and ran the clubs.[55] In 1952, following the arrest of
curfew violators at a local drive-in, San Gabriel police helped found the Road
Rebels for teen customizers. Still, the boys wrote their own bylaws, requiring
a two-thirds vote of the membership for new members to join, and a monthly
safety inspection of members' cars.[56] As an alternative to street and speedway
racing, some clubs sponsored reliability runs, single cars traveling over a long
course on roads with various driving conditions. The winner was the driver
closest to the "official time." This competition stressed driving skill and safe
and sturdy vehicles, rather than power and speed. Similar were organized
"road-e-o" contests in which teen drivers tested their skill in driving at safe
speeds through obstacle courses of pylons and flags.[57]

The Downshifters club of suburban Westport, Connecticut, was started in
1956 by seven boys still in junior high, with the sponsorship of the local YMCA
and the NHRA. Its members proudly wore the NHRA insignia on their club
clothing, and adhered to the organization's rules. The "Y" provided a club garage and helped equip it with a cable hoist, welder, torque wrench, and other
shop tools. The local driver education teacher talked to the club about safety.
Goody two-shoes to the end, members were fined for swearing at meetings
and put on "probation" for speeding tickets. As members aged and entered
adulthood, the Downshifters became a social club that undertook fundraisers
for charity, much as did the Lions or Rotary clubs.[58]

Hot rod memoirist Robert Genat recalls that youth car clubs in the 1950s
shared tools and worked cooperatively on "rail jobs" to enter in track races. All
this offered members an education in the arts of customization and rebuilding
before investing in their own vehicles. Other "clubs" were loose and ephemeral
groups that gathered on cruise nights. New Englanders Arnie and Bernie Shuman remembered that many clubs in the 1950s met in local barns, equipped
with little more than a welding torch.[59] Most teen car clubs were white and
came from small or middle-sized towns, but in 1952 a high-school group from
Los Angeles called the Juggers included some African-Americans.[60]

Inevitably, not all youth car clubs in the 1950s followed the NHRA script.
The Shuman brothers recall how the Piston Pushers of Concord, Massachusetts, after meeting in the barn of a member's dad, "blasted outside into the
fresher barnyard air, [where] they behaved like the crazed teenage car junkies
in the B movies shown at drive-ins." They headed for the Sunshine Diary,
where "they would posture and ogle the young girls serving ice cream, make
lewd comments, and eventually be thrown out by the owners." In 1953 this

thirty-member club split in two over the question of street racing. One faction quit the club in opposition to this illegal activity, forming a new group, the Ty-Rods. Led by an older member, Carrol Sleeper, the Ty-Rods imposed the NHRA rules (even requiring new members to obtain the endorsement of a local police officer) and raced on drag strips, not streets. However, even the Ty-Rods pulled pranks like sneaking up on couples at make-out spots on dirt roads in the woods, and spraying water on them from a pickup truck before speeding away. Started mostly by high-school students, most clubs eventually broke up as their members drifted away into the armed services (at a time when most youth were conscripted for two years), jobs, or college. While some hot-rodders became mechanics, a few became engineers or businessmen.[61] None of this should be too surprising. The clubs provided a male-bonding moment in their lives prior to the inevitable diaspora of adulthood into families and social stratification.

Still another car club, the Cal-Rods, illustrates the complex relationship between youth and adulthood. By good fortune I met the organizer of this revived teen car club, Vic Cunnyngham of Orange County, California, in the summer of 2016. He introduced me to a number of the "originals" from the club, which was founded in 1954 in the small town of Baldwin Park, now part of the vast complex of eastern Los Angeles suburbs. The housing in Baldwin Park was mostly new in the mid-1950s, and members of the Cal-Rods came from skilled working-class or small-business families. The high school was nearly all white, except for two daughters from a black family. A few Mexican students were in a "gang," I was told by an "original," but were not violent.

Don Scurti, the son of a tailor, was infatuated by hot rods from his job sweeping up at Bob's Auto Parts, a business he would buy years later. With the initial assistance of two adults, Scurti, then sixteen years old, organized the Cal-Rods. At first there were about ten members, many of them related to each other or to members of the gymnastics team. They adopted by-laws, associated with the NHRA, and heard talks from the local police about automobile safety and traffic laws. Members paid dues of twenty-five cents at each meeting. One rule of the club was no drinking at club functions or while wearing club garb. The adults involved approved of the club as an alternative to letting local boys fall into juvenile delinquency. Early members claimed that they were typical of this lower middle-class community, were not hostile to school (though many didn't go beyond high school), and had received at least average grades. They never saw themselves as "greasers," though they had hot rods typical of the era and some wore ducktail hairdos.

One of the adult sponsors, Pete Peterson, a gas station owner, offered the club a local barn on the condition that they fixed it up. In their barn, the lower level of which they equipped with auto shop essentials, they jointly built a "rail job," a stripped-down race car built on a Model A engine, and equipped it with two carburetors so that it could reach one hundred miles per hour. They also rebuilt a 1934 Ford roadster that they entered in a local car show.

Like the Ty-Rods, they weren't always on the straight and narrow. Several members conceded that they had street raced at a nearby park, and even admitted that members had "borrowed" lumber for their barn clubhouse at night from a construction site—for which several, when caught by the police, were obliged to submit to community service. Some gathered for "garage parties" at the homes of members whose parents were away—a smart alternative to gathering in living or "rumpus" rooms, where drinking teens might break or stain something.

Still, the Cal-Rods were a pretty tame lot, well organized and closely attached to the world of adults. One Cal-Rod member commented that he wore a "one-button powder blue suit" to dances with the iconic '50s dark blue suede shoes. Virtually every member (as well as most boys at Baldwin Park High) had a car, essential for any degree of independence in a spread-out suburb with no public transportation. And knowing something about repairing or rebuilding cars was highly valued when these teens began with junkers. Inevitably, most left the club shortly after high-school graduation and marriage, which usually came at the same time. And the club broke up within a decade, with conflicts over new leadership and the loss of the clubhouse.[62]

Most of this confirms the stories of other car clubs of the era, but the Cal-Rods were also distinct. First, instead of being small, meeting in a parents' garage or a local shop, they had a well-equipped barn as a clubhouse (moving to a second one a couple of years later); and instead of cruising, they met at a local drive-in, the In-N-Out Burger, which was later expanded into a prosperous chain. Their club grew quickly, and though they were not associated with the high-school extracurriculum, they were, all agreed, more respected than the members of other smaller, more ephemeral car clubs (the Ratchets, Nerfers, Deckers, Wambomies, and Loafers), about whom the "originals" recalled little.[63]

Most interesting, the Cal-Rods had from the beginning a female "auxiliary" that met separately, called the Cal-Rodettes. Originally there were nine Baldwin High girls who met at the home of Sharon Davis, not wanting to be left out of the fun (according to another Rodette, Jeri Silva). They had their own rules, even fining a member for drinking a beer with a boy from a different club. Several Rodettes were the girlfriends or sisters of Cal-Rod boys. They took part in painting and light carpentry improvements at the barn but, following the gender code of the time, didn't work on the cars. And upstairs

FIGURE 3.4. A group picture of the Cal-Rods and the Rodettes of Baldwin High School (about 1955). This group is unusual in its mix of male and female, but otherwise it is like other teen car clubs of the era. From the collection of Sharon Davis. Used with permission.

in the loft, the Rodettes joined the boys in dancing to a jukebox, relaxing on the couch, drinking Cokes from a vending machine, and sharing good times at parties that sometimes featured a band led by Scurti, who sounded like a "good Louis Prima" as he sang songs with altered lyrics that were not always on the "up-and-up." The Rodettes were also important contributors to joint charity activities, and were especially noted for their fund-raising for the City of Hope. They also joined the boys in car-related games—scavenger hunts and poker runs, the latter of which involved driving around town guided by chalk markings on the road to gather cards, which at the end of the run would be compared to determine the best "hand." The Cal-Rods and Rodettes also had picnics and dances. On weekends there was always someone at the clubhouse to socialize with.

What seemed to make this unusual arrangement work was the fact that many of the original Rodettes were friends to begin with, as were several of their mothers, and even hung out informally at those home of one of the girls. Her mother was perhaps ahead of her time, occasionally organizing "taco parties" at which she would let her bathtub be filled with bottled beer and ice. Of course, the mother collected the boys' car keys, returning them only when they were "all right." The club name would not be sullied by these "taco parties," because they were not club events.

At a time when teen girls regularly "went steady"—in this case, often with one of the Cal-Rod boys—there might have been jealousies and other conflicts. But the members I talked with didn't recall any. One explanation was that they weren't "intimate" with each other, unlike some of the other girls in the high school, who "went all the way." Even though some Rodettes engaged in "petting" at drive-in movies or parking sites, their self-control or naiveté regarding sex made breaking up or changing partners less difficult. Most married soon after high school, and usually stayed married. All of this conformed to the gender code of the 1950s (as we shall consider fully in chapter 4), in which males called most of the shots and most members were in couples. Still, the Rodettes (at least the core members) were a kind of sisterhood, often friends through life.[64]

Of course this is an insider's story, recalled in nostalgia. As in most teen tribes, others were excluded, if not maliciously. Still, the story of the Cal-Rods and Rodettes suggests something of the history of the hot-rod culture, posed between youthful liberation and the quest for adult respectability.

As promising as the new teen car clubs were in cooling the hot rod, there remained tensions between adult authorities and young car enthusiasts, especially over the question of where to draw the line regarding racing. A major goal of many clubs throughout the country was to gain access to drag raceways, of which, as we have seen, the NHRA and many officials approved. Drag strips were off the streets, and the contests, though exhibitions of power and skill in managing rapidly accelerating vehicles, were contained to a quarter mile. The main ingredient for winning was the work and skill in enhancing the stock car's ability to reach high speeds in a few seconds. Drag racing was well regulated by adult clubs after 1945, with standardized components: course length, inspection area, timing equipment, and scales to weigh cars for different classifications. Ideally, the strips also adhered to safety and legal requirements: barriers, a control stand, an ambulance, prohibition of alcohol consumption, a full complement of officials, and of course insurance. Because of its short duration and confined course, drag racing was widely regarded as a relatively safe alternative to paired street racing.[65]

There were plenty of sites for drag strips, especially abandoned World War II–era airplane landing strips. Adult-sponsored strips may have started in California, but they quickly spread nationwide. In 1951, high-school hot-rodders on Long Island petitioned a local township to use public land for a strip. Two years later, a track was opened at Glen Cove with the collaboration of local police, who saw it as an alternative to juvenile delinquency and drinking.[66] Local efforts like this led to 130 strips in forty states by the early 1960s, according to the NHRA.[67] The drag strip was a classic expression of redirecting the competitive and aggressive urges of youth from the dangerous and defiant to the safe and sanctioned—a path to adulthood embraced by adults.

Still, police often opposed these drag strips, fearful that they would attract public drinking or gang fights. For opponents, the guiding principle was an old psychological principle that any toleration of a negative desire—in this case, to race—was unquenchable and naturally led to its extreme form, as in the theory that any taste of alcohol culminates in drunkenness. In 1956, delegates at the Chicago meeting of the International Association of Police Chiefs voted to outlaw drag strips. The statement from the association made it clear: drag races "tended to inspire participants to carry the practice to the public streets." [68] For many adults, teens at the wheel, even when contained in clubs and drag strips, remained a threat to public safety. Yet the strategy of co-optation and containment generally prevailed.

Drivers' Education: Maturity as Civilized Automobility

The taming of the rodding culture was only a part of a broader campaign to domestic the teen driver. The larger problem was the more extensive group of high-schoolers just emerging from childhood, frequently eager to assert their independence from and even rebel against adults. School officials recognized that for their young charges, the driver's license, often more than a diploma, marked their entry into the adult community. As the historian Cotten Seiler notes, the "republic of drivers" was a community that affirmed liberty and choice of movement for its members, while also requiring them to adhere to an extensive list of rules. Holders of automobile licenses had embraced restrained liberty, and thus gained entry into the community of grown-ups. The significance of this recent change in American life was captured by a California state guide for drivers' education (1948) in which civil engagement and automobility were intertwined:

> Training in civil competency and social responsibility in our democratic culture requires that youth and adults be prepared to live safely and sanely in an age that has become increasingly mechanized. . . . [The car] affects directly or indirectly the life of every person in the state and nation. . . . [and thus youths need] to develop proper understandings, appreciations, attitudes, and skills in the use of automobiles on streets and highways.[69]

Though the age of sixteen or even fourteen had become the standard point of entry into this community of drivers, authorities often saw this age as problematic. In an early driving manual, Robbins Stoeckel, a former commissioner of motor vehicles in Connecticut, and two Yale professors, Mark May and Richard Kirby, note: "Children . . . at the age when they are aspiring to be adults, if allowed to indulge in adult occupations on the same level with adults, are likely to become overconfident and unable to make allowances for their inexperience in the conditions of life which must be met on the road." The advantage of adults in driving was that they "have perhaps learned by experience more about [their] own limitations." This "immaturity," marked by the denial of limits rather than a simple lack of capacity to be a skilled driver, made teen drivers problematic. This text went further by identifying this failure to recognize limits as a "lower-class" trait resulting from an "inferiority complex." Such people "compensate for their status . . . in the way they drive their automobiles. . . . . It may result in the most vicious type of reckless driving. The craving that such persons have for superiority over others urges them to express their desired importance in the world by dashing madly through traffic, cutting in and out . . . from which they derive a great deal of satisfaction."[70] The right to drive a car might not be denied to a sixteen-year-old, even a "greaser" from the working class, but these writers clearly saw this freedom as a negative consequence of the democratic revolution in mass automobility. Still, they insisted that the right to drive had to be earned and could be revoked, more easily than the right to vote and other rights of adulthood, if the driver failed to follow the thicket of rules governing driving.[71]

This point of view may well explain why public safety and educational authorities demanded rules of initiation into the community of automobilists, a rite of passage that was intended to be complex and ultimately became deeply ideological, biased by age and class. That initiation demanded much. It required an understanding of the mechanics of the automobile and personal skill in car maintenance as well as in driving, so that a complex set of motor and intellectual skills became virtually habitual. But underlining all this was the expectation that driving was a marker of emotional maturity, and a challenge to a psychology and culture of youth that rejected the ethos of the "republic of drivers." And this meant confronting the mentality and community of the "bad" hot-rodder in driver training.

Yet this drivers' education did not come quickly or without resistance. In the early years, automobile dealers offered brief instruction on car operation to buyers, and provided toolboxes with often detailed repair instructions, but only brief driving manuals that explained just a few rules of the road (e.g., speed limits, passing on the left). In 1903 the YMCA of Boston, long an innovator in vocational education and sports instruction for young men, still offered only courses in car repair, not driving instruction. For many years, high schools failed to offer students training in driving and traffic law. Driving was to be self-taught or learned in the family, like riding a horse. As we have seen, Americans were relatively slow in imposing restrictions on driving. However, with the doubling in the number of cars on the road each year after 1900 until

FIGURE 3.5. Driver education car with a dual steering wheel in Texas (1948). *San Antonio Light* Collection, University of Texas at San Antonio. Used with permission by Zuma Press.

1917, when there were already five million vehicles in service, and with the increased speed and weight of cars, it isn't surprising that licensing gradually became more rigorous. At first this meant traffic safety training in the schools; though that began only in 1926 (establishing safety patrols at crosswalks near schools, for example).[72]

Driver training was first formalized at the high-school level, many claim, in State College, Pennsylvania, in 1934. Amos Neyhart, a professor at what would become the Pennsylvania State University, acting with financial support from the AAA, introduced a course consisting of eight hours of on-the-road driving instruction along with classroom learning. By 1935, New York and Chicago school districts had introduced driving courses in high schools. Lane Technical High School in Chicago pioneered the use of "dummy cars" for simulated driving in class. These programs gradually extended throughout the nation, but as late as 1947, only 3,055 high schools offered some form of driver education—about 12 percent of the roughly twenty-five thousand high schools in the country. The number of participating schools rose to 8,218 by 1951, due in part to the active prompting of groups like the Association of

Casualty and Surety Companies, which initiated the National High School Driver's Education Onward Program in 1948. Still, of these schools, only 6,071 had on-the-road training, often an expensive extra for small or financially conservative school districts. It was only in 1965 that as many as thirteen thousand high schools offered instruction to an estimated 1.7 million students and still only 68 percent of these schools followed the standard of thirty hours of classroom instruction and six hours of driving.[73]

The costs of driving instruction surely slowed the introduction of these courses in the schools, but school boards and faculty sometimes resisted the introduction of "nonacademic" vocational courses, and often saw driver training as a private matter rather than a public concern. Educators, insurance companies, and safety officials combated these attitudes. In 1937, Philip Attwood, a science teacher from Northern California and the author of a driver's training manual, made a common appeal: While few could predict what the student would do for a living after high school, he noted, virtually everyone would drive a car, thus justifying universal drivers' education. The claim that 94 percent of car accidents were the result of driver error further made drivers' education a matter of public health and safety. Attwood also saw this class as an essential component of "consumer education": training in the purchase of cars, parts, and automotive services in the jungle of sometimes false advertising and dishonest salespeople.[74]

These arguments recurred frequently, especially after the war. In 1946 the AAA noted that sixteen-year-olds had nine times the fatal accident rate of drivers from forty-five to fifty years old. The next year, Herbert Stack, an official in the National Commission on Safety Education (NCSE), insisted that it was essential to instill good driver habits in the "formative years when sound safety habits can be established." The NCSE added in 1950 that driver training was to develop "strong attitudes of social responsibility." Joining the AAA in promoting driver education were the National Safety Council and the national PTA. The insurance and automobile industries awarded grants to various commissions to promote this crusade. In a rather more alarmist fashion, the popular national magazine *Saturday Evening Post* insisted in 1949, "Our youngsters don't have to be killers," and claimed that the schools had a responsibility to do "something to regulate youthful exuberance and eliminate irresponsibility at the wheel." High-school students needed at least eight hours of behind-the-wheel training along with twenty hours of classroom instruction to instill "proper attitude and respect of the motor vehicle. . . ."[75]

Drivers' education became something of a crusade for a wide range of authorities: automobile drivers' organizations like the AAA, the car insurance industry, nonprofit public interest groups, and especially progressive educators. Drawing on avant-garde trends in teaching techniques, advocates like Amos Neyhart and F. R. Noffsinger set out a detailed outline of a high-school driver's course in 1938. Insisting on systematic training rather than informal learning from parents or other family members, they proposed that students receive "practice[in driving]as in a sport" and "tests for excitability, reactions to unusual conditions," so that students could evaluate for themselves their capacity to drive. They equally insisted that students learn the details of auto maintenance as future consumers, but also simply because "to do intelligent driving it is necessary to know how the automobile runs." This included a surprising emphasis on mechanical details (an interesting appeal in an age when many still assumed that they should understand how their machines worked). But even a more important goal of driver's education was to discourage unsportsmanlike behaviors like insisting on the right of way, showing off, hogging the road, and "resenting laws and other restraints." The central objective of driver's education was "to create a desire on the part of the student to obey the traffic laws, based upon reason and respect for law."[76] At the core was the call for freedom with civil constraint.

These ideas permeate driver's education texts introduced from the later 1930s. The most influential of these was *Sportsmanlike Driving*, first published in 1936 by the AAA with input from a wide range of traffic engineers, public school officials, college educators, and psychologists. The chapter order says a lot about the assumptions and goals of the AAA. Beginning with a chapter titled "The Driver," the authors focused on preparing the youth psychologically for getting behind the wheel; the second chapter, "Driver and Pedestrian Responsibilities," continued this emphasis, focusing on rules of traffic; the third, "Society's Responsibilities," offered a surprisingly academic treatment of the history of the car, highway design, and ongoing legal and legislative issues. Only at the end was there the chapter "How to Drive," including the mechanics of the car as well as instruction in steering, gear shifting, and vehicle maneuvering.

Sportsmanlike Driving assumed that practical behind-the-wheel training would follow, but it was mostly about instilling proper attitudes and creating a counterculture to the "bad hot-rodder." The book's title was also significant. The authors, recognizing the growing role of organized athletic games in American high schools, adopted the point of view of the tough but understanding coach who made "men" and "women" of "boys" and "girls" by offering as a path out of childhood an alternative to the culture of the youth-led peer group, be it the street gang or, in this case, the auto-mobilized cruiser and racer. "Sportsmanlike" driving meant attaining manual and mental skills and knowledge of the game, including a full understanding of the other "play-

ers"—in this case, other drivers on the road. It also meant "fair play": courteous behavior, even going beyond the legal requirements, thus reducing accidents. Though modified, this text went through six editions by 1970.[77]

The 1936 edition of *Sportsmanlike Driving* opened with the crucial role of
the driver: While "the automobile is an unreasoning, irresponsible instrument
with awe-inspiring power. . . . The capable driver appropriates this power to
himself . . . , controls it at will and converts it into a safe instrument of general
good." But that driver, especially if a youth, too often exhibited the excessive
self-confidence of the child striving to be a grown-up by displaying the attitude that driving was a "cinch." The student had to understand the power of
the modern car and the limits of the roads, pedestrians, other drivers, and
especially him- or herself. This required not only the acquisition of technique
and a knowledge of the rules, but "wise habits" and proper "attitudes."[78]

The manual challenged the audaciousness of the child wanting to be
grown-up: "Conceit and a childish urge to 'show off' are likely to make us see
things out of proper relation and proportion, . . . indications of not growing
up—of being too immature to hold a license and drive." The worst attitude
was expressed by "egotists" who, like babies, "are normally self-centered." Such
people had uncontrolled emotions, "another sign of immaturity." Egotists cut
in, hogged the road, double-parked, and, most of all, "fail to see that traffic
laws are for the social good, and express this by boastingly breaking as many
laws as possible." In particular, the egotist acted like an unmentioned hot-
rodder, "boasting of his car's speed and power, . . . painting his car with 'loud'
colors and smart remarks and plastering it with stickers," as did some early
hot-rodders. Perhaps most of all, the egotist was "willing to turn the highway
into a race-track." Echoing Stoeckel and the Yale team in their assessment
of the inferiority complex of working-class youth, *Sportsmanlike Driving* insisted that such people were "trying to make up for their failure to achieve
certain desires. . . . The little, unimportant fellow looks for a chance to appear
powerful." Mature drivers not only controlled their emotions and egos but
recognized the rights of others on the road—a perfect expression of "good
sportsmanship." Again and again, correct driving was equated with maturity.
A driver must be focused: "Unless the driver can control his own attention,
he cannot control his car. To be able to control attention is a sign of growing
up—of becoming mature. A baby cannot do it." [79] Later versions of *Sportsmanlike Driving* changed little in this approach. The sixth edition (1970) similarly stressed getting "prepared to drive," problematizing an activity that many
youth were eager to get to. Authors of the 1970 edition lectured the reader to
avoid the temptation to play the "fearless daredevil," and took the mature view
that a "car is a means of transportation, and not just a toy for showing off."[80]

This general formula was followed by other driver education texts, including Maxwell Halsey's *Let's Drive Right* (1954)[81] and Harold Glenn's *Youth at the
Wheel* (1958). The latter, written by a Long Beach high school teacher, tried to
scare readers with statistics on accident and death rates of young drivers in the
United States (8,200 dead and 365,000 injured in their cars in one year), but
made a rational appeal for young drivers to improve their chances of staying
"alive and out of jail" by avoiding the "personality traits of drivers habitually
involved in accidents."[82] This appeal to enlightened self-interest in the pursuit
of personal freedom once again confirmed the ideology of the "republic of
drivers." But like the other manuals, Glenn made another appeal, offering a
counter-definition of growing up in contrast to that of the hot-rodder. Good
drivers, Glenn told his juvenile readers, were like professional drivers, safe and
courteous; while "cowboy driving" was "kids' stuff," and the egotistical driver
who sped and squealed his tires "when he has an audience" was often insecure,
even schizophrenic and in need of psychiatric help, just like the youth who
"dresses in loud colors, is late to class." Just in case Glenn hadn't made his
point, he included a cartoon of the show-off driver in a baby hat.[83]

This message to kids in cars appeared also in popular and probably more
influential media—especially the teen novel. Perhaps the most notable is
Henry Gregor Felsen's *Hot Rod* (1950). Written by a Marine Corps veteran
who edited *Leatherneck* during the war, Felsen dashed off this hortatory tale
on the suggestion of the Iowa Safety Commission. *Hot Rod* was the first of
six books that Felsen published for car-crazy boys, designed both to attract
a teen audience and to preach the gospel of adult responsibility. *Hot Rod* was
set in small-town America, where so many hot rodders came from, and was
built around the coming of age of Bud, a seventeen-year-old orphan who
lives with a bachelor uncle and works at the local service station. Bud is the
classic lonely hero, set in the modern world of the emerging hot-rodder. With
no social standing and indifferent grades in school, his self-esteem is built
on his one emerging talent: his mechanical skill in building the fastest car in
town, and especially his ability to handle it at death-defying speeds on country
roads. Like other boys his age, he is caught in a web of conflicting desires and
influences: wanting prestige for the one thing he is good at, driving, he finds
himself in competition with other town boys and is goaded into a road race,
fearful of losing face with his peer group if he is labeled a "chicken." He is also
eager to win the attention of an attractive but fickle girl who cares only for
being attached to the hero of the day, and who dreams of Hollywood stardom.

Against these obviously troubling values stands an understanding teacher,
intent on winning school board approval for driver's education, and an equally
sympathetic local cop. After defeating his rival in a death-defying race along

FIGURE 3.6. Cover of the popular teen novel *Hot Rod* (1950), revealing the hero and his thrilled female friend before he sees the light and becomes a mature driver.

winding country roads, Bud is arrested for speeding after a police chase. Instead of seeing him go to jail and become a hero to his immature peers, the
teacher and cop arrange for Bud to compete in a real test of manly driving:
the "Roadeo," a competition in driving skill rather than speed, in which the
winner earns a college scholarship. The story builds to a climax as Bud learns
about the dangers of racing when underaged kids who admire him kill themselves while joyriding. As the cop and teacher expect, Bud loses the Roadeo
to a cautious competitor, Chuck. Downcast by his failure—and losing his girlfriend to Ralph, a rich kid—Bud withdraws from the crowd. A group of teens,
led by Ralph and including the reluctant Chuck, pile into a hot rod for another
speed game, which inevitably culminates in a crash, killing all but the seriously
wounded Chuck. The cop and teacher talk the downhearted Bud into speeding
Chuck to the hospital in his hot rod, finally making good use of his automotive
skill and restoring his own confidence by saving Chuck's life. Chuck is unable
to go on to the state Roadeo, so Bud stands in for him, and naturally wins—
using his physical skills, but "Chuck's brain" of common sense.

Though it grows preachy by the final chapter, *Hot Rod* never demonizes the
hot-rodder. In fact, the novel lures the adolescent reader into the story with
its exciting discourse and sympathetic portrayal of the working-class Bud. At
the end, Felsen makes the book a tale of Bud's enlightenment, embracing the
driver's education ideology. And, adopting the attitude of adults who supported regulated drag strips and supervised hot-rod clubs, Felsen also offers
this closing commentary: "Young people need a chance to have fun and blow
off steam in some other way than in cars. School sports help, recreation centers
help, and so on. . . . Some youngsters need more action and excitement than
others. That's the way they're built. We have to find outlets for that energy. We
just can't tell them to sit still and be good."[84] Maybe some need drag strips and
garages to soup up their cars.

Hot Rod was just one of many coming-of-age car novels for American boys
that appeared in the 1950s and '60s. Most seem to have had similar charac-
ters and story lines: a good teen hot-rodder, often mistaken for a delinquent
by adults, is pitted against a bad hot-rodder who defies authority, commits
crimes, and, most of all, breaks the rules of orderly hot-rod competition, only
to lose in the end. All this was entirely in tune with the rhetoric and ethics of
adults who sought to cool the kids' hot rods. William Gault's *Thunder Road*
(1952) features Barney, a veteran mechanic whose talk of Marmons and Stutz
Bearcats that back in the 1920s could go eighty or eighty-five miles per hour
is met by laughter from the boys who hang around his shop. They brag that
their rods can do that in second gear. Barney replies, "If you live to become
fathers, your sons will laugh at you when you talk about speed. They'll have

jet engines." Readers learn that progress favors the young, even if it splits generations. Still, the teens respect Barney. He serves as a mentor to the good teen hot-rodders who win a track race against Rocky, the inevitable arrogant, out-of-control antagonist.[85]

In the 1960s Robert Bowen cranked out a series of teen hot rod novels. *Hot Rod Rodeo* (1964) sets the law-abiding Larry, who happily runs errands for his mom and wants to participate in an auto roadeo, against Curly Durkin, a juvenile delinquent who has done two stretches in reform school. Durkin peevishly enters the roadeo, but his wild driving wreaks havoc on other participants and reveals his lack of skill. Larry shows great self-control across the obstacle course, while Durkin is disqualified. The sequel, *Hot Rod Patrol* (1966), is equally predictable: The seventeen-year-old Ted asks the mayor to authorize a drag strip for his small hot rod club. While the mayor recalls his own days of tinkering, remembering "wistfully" that he "never owned a hot rod," the city council refuses. Ted accepts his elders' decision, but his fellow hot-rodder Sloan rants against the adult authorities and quits the hot-rod club when it accepts the mayor's offer to form a "hot rod patrol" to warn speeders and take license plate numbers of scofflaws. The rich father of another irresponsible kid, Lee, uses his newspaper to attack the "juvenile stool pigeons" on the patrol. The good kid, Ted, is accused of a crime: running another driver off the road. But it is a case of mistaken identity, and in the end Lee is nabbed for drunk driving. As did the Felsen classic, these stories of good and bad hot-rodders enticed youthful readers with much discussion of the details of customization and racing, but never avoided the heavy moral message.[86]

Theatrical hot-rod movies in the 1950s and '60s (as opposed to propaganda shorts produced with police and NHRA support) shared many of these themes, with a bias toward thrills rather than morality.[87] The often garish advertising for these films featured sexually alluring females, speed-crazed dragster males, and taglines like "Murder . . . at 120 miles per hour!" (*Dragstrip Riot*). While these posters appalled adults, the movies attracted teens, many of whom viewed them on dates at drive-in theaters. Still, movies like *Devil on Wheels* (1947) taught the dangers of speeding. *Hot Rod Girl* (1956), the title of which had nothing to do with the story, featured a "good" hot-rodder who accepts the contained thrill of an approved drag strip and is cleared of a manslaughter charge committed by a "bad" rodder. *Teenage Thunder* (1957) included a version of "chicken" as a bully cajoles a good if "troubled" teen, Johnny, into a head-on race; but the real story is about how Johnny's emotionally distant businessman father learns to relate to his teen son and to understand his enthusiasm for hot rods after Johnny beats the bully in a race at the drag strip.[88] The lesson was there to be learned in these films, even if many teens were drawn to them for the excitement of roaring engines, spinning tires, and flashing lights.

To many adults, the teen's hot rod posed a major threat to the postwar social order and to the ethos of the "republic of drivers." As a result of the mobilization of men during World War II and the affluence that followed victory, the teen gained an unprecedented autonomy, even from the racing and customizing world of young veterans. Inheriting the drive-in car culture of their elders, teens gathered to test their stripped-down and souped-up ja-lopies, to the increasing consternation of the police and authorities. Alarmed by hordes of sometimes unsafe and often overpowered hot rods operated by speed-crazed youth on American roads, these adults panicked. Teen hot-rodders threatened the regulated freedom in licensed automobility, where the only thing preventing crashes by tons of fast-moving metal was universal compliance with a maze of regulations and the willingness of drivers not only to obey the rules but to drive defensively.

Yet, rather than engaging in a massive repression, or even raising the driv-ing age to eighteen as was common elsewhere in the world, the authorities in the United States were surprisingly permissive. This may have reflected the small-town (if often suburban) setting of encounters between most hot-rodding youths and police, many of whom shared the sympathetic, even pa-ternalistic attitudes of the teacher and cop in Felsen's novel. And the pre-dominantly white skin and sometimes middle-class parentage of young hot-rodders convinced police and judges that the moral panic over kids in cars could be contained.

Allied in this cause were returning war veterans, intent on transforming the sometimes outlaw hot-rod culture of their own recent youth into a re-spectable adult hobby—countercultural to the mainstream world of Detroit's family car, but increasingly a well-ordered and in fact highly commercialized pastime of men moving up in society. In the confined but still thrilling rituals of drag racing, customizing, and engine rebuilding, cooling down the hottest of the hot rodders, Parks, Petersen, and many others offered an alternative to the risk-taking, adult-defying world of Bud in *Hot Rod*. Even more, some adults saw the teen driver not merely as a threat to the vehicular social order, but as an opportunity to inculcate a code of maturity in the age of the auto-mobile by introducing an elaborate set of values and behaviors that defined growing up with cars and the acquired right to drive them. Yet, as we shall see next, the car and its use could not be so easily contained. The motorized ve-hicle inevitably became central to the creation of a unique youth peer culture built around cruising and a "courtship" culture of "parking."

Cruising and Parking: The Peer Culture of
Teen Automobility, 1950–70

I recall seeing at the age of seventeen, on Friday nights in the spring of 1964, dozens of teen cars crawling in a circuit down Riverside Avenue and up Main Street in downtown Spokane, and feeling left out because I was driving my mother's 1956 Ford Station Wagon (no chick magnet, for sure; not that I was one) rather than the much favored 1955 or 1956 Chevrolet sedan. Of course, Riverside and Main were only one of a great many cruise routes that by the 1960s had become the stage on which millions of American teens displayed themselves and their cars. Southern California had courses that wound their way through the suburban towns of Los Angeles—Colorado and Van Nuys Boulevards to the north and Whittier Boulevard to the east, especially. There were also many other local Los Angeles routes in suburban towns like Bell, Covina, Compton, Downey, Hawthorne, Pomona, Pasadena, Riverside, San Bernardino, and Wilmington—many anchored with a distinct drive-in or two, and often the rendezvous for teen cruisers in the years after World War II when cruising took off.

Southern California was hardly alone. After the war, the main streets of market towns from Springfield, Illinois, to Newark, Delaware, attracted kids from rural areas or hamlets. In 1964 even Bellefonte, a county seat in rural central Pennsylvania with a population of about six thousand, was so crowded on Friday nights that it took an hour to traverse a ten-block course. And while a smallish city like my hometown of Spokane (about 175,000 people in the 1960s) had one central cruising course, larger towns like Columbus, Ohio, had neighborhood routes that separated ethnic and class groups, each with its own teen parade route.

But the teen's cruise was only part of the space and time carved out of the adult's world of public exchange. The kids also found private places in cars, relatively free from the peering eyes of parents and adult authority, which served as sites for the ritual of "parking" (petting or necking in cars). Many of the "parking" places were at the tops of hills, offering a "view" of the cityscape below (a not too subtle ruse when the real object of attention was much closer). These outlooks were where teens went to "watch the submarine races," a whimsical euphemism for a couple making out in a car. The steep route of Mulholland Drive north of Hollywood was just one such site, known across America as the place where Bob Cummings played the role of a "wolf" photographer of beautiful women in a 1950s TV sitcom). But my interviewees at car shows also recalled Signal Hill in Bellflower, another Los Angeles suburb, as a renowned site for making out. Others parked near the airport to "watch" planes take off and land. Often little more than a pull-off on a country road provided teens with a place to park in relative seclusion. Less private, but plentiful in the 1950s and '60s, were drive-in movie theaters where dozens of teens could neck in semidarkness while ostensibly watching a teen hot-rod or monster movie. Cruising and parking offered teens and youth opportunities unknown before the advent of the car.[1]

Beyond the mostly male realm of customizing and racing was another realm of youth in cars, where a distinct high-school peer culture thrived. On roads and in the backseats of cars, mid-twentieth-century American teens found settings of competition, communion, and sexuality. There they learned how to be one of the boys or girls, discovering the rites of social and sexual disclosure and much else. These rituals of automobility both prepared the young for modern adulthood, yet also often deferred and evaded that future. This chapter will explore how cruising defined teen male competition, and how parking transformed courtship and dating in ways that especially affected females. A little background on the postwar teen, necessarily brief and only suggestive, will be helpful in understanding the social meaning of coming of age behind the wheel.

Setting the Stage for the Cruise and Parking

During World War II, while Americans were focused on the serious job of victory, at the corner of their collective eye they noticed a troubling sign. Youths with money earned in a booming wartime economy were spending it on themselves and living it up, or so many adults thought. In 1942 the famous American sociologist Talcott Parsons coined the term "youth culture" to describe what he saw in American teens, who seemed fixed on consumption and a hedonistic denial of responsibility, living in "a self-contained world of juvenile preoccupations." This was an inversion of adult roles, which routinized work and the acceptance of family duties. After 1945, social observers increasingly saw youth as a "class" removed from the world of work and adult expectations.[2] In 1961 the sociologist Jesse Bernard reaffirmed this concern: some nineteen million children born between 1942 and 1948, an "advance guard of the great baby boom," had become teens and youth by 1960, a "leisure class of youngsters" created by affluence and an economy dependent on their spending. Yet Bernard also recognized that about half of working-class youth had left that leisure class for work and even parenting by the age of eighteen, and that the peer culture was deeply fragmented. What divided them was not, at least not overtly, politics or economics but "taste" in movies, clothing, and hairstyles. At one point, "collegiate" boys in high school wore tan raincoats, corduroy pants, and crew-necked sweaters, while their working-class counterparts wore flannel shirts and baggy pants. College-bound girls dressed in button-down blouses with pilgrim collars while working-class females wore blouses with long-wing collars under Ban-Lon sweaters. It was through these seemingly superficial differences that teens grouped themselves and excluded others, often in after-school cliques. Usually the more affluent teens prevailed in the pecking order, alienating the working class from the dominant high-school peer culture.[3]

Some evidence of these observations was gathered in a series of national surveys of 2,000 to 2,600 high-school students undertaken at Purdue University in the generation after the war. The impact of the peer culture was evident in the results of a 1948 survey, which found that 56 percent of girls and 37 percent of boys believed that there were cliques in their schools (an interesting gender difference). In the 1959 survey, only a quarter of high-schoolers agreed that fads in fashion were "silly." Reaffirming the role of youth peer culture, 59 percent agreed that the only way to develop one's personality was to have a lot of friends. In fact, 46 percent of boys and 44 percent of girls in that survey complained that they didn't go out on enough dates.[4] The postwar high school was fun for some but torture for others, offering valuable lessons in getting along and sometimes moving up, but also producing stress, disappointment, and humiliation.

It was in this context that the postwar teen car culture emerged. Though in 1960 about 1.5 million teens owned their own used cars, two years earlier 5.9 million had held drivers' licenses and had presumably access to vehicles.[5] Even as early as 1949 in the Purdue survey, parents were surprisingly permissive about letting their of-age offspring use the family car: 30 percent of fathers "usually" gave in to their pleas, and another 55 percent allowed their kids access to the car "sometimes," while mothers turned over the car with corresponding rates of 23 and 65 percent. Still, upholding a double standard, parents were more generous to their sons (30 percent of both parents saying yes "usually") while they were more restrictive with daughters (only 16 percent of dads and 18 percent of moms letting them drive the family car on a regular basis). In 1949, girls were more often expected to be "homebodies." A 1962 survey reported that 47 percent of high school students rode "around in a car with friends during the evening" at least once a week.[6] For all the imperfections of the Purdue surveys, they show a teen peer culture heavily defined by the car. A new world of relatively autonomous and free-spending youth had emerged, and from it arose a distinct culture of cruising and parking that transformed youth and the transition to adulthood.

It is difficult to determine when for teens the informal activity of "driving around in a car" became cruising along a prescribed route. In his famous "Elmwood" town study of the early 1940s, the Yale sociologist A. B. Hollingshead describes the evening "driving around" of high-school kids as "restless, random movement from one public place to another." Seeing girls on the street, boys would "drive by them slowly [and] whistle. . . . as one clique or another seeks excitement and girls." Sometimes, when boys found "girls willing to go for a ride," they drove out of town along country roads, "where they pet with varying degrees of intensity."[7] All this suggests some of the basic practices of cruising and parking, even though the sexual contacts were likely unusual and not "dates." In any case, the teen culture would fully develop only after 1945, often to the exasperation of parents and authorities.

Cruising Guys and Their Routes

The cruise helped to define the world of mechanized and mobile youth during the two generations after World War II. In his popular memoir of hot-rodding, Robert Genat recalled how he learned about the art of cruising in 1960 from his older brother when he was sixteen years old in Allen Park, Michigan, a suburb southwest of Detroit. Riding with his brother in a 1958 Chevrolet hardtop fully equipped with a 348-cubic-inch engine, exhaust cutouts, Sun tachometer, and twin glasspack mufflers which added a "throaty rumble that let everyone how this wasn't daddy's car," Genat arrived at the local A&W drive-in, thrilled to be in "the kind of car every guy wanted to be seen in." The excitement was enhanced when his brother taught him the fine points of the "art of cruising," as in how to master the right speed to pass through the drive-in, and how to catch "a reflection of the car in storefront glass" windows, presumably to impress admiring bystanders. These posturing gestures were central to cruising culture—a distinctly (mostly) male world of presentation and procession. Genat's world of dos and don'ts was well established by 1960:

Never be seen in a four-door family car, especially a Buick or a Nash; never let the car's engine stall; keep the windows all the way up or down; and maintain a look of cool indifference. If possible, you should show up with customized hubcaps, a tachometer on the steering wheel column, and even a reverberator unit added to the radio. Genat recalled how this combination was a sure-fire "chick magnet." While males went out in pairs or even singly, only females appeared in larger groups. The driver and his car were supposed to meld into a single image. The car did the speaking, overcoming the driver's youthful shyness.[8]

Over and over in interviews of men and women who participated in cruising from 1950 to the early 1980s, I heard a similar story: Cruising was mostly about males and their cars. A man who cruised around Covina, California, in the late 1950s recalled cutting a hole in his car's muffler in the hope of getting attention on the road or at the drive-in; he normally kept the hole plugged to avoid getting a ticket from police, but opened it when he wanted the noise to let everyone know that he had arrived at the cruise. Others simply removed a car's air filter for the same effect.[9]

Of course, the point was to meet members of the opposite sex, or so was the claim. A man born in 1953, from Williamsport, Pennsylvania, noted that in the back of every gearhead's mind was the notion that "the car was just a tool to attract the opposite sex."[10] While many boys certainly had their eye out for females, a man who cruised in the early 1960s admitted that, though he cruised across suburban Los Angeles "all night," he perhaps optimistically estimated that he had met girls 10 percent of the time. Another male teen who cruised San Bernardino in the same era admitted that, though there were "some girls around," even some who had their own cars, he was "too inept to pick one up." Another man, who cruised San Bernardino in the late 1950s, claimed that he lacked the money to take out females, though he owned three cars in his senior year of high school. It is pretty obvious what was more important to him.[11] Of course, teen males often took girlfriends or dates on the cruise with them. Nevertheless, a common story was that after the girl had to be brought home—often by 10 p.m., the common curfew time—the boys stayed out on the cruise past midnight.[12]

Ultimately it was the car itself that was central to the cruise, not the lad or even the hunt for the female. In a published memoir, a man recalled a typical exchange from his teens in the late 1950s: Upon entering a drive-in parking lane, a carload of boys would ask the driver of the car next to them, "What you got in it?" And then, if the other car's engine was a match with theirs, they would propose, "How about a little go?"— meaning a race. A small-town boy from Hamilton, Ohio, recalled how even in the late 1970s he was the center

FIGURE 4.1. A film still from *American Graffiti* (1973), depicting a famous scene of cruisers stopping at Mel's drive-in.

of attention on the local cruise with his 1930 Plymouth coupe, a "very radical hot rod and the fastest street car in town.[13]

As the Chuck Berry song suggested, cruising was about having "no particular place to go." And until the energy crisis of 1973, fuel, even for gas-guzzling hot-rods and muscle cars, was amazingly cheap. A man who cruised in Bellflower, California, in 1959 remembered that gasoline cost only twenty-five cents a gallon, and that with the two dollars he earned for mowing two lawns he could cruise all night despite low gas mileage. Again, this kind of activity was not restricted to the suburbs. A small-town Iowan recalled how in the mid-1970s, he and his buddies would "drive around on gravel roads and smoke stuff and drink," seldom with girls. Another rural cruiser from Southwest Missouri on the edge of the Ozarks (born in 1947) told me how he took his car on roads "as crooked as a pig's tail," driving as fast as he could for the fun of it, and surviving "some very, very close calls . . . that first six months of driving legally. The moonshiners had nothing on me and my buddy."[14] A cruiser from the early 1960s recalled how he spent weekend evenings with a band of teenage boys in the small town of Columbus, Wisconsin. Each boy contributed fifty cents to fill the gas tank and they cruised aimlessly, seldom finding girls, and telling each other "many times that we ought to be doing something better than cruising our lives away."[15] The seeming aimlessness and shallowness of this male rite is a story told again and again from the 1950s to the end of the century. It makes one wonder what really sustained cruising for so long, other than boredom and a teen lack of imagination.

But surely there's more to it. Ultimately, I think car cruising was a vehicular extension of the village stroll around the town square or up and down Main Street. And it improved on that ancient rite because the mobility of the car freed youths from the gaze of parents and family, who were often nearby and in control at the village promenade. Instead of walking, teens drove slowly up and down a wide, usually straight street, ideally one with many stoplights, all to create opportunities to meet other cruisers or bystanders. The route itself was often important. Los Angeles, the mecca of automobility, with three million cars by 1955, had well-established venues of boulevard cruising. These included Van Nuys Boulevard, which ran north of Hollywood; Colorado Boulevard, between Glendale and Pasadena); Sunset Boulevard, which traversed Hollywood; and Whittier Boulevard, especially in East Los Angeles and the eastern suburbs. All these routes on cruise nights were sites of diversity, excitement, and sometimes conflict. By the late 1970s, Van Nuys Boulevard was especially famous for its long-standing tradition of a Wednesday night cruise attracting perhaps up to forty thousand cars.[16]

Other cities had their hallowed routes as well. Detroit's Woodward Avenue, an almost ten-mile route on the eastern edge of the city extending to Royal Oak, was also a mecca for cruising youths. Until the early 1970s, Detroit teens just out of high school easily found jobs, especially in the car factories, so many could purchase cars, even new ones. Suburban cruise routes were also found on Forest Lane in Dallas and Lindbergh Boulevard in Saint Louis; smaller cities and even rural market towns that pulled in kids from neighboring villages and farms also had their weekend routes along the main streets.[17] A cruiser (born in 1968) who appeared late on the scene from a rural region south of Kansas City wrote of a "giant trail through town (six miles)" that he drove "over and over to fast food chains and the local square."[18] Different regions had their own traditions and names for cruising. In Idaho, cruising was called "dragging the gut." In my home town of Spokane, they called it "tooling the town"; an African American reference librarian at the Library of Congress recalled to me the practice of "promming" in Birmingham, Alabama, as a youth.

These routes, often well lit by streetlights and commercial neon, were alluring at night, even glamorizing cars with their headlights, often distinct rear lights, polished chrome, and lacquered paint jobs. And for youths only recently liberated from the humiliation of riding in the backseat of their parents' cars, the thrill of weaving through a labyrinth of vehicles driven by people their own age was unsurpassable. Breaking the routine of the procession were regular stops at drive-ins and empty store parking lots where informal clusters of the peer group gathered. Genat recalls that the core of Detroit's Woodward Avenue cruising route was between the Totem Pole Drive-In, in Royal Oak, and Ted's Drive-In, near Bloomfield Hills.[19] In the East Bay towns of San Leandro and Hayward, California, teens in the 1960s gravitated to "the Strip," along East 14th Street, noted for Prang's Coffee Shop and Karl's Drive-In. In 1969 a journalist described the action in Tucson, Arizona: "Cruisers, like moths and June bugs, eventually congregate around brightly lighted areas [like Johnnie's Drive-In]."[20]

Although the A&W chain of drive-ins attracted many kids with its root beer and burgers, most of the teen cruiser hangouts were locally owned and operated, at least at first. Harvey's Broiler in Downey, California, a suburb just southeast of Los Angeles, was a hangout for thousands on weekends from 1958 to 1968. At its peak of popularity, the crowds were so large there that it took twenty minutes just to drive through the parking lot. The Clock—a drive-in in Bell, California, south of Los Angeles—was famed for its links with customizers Ed Roth and Larry Watson, and was the site (according to one interviewee) where Latino/a hot-rodders encountered the paint and interior jobs that influenced the lowrider car culture of the late 1960s and '70s.[21]

The cruising tradition had hardly changed in the 1970s or 1980s. The "Strip" in the East Bay town of San Leandro in Northern California was a place to "be rowdy," according to a 1975 newspaper investigation; it was a place to go when you had no other, and many didn't. In another newspaper interview, a high-school junior considered the idea of a boardwalk as an alternative, but feared that it would bring tourists: "I wouldn't want *that*, either." The police recognized that there wasn't likely to be any alternative to the "Strip," and admitted that they only went after the troublemakers.[22] Similarly permissive was the scene on Van Nuys Boulevard on Wednesday nights, described in a November 1977 report. By then, up to twenty-five thousand youths cruised the boulevard or stood on street corners to watch the parade. A seventeen-year-old admitted, "I come down here because it's a lot better than staying at home. . . . It's the only place you can come totally broke and still have a good time." And even the chief police officer in Van Nuys could say, "It's a great American tradition out here Wednesday nights." By the 1970s, partly replacing the old hot rods and muscle cars, "wildly painted vans seem to be a favorite,

complete with plush carpeting, CB radios, and even refrigerators." A new generation of kids had appeared, with a new taste in vehicles and new technology,
but that didn't alter the ritual of the cruise.[23]

Smaller regional centers of cruising were also common into the 1980s. By
1982, for example, Goshen, Indiana, normally a quiet market town of nineteen
thousand, had a long tradition of summer weekend cruising on a five-block
circuit. Some said it dated from just after World War II, when Bower's Drive-In
famously offered good cheap burgers and Cokes, attracting teens in cars from
surrounding towns. In 1982, the local police claimed that Goshen drew cruisers from a one-hundred-mile radius. "Flame-painted vans and pickup trucks"
with blaring tape decks annoyed local merchants, who gave up on attracting
any customers on Saturday nights. A local reporter observed "two or more
halter-clad girls standing in the truck bed, holding on to the roll-bar and wav-
ing like Rose Bowl queens." As elsewhere, officials were tolerant, though, in the
hope of stopping loitering and fights, they prohibited cruisers from parking
on the streets on weekends.[24] A report of a cruise night in Cedar Rapids, Iowa
(1983), captures some of the simple adolescent sociability of the ritual: "On
one recent night about 100 youths . . . lined the street. . . . The majority seemed
satisfied with talking, yelling obscenities at both friends and foes, trying to
pick each other up, and horsing around." But soon two cops, acting at the
behest of local merchants, demanded that the kids disperse; as the teens got
back into their cars, they promised that ten minutes later they would be back.
Of course, they were.[25]

Racing and Boyish Games

At many cruise sites, a dominant feature was racing. While it was first re-
corded on Woodward Avenue in Detroit in 1895, competitive teen racing took
off there in the late 1940s. Sometimes even engineers from the car companies
competed in these races.[26] Impromptu racing took place at designated spots,
often after midnight, arranged during the many cruise encounters between
souped-up vehicles and mostly male duos, each consisting of the driver and a
pal who rode "shotgun." In South Chicago in the late 1950s, there was a two-
lane, half-mile stretch of blacktop behind Sammy's Drive-In that served as a
handy racecourse. Drivers selected two judges, one standing between two cars
ready to signal the start of a race with a dropping of arms and another judge at
the end to declare a winner. In the late 1960s, racing was reportedly more viral
at Johnnie's also south of Chicago, where teens would bring "booze to mix
with their Cokes," sometimes engage in fistfights, and race their muscle cars.

Many races began in seemingly spontaneous encounters at stoplights, where two competitors would challenged each other to a race to the next stoplight.[27]

Most of the men that I or my associate John Hoenig interviewed in the Los Angeles area repeatedly stressed the priority of racing. A cruiser from San Bernardino who had been active in the late 1950s recalled that if you had a fast car, the word got around and rivals would come looking for you. As elsewhere, the races would often take place on service roads. The kids from Baldwin Park raced on then deserted Sixth Avenue, a long, straight road. Teens would usually get "off" a few races before the sheriff showed up. Some cruisers even kept "slicks" (treadless tires, thought to be good for quick acceleration) in the trunks of their cars in anticipation of an opportunity to race.[28]

Several ex-racers reported on how surprisingly tolerant the police were. A Latino who had cruised in the late 1950s recalled that a policeman named Joe was friendly to everyone. He just wanted racers to stay away from town, where they could hurt someone. Teens competed in the open spaces between towns in the Riverside area, where orange groves were common. When one cop asked a gathering of hot-rodders what they were doing, they claimed that they were "smudging" (burning small pots of oil to keep the oranges from freezing in cold weather). The officer replied, "I hear your smudge pots"; apparently he was willing to overlook the noise of their cars preparing to race. This tolerant attitude, however, was not often shown toward teens who were not not known by police. A cruiser from Downey, southeast of Los Angeles, recalled that in the late 1960s police pulled over teens whose cars lacked fenders only if they were not from Downey.[29] At least in those early days, police often knew the cruisers personally, because most youths remained in their own towns and drove on routes where the police themselves may have cruised only a few years earlier.

This generally positive relationship with law enforcement was duplicated throughout the country in the 1950s and '60s. Especially in rural areas and small towns, the police were scarce on cruise routes, either because they had other duties or simply because, being outnumbered and having personal ties with the cruising kids, they chose not to take them on. A man born in 1947 recalled that the town marshal in a small resort town of southwestern Missouri was "invisible," except when the tourists came. Normally, he patrolled the busy highways that the teens avoided. A rural Wisconsinite (born in 1958), whose son later became a police officer, bragged that he succeeded in outrunning the law while racing on country roads—and that though he had been caught a couple of times, he had received no tickets because he was such a "good talker."[30]

The police, however, were less tolerant of teens who drove in cars that looked like hot rods, or who were racing in more densely populated areas. A female driver from near San Antonio (born in 1983) claimed that police didn't bother her until she started cruising in a Firebird (a small muscle car). The patrolman, she surmised, "must have assumed I would be male." Much earlier, a man from San Diego (born in 1940) remembered the cops as "Grinches" who "gave out tickets like toilet paper, mostly for equipment violations." He claimed that he had to join the army as a late teen because he'd lost his license due to too many traffic tickets. Still, police pressure, at least until the late 1970s, was pretty mild. Sometimes, as a small-town Ohioan (born in 1959) recalled, cops would stop near cruisers in parking lots not to harass them, but to check out their cool cars—a memory shared by a man born in 1968 in suburban Kansas City, who said that police "always admired cool cars; heck, that's what they do all day was to cruise."[31]

Still, despite this somewhat permissive climate, police surveillance and increased traffic gradually discouraged racing. Other games, dating from the 1950s but still practiced in the mid-1970s, became substitute activities. These included "popping wheelies" and leaving patches in parking lots as youths displayed their skill at fast acceleration and gear shifting. Another game was "dancing the car," accelerating and breaking in time with music blasting from the vehicle. Also surviving into the 1970s was the tradition of "mooning" (cruisers baring their backsides, often against a car window) as an act of contempt toward onlookers (winning special honor if done to an authority figure, such as a schoolteacher). In another "famous" tradition, the "Chinese fire drill" (something I admit to have done on a dare as a teen), a car would stop at an intersection or even in the middle of a street and its occupants would get out, run around the car, and get back in, occasionally leaving someone behind when the car roared off. Probably most common was catcalling, shouting insults to others from the safety of a speeding car.[32] In the early 1970s in a small mid-Michigan town, a cruiser recalled how after 11 p.m. the local town

> would roll up the sidewalks. We would park along the side of the street downtown and just talk and do a little drinking. . . . One [cruiser] left his Cutlass parked and went to get booze in another car. We lifted the back of his car up and put it on cinder blocks. He was roasted when he got back and fired up the car to leave. He put it in gear and the back tires could just spin. Took him about 15 minutes to figure out what we did. It was hilarious![33]

These rather aggressive games sometimes went further—in paired fights or even brawls. A seventy-year-old man I met at a Los Angeles LA Roadster show in 2016 admitted that when he was in high school in 1963, he went cruising around Compton as much to see the fights as to get a "piece of ass." This man had a colorful perspective on cruise-related fights. He was convinced that the cruisers from Compton had been poorer and tougher than those from neighboring Downey. Compton teens wouldn't dare go to class without switchblade knives, while Downey kids actually went to high-school dances, chaperoned by teachers. And teens from different towns did not invade each other's turf unless they were looking for a fight. The boys from Wilmington, south of Los Angeles near Long Beach, were especially tough, he claimed. Mostly sons of stevedores, they usually had dropped out of school in the eighth grade and were famous for fighting dirty. Their only rivals were the "Okies" (presumably migrants from Oklahoma) who lived in Bell Gardens. The Okies "were the only ones who could go to Wilmington and win."[34]

Curiously, the culture of the turf-defending city gangs, common in the East, blended with the cruising culture of the West. And, though suburban, the towns surrounding Los Angeles were still separate in this era, often divided from each other by farmland or orchards and composed of ethnically and economically distinct communities. My friend from Compton recalled how the emerging surf culture of the early '60s, made famous by the singing group the Beach Boys, was divided between the Heads (real surfers, with the right cars to match) and the Grammies (rich kids who pretended to surf but were really "dirt surfers," who carried the equipment and wore the fashion but were essentially fakes driving their dads' luxury cars). The cruise culture reproduced the ethnic and class conflicts of the broad society.

Cruising Girls and Cruising for Girls

Still, the most common activity was simply the automotive stroll along a path guaranteed to provide regular, if sometimes serendipitous, contact with others. The scope of male cruise encounters was always limited: going from drive-in to drive-in, occasionally running into friends or interesting strangers, showing off a new paint job, challenging a new hot rod on the strip. But cruising was also an opportunity to meet new people, especially of the opposite (or favorite) sex, from other high schools. This meant that females played an important role in an otherwise male-dominated world of cruising. A high-school friend of mine recalled how in 1964 he "tooled the town" in Spokane, fighting the traffic to get to the outside lane for a chance to call out to a carload of girls and possibly arrange a rendezvous with them on a side street. The cruise was where you heard about parties at the homes of absent parents, and where boys maybe even got girls' phone numbers.

As we have seen, this was not easy for most boys. As an interviewee in an oral history project of South Chicago youth in the 1950s noted, "So many [girls] would cruise together the possibility of pairing off was practically nil." Those guys who did get dates would show them off at the drive-ins as "proof that you had at least gone out with the girl you'd be telling stories about."[35] All this suggests that the cruise ritual was as much about near contact as about actual encounter; it was about the tease, the play of pretending to be a grown-up in a heterosexual world of dating and sex, when in fact many cruisers had neither the knowledge nor the skill to undertake the risk of self-disclosure in a real sexual encounter. The car, the movement, and the rules of exchange on the cruise all created a culture of the "almost."

This raises the question of the role of young women in this world of male presentation, procession, and posturing. The fact is that females on the cruise over many decades were more than pickups and dates. A few joined the boys in priming and painting their own cars, and some even participated in street racing from stoplight to stoplight. A woman from suburban San Antonio, who was late to the cruising game (born in 1983), as a teen had customized her Pontiac Firebird with her father. She remembered how at sixteen she had listened to "silly songs" that she played over and over, cruising with girlfriends "while we enjoyed our new freedom that day." A woman from Virginia, also born in 1983, recalled the thrill of driving her parent's 1984 Subaru Brat with her girlfriends around 2000 "so they could wave to people in town. I felt so cool." But this female assertiveness occurred much earlier. A male from southeastern Los Angeles, whom I met in 2016, reported seeing teen females "drop their pants" at stoplights in the late 1970s, "mooning" boys with much laughter. The females with their own "cool cars" who could "talk the talk" of the car culture were attractive to the males on the cruise. Somehow, he said, their entry into the "man's world" of cars at that time of emerging feminism made them more "sexy."[36]

And this behavior wasn't restricted to the comparatively liberated females of the 1970s and later. In the late 1950s, teen girls on the Southeast Side of Chicago drove by the red-light district to hoot at prostitutes on the street.[37] According to Bonnie Morris's collective memoir of Los Angeles cruisers in the 1950s, there were rules that distinguished "cheap girls" from "good" ones (the former, for example, "made out" on the beach). One former member of Morris's gang recalled cruising Sunset Boulevard with other teen girls, worrying that her companions were a little fast and that they might "lose control." Another went cruising with her "dirty dozen" girlfriends, catcalling guys and drinking beer on Hollywood Boulevard. She was "clearly on the edge." But, she recalled, "we were good-looking enough and sharp enough and popular enough so that nobody really called us on it"—an interesting observation

FIGURE 4.2. This image of a group of teen girls at a drive-in in Gary, Indiana (1957), suggests that the cruise wasn't for boys alone. Still, unlike the boys, the females traveled as a group and were probably driving a parent's car, not a hot rod. Photograph by John Vachon. *Look* Magazine Photograph Collection, Library of Congress, Prints & Photographs Division. Reproduction number LC-57-7134-CC, frame 34. Permission: Ann Vachon.

about the link between "beauty" and class. She didn't hang out with the "debate club," but, like others, could play the "good girl" by not appearing too "cheap."[38]

That didn't mean that girls in the cruise culture only postured. James Lane's oral history of youths around Chicago's Southeast Side and Northwest Indiana in the 1950s reported stories of teen girls meeting boys at drive-ins to flirt with them and even, to use modern parlance, "hook up" with them "without having to let their parents scrutinize them." And, at least according to common belief, car hops at some drive-ins, known by their dress and reputation as "hot chicks," accepted dates from teen male customers.[39]

This image of the crazy girl cruiser needs to be tempered. Doubtless more common was the experience of a woman who in 1968 had graduated from high school in St. Marys, a small town in rural northwestern Pennsylvania. Her dad, who owned a body shop, insisted that she learn about basic car operation and maintenance before getting a license. But he held to the double standard, refusing to let her get into cars with boys. When she was in her senior year of high school he gave her a car, but it was a very unfashionable Rambler. Naturally, she didn't cruise in it, but instead went with friends in other cars to meet guys at the town center. She even recalled going to drinking parties in the woods near a strip mine. At one such event, forty to fifty kids partied until the police arrived and forced them to scatter.[40] A woman shared with me a similar experience that took place much later, in the early 1990s, near Winchester, Virginia. While at the mall, she looked for parties of cruisers, which were generally held in a "middle of a field. It really was freedom, having your own car and being able to access these parties that were way out of town," free of adult control except when the cops would "come to the field to bust a kegger party."[41] It was a predictable mix of adult control and group rebellion.

Across the decades, female teens often piled into a parent's big family car (even a station wagon) to cruise. They might call out to boys, but they had protection in their numbers.[42] Group cruising also helped girls avoid the loss of reputation that cruising in the male fashion would have brought. In a 1960 Purdue survey, half of high-school girls had access to their family car, but only 3 percent owned their own. In a 1962 survey, 81 percent of high-school girls claimed to have "ridden around in a car with friends during the evening" at least occasionally, and 41 percent did so at least weekly.[43] Still, fathers often refused to let their daughters take the driver's' license test until they were at least seventeen, and few of those daughters had the jobs, and thus the money, to buy a car. The leader of the pack was still a guy at the wheel. As one woman in Lane's study put it, "The guy with his own car got the girls. . . . When a guy with his own car picked me up, he didn't have to ring the doorbell; he just revved his engine."[44] Despite a minority of hot-rod girls, this was still a male world, and not much changed between the 1950s and the 1980s.

Even as late as 2003 and 2004, along Santa Clara Street in San Jose, cruising young men hooted and catcalled groups of females on foot and in cars. This rite of sexual posturing often involved girls gathering attention in fashionable and revealing clothing as they stood or parked on the street wearing looks of "cool indifference"; this sometimes led to encounters that in turn spilled into male aggression, such as jumping into girls' cars. Amy Best interviewed female cruisers who were convinced that "guys are really aggressive during that time. [It's like] cruising gives them the right to act that way. . . ." Recognizing this danger, females entered what they perceived as male-dominated cruise zones in large groups, and even when they talked with males, they often enjoyed faking interest and giving them false phone numbers.[45] Though the boys were more aggressive than in the past—possibly a sign of more tense relations between the sexes by this time—in most ways these encounters between males and females on the cruise had hardly changed across the generations.

The cruise was an opportunity for the young of both sexes to break from the dependency of childhood, and thus it was always a threat to the prerogatives of parental authority and to adult-controlled public space. Because cruising intruded on vital public roads—often highly valued commercial and official spaces of central business districts—and sometimes disrupted traffic, local merchants sometimes demanded that police control or even ban it.

In the 1950s, notably, officials were not shy about insisting that parents limit their offspring's driving. For example, when twenty-nine teens were arrested in the small town of Boyertown, Pennsylvania, in 1959 for racing on the country roads, the local judge sent them home with letters to be signed by their parents, warning them that racing would in the future lead to punishment or even death. Southern California curfew ordinances prohibited young teens from being away from home after 10 p.m., and sometimes fined the parents for violations. The rules were seldom enforced, but a crackdown in Long Beach, California, in February 1956 resulted in fifty-four parents being fined.[46] Yet what is remarkable is how rare and sporadic these crackdowns were, as police repeatedly reassured the cruising public that the goal was not to ban this ritual but to tamp down conflicts and congestion. As we shall see in a later chapter, this would change by the mid-1970s.

Making Sense of the Cruise

The cruise played a contradictory role in American family and public life in the 1950s and after.. Academics and journalists have long associated cruising with male working-class rebellion against increasing marginalization in postwar America. But in 1960 Ralph England offered a somewhat more subtle analysis. Following sociologist Talcott Parsons, England argued that teen culture, with its own code of behavior, is separate from adults, even as this autonomy is shaped by adult values and commercial interests. The result is that teens embrace "distorted and caricatured fragments from the adult culture." Thus, the adult's car, a symbol of "responsibility," becomes a "plaything," and the competitiveness esteemed in adult society becomes a justification for racing.[47] The anthropologist Charles McCormick offers a similar if less negative argument: cruising was an expression of teens adapting to adult culture, seeking to confirm their "adult" status while also challenging predominant adult values. As a result, youth displayed contradictory behavior and attitudes, while adults expressed deep ambiguity toward cruising and its impact on their offspring's growing up.[48]

First, adults usually recognized that cruising was very similar to their own teen rituals. Cruising picked up where traditional strolling around the town square had left off as a ritual of display and courtship. It shared a common theme in American culture: a glorification of motion for its own sake. And, for parents who had matured after 1945, the cruise had often been part of their own teen experience. Finally, it shared another characteristic with adult traditions: the cruise was an escape from the city center, at least in its later suburban forms. All this made for a measure of adult toleration of the practice.[49]

Yet the cruise was also where youths protested their marginality and pow-erlessness in the adult world, and did so with that quintessential symbol of growing up: the car. This is understandable because, after all, the teen, as dis-tinct from both children and adults, emerged as a recognized social category at the same time as the car, in the early twentieth century. The modern exten-sion of schooling into high school and beyond sheltered youth from market work. But this "moratorium" on maturity, as Erik Erikson famously noted, also produced psychological tensions, especially identity crises resulting from the uncertainties of "belonging" in an emerging peer culture.[50] This meant not only a sometimes awkward teen and youth autonomy, but also rebellion, especially when teens were placed in a subordinate class or race. As a result, young people imitated and anticipated future adult gender and class roles while also protesting adult authority. In this way, the American teen's access to the car was not primarily a transition from childhood to adulthood. Instead, the car, especially on the cruise, provided "freedom" from childhood, but also a means of rebelling against adulthood.

This inevitably produced tensions between youth and adults. In particular, parents worried that familiar rites of passage into adulthood were disappear-ing. Inevitably, adult authorities attempted to restore control over youth through organized sports and the high school extracurriculum, but also, as we have seen, by taming the youth hot-rod culture. At the same time, youths appropriated the adult freedoms and privileges, denied to children, that they won through the driver's license, while subverting those same values on the cruise.[51]

In many ways this was not really new. The centuries-old customs of youth misbehavior—the rowdiness of mumming and "turning the world upside down" at village festivals—shared much with cruising behavior: disregard for traffic rules, the takeover of commercial and family space, and defiant and un-civil games like mooning and catcalling. Both the old and the new were forms of play that were traditional and imbued with conservative values (stereotyp-ical gender roles, for example), but also defiant and disruptive. The cruise is, of course, different from traditional "sowing of wild oats." The older traditions were seasonal, even confined to holidays or festivals—temporary suspensions of the rules. Cruising, like modern leisure, became a weekly event. But both kinds of activity were highly ritualistic.[52]

The cruise embodied the thrill of initiation into adult society, and of free-dom from adult constraints. Usually that pleasure was transitional, given up after a couple of years, with marriage or—until the end of conscription in 1973—with induction into the military, even if its appeal survives in "road movies," or returns for some, later in life, as nostalgia in collecting old hot rods.[53]

However ephemeral the cruise may have been, it was a serious intrusion of youth on the adult world. Indeed, youth appropriated adult space on the commercial strip. Significantly, the site of this teen defiance was not the playground or the youth's bedroom, places ceded by and ultimately controlled by adults.[54] Youth knew better. In the United States, when a kid turned sixteen and qualified for a driver's license, the car allowed the teen to colonize roads and parking lots, quintessential adult spaces. This act separated the teen from children, but also expressed defiance of adults. That commercial strip held a particular attraction because it was not only a center of adult public life, but had been created to intensify sensations and stimulate the desire to consume. These strips were "action spaces," the most exciting sites of adult life. They were sites of escape from what was often boring about being an adult: work and domesticity.[55] Commercial strips were attractive to teens precisely because they anticipated adult life or, more accurately, a part of it that was presumed to be more exhilarating and dramatic than the teens' own pasts as children.[56]

Yet teen cruisers also transformed these routes, and this was essential to their rebellion. They usually used them not to shop or dine, but to engage in a series of peer rituals for which the roads were obviously not designed. The car on the cruise made breaking the rules—for example, by drinking in the back seat—fairly easy. When cruisers gathered in large numbers, they could, with a bit of risk-taking, flout the police. Cruisers could make lewd comments to members of the opposite sex, dress and act sexually in tight clothes, and make suggestive gestures. But this was more than mere defiance of adult norms. Kids in cars could present themselves to each other in ways very different from what prevailed in school hallways or in class. The cruise route was a place where teens could be free of any reminders of homework, vice-principal–patrolled hallways, household chores, quizzical parents, and disapproving eyes. As teens crowded into spaces poorly controlled by adults, they could be "themselves." No longer obliged to sit up straight as in class, cruisers could be "cool," slouching in their cars. Finally, like the nineteenth-century urban *flâneurs*,[57] youths who purchased a look and identity in avant-garde clothing and displayed it on the anonymous street, modern cruisers could display themselves through their "cool cars." The cruise transformed adult spaces into teen spaces.[58]

Along with space, the cruise transformed and appropriated time, liberating a few hours every week when teens suspended or challenged the normal routine of commerce. It was a time for short bursts of serendipitous encounters, a break from long and often arduous durations of academic concentration. To the outsider the flitting from one drive-in to another, the traversing of the same route a dozen or more times an evening, may have seemed pointless, but to the cruiser it was often time spent free from the "chains of everyday life."[59]

In all, the cruise both imitated and mocked adult life. Adults quite naturally reacted to it with similar ambiguity. For two generations or so, authorities recognized in the cruise a game similar to the one they had played as teens, a putting on of adult life with usually a modest degree of "prankish" rebellion. Elders could tolerate the "stylistic other"—as McCormick called those teens who displayed generationally distinct dress, hair, music, and car preference—because most of them recognized that these minor acts of rebellion were a part of youths' need to differentiate themselves from those who had preceded them (though many adults resisted this insight). Yet, as we shall see later, the "structural other," those cruising youths whom adults in charge didn't recognize as "their own" children—youth of different classes, ethnicities, or races "invading" the route—were often not accepted, and were even persecuted.[60] When the cruise was contained in space and time, and when the "crowd" did not overwhelm or threaten adult merchants, cops, or residents, it often was tolerated. In the long run this toleration broke down, first in populated anonymous places, but later in small-town and rural areas. Still, the mobility and freedom provided by the car on the cruise took a long time to abandon. The cruise was a site of liberation as well as risk, a time and place that adults accepted but ultimately could not tolerate. This ambiguity was even more apparent with regard to a second rite of the teen car culture: "parking."

Parking: Dating and Danger

Just off major roads, often at scenic lookouts, young couples found the privacy to "neck" in parked cars. A little-documented part in the history of the twentieth-century "dating" culture, the ritual and myths of parking bring together the evolving story of the automobile and youth sexuality. In the early twentieth century, dating had become a ritual of unsupervised and open-ended but quasiformal public recreational encounters between the sexes. It gradually replaced home-centered, parent-supervised courtship. In contrast to the older courtship system of the middle and upper classes, in which sexual contact had usually been limited and delayed until after marriage, dating led step-by-step to increased intimacy, and even intercourse, prior to nuptials. As the mid-century sociologist Paul Landes observes, with modern dating, "mate selection" rested almost entirely on "teen-agers themselves."[61]

But dating itself changed over time. As historian Beth Bailey notes, its practice shifted to younger couples. An early feature of dating was a succession of casual partners before any pair bond decision. Another part was the so-called rating-and-dating system that minimized intimacy and encouraged participants to choose partners based on social status. This was partially supplanted in the 1940s by a dating system that featured early decisions to "go steady," a ritual in which couples met exclusively for a prolonged period, which sometimes led to engagement and marriage, and which often involved a gradual progression toward "advanced" sexual relations. The date, with its sexual implications, and its shift from older to younger youth, coincided with the emergence of a high-school based peer culture in the 1930s and '40s. The result was that the cauldron of raging teen hormones was far more heated with the liberating mobility and seclusion of the teen-driven car.[62]

By the 1950s, teen dating had become a preoccupation of survey takers and sociologists, social commentators, and advice givers. The Purdue Opinion Panel found that young Americans were comfortable with dating, even going steady, although parents often did not agree. In a 1949 survey, 44 percent of teens approved of "going steady," and almost 90 percent of boys and 75 percent of girls thought necking or even petting was at least sometimes acceptable. By contrast, only 58 percent of their mothers accepted going steady for boys, and fewer still (39 percent) approved of it for their daughters. For fathers, the numbers were even lower for their daughters (32 percent) but higher for their sons (70 percent).[63]

By 1959, only 17 percent of high-schoolers thought that they were too young to go steady, and fully 65 percent of twelfth-graders admitted to having embraced the practice. Almost half "probably accepted" the idea of high-school seniors considering marriage. By 1961, 48 percent of teens surveyed thought that fourteen-year-old girls were ready for dating, as compared to only 16 percent in a 1948 survey.[64]

These findings were confirmed by Gilbert Youth Research in 1956 in a study that found that Chicago girls began dating at fourteen and a half, on average, and that they believed going steady was acceptable at fifteen years of age. Boys agreed with them, and in fact preferred going steady to the insecurities and stresses of finding girls to ask out.[65] All this meant that the age of access to the car keys coincided with a lowering of the age of romance.

This trend toward earlier dating and going steady surely increased the anxiety of adults, especially as the practice was descending to junior-high-school kids. No doubt parents would have preferred that their offspring continue the more casual and less sexually and emotionally charged rating-and-dating system they may have experienced as teens.[66] When the sociologist Ira Reiss in 1960 noted a trend toward "petting with affection," if not necessarily "going

all the way," among older teens in "steady" relationships, he was only stating
the obvious.[67] What parent would not be disturbed, especially when sex at
younger ages was combined with the privacy and mobility of the car?

This made all the more important the imposition of a number of widely
accepted but unwritten "rules" along the way to "going all the way." Winifred
Breines's memoir of her teen years in the late 1950s recalls the progression: a
good-night kiss on the second or third date, kissing and fondling above the
waist and "on the outside" if "pinning" (going steady) was imminent, and
"inside" and below if already pinned. Boys had an elaborate progressive set
of expectations: From fondling a covered breast, to French kissing and un-
covering the breast, to "dry humping," followed by digital insertion. For boys,
petting was often a rating game, like the original meaning of the term "make
out" (dating from 1944) that referred to business success.[68] The more one "got,"
the greater one's prestige among peers. But of course this went along with an
attitude that girls who "gave in" too early in the progression were not "steady"
or girlfriend material. Inevitably, this put the girl in a bind. To be a success, she
had to be popular with boys, but this meant to be "pleasing without giving too
much of herself." As the anthropologist Margaret Mead explained, "the boy is
expected to ask for as much as possible, the girl to yield as little as possible."[69]
The rules changed, of course, when a couple went "steady," and even then, in
the 1950s, many girls remained "technical virgins."[70] All this inevitably was
confusing and stressful for both sexes, but especially for the female. And it
became all the more so in the private and unprotected setting of the car parked
in some dark and even remote location.

Not surprisingly, the automobile as a potential site for "premature" youth
sex was at the heart of a postwar "moral panic" over teens with cars. In the
1950s, widely publicized teen "going wild" films (see chapters 3 and 5) exploited the widespread perception that parents and adult authorities were
losing control over youth not only in cities, but also in the presumably upstanding confines of suburbia.[71] Lurid reports of teen sex clubs appeared in
the *Chicago Tribune*, involving both urban (probably black) teens and white
middle-class suburban teens meeting in cars gathered at remote sites.[72]

But a greater concern was the dangers of "lovers' lanes" and their attraction
to teens in vehicles. These sites and the goings-on there have a long history,
rooted in the development of the "closed car," which replaced open-top vehicles in the decade after 1918, and the opportunity that such an auto presumably provided "loose women" as a "room protected from the weather [that]
could be moved at will into a darkened byway or a country lane," as the famous
chronicler Frederick Allen wrote in 1931.[73] As early as 1920, a news report told a

FIGURE 4.3. A young couple necking in a car after the prom (1953). Used with permission of Getty Images.

lurid tale: a Chicago dry goods merchant having sex with a married woman in his car was killed by a robber.[74] In 1928 a thirty-two-year-old lawyer who lived with his mother shot a "stenographer" and himself while they were parked together on a lover's lane in Brooklyn, apparently when she refused a kiss. Other stories of the robbery or murder of unsuspecting couples on lover's lanes appeared in the press from the 1930s through the 1950s. In October 1955 a gang of five teens robbed ten cars on a lovers' lane in Palos Verdes, California; they were finally caught after ripping the clothing from a thirteen-year-old girl and subjecting her to "multiple attacks" (presumably a euphemism for rape). An especially prominent case was that of Carl Chessman, who accosted teens on a Los Angeles lovers' lane in 1948. He was sentenced to death—and executed in 1960 after a long, well publicized appeal—for kidnapping and forcing two females into "acts of sexual depravity."[75]

Perhaps the most famous example of the terrors of lovers' lanes is the case of the "Texarkana Moonlight Murders," in a border town between Texas and Arkansas in early 1946. Beginning with an assault on a parked couple and the rape of the young woman, the "Texarkana Phantom Killer" later attacked three more couples (two parked on country roads), killing three men and two women. These events sparked a panic as local people armed themselves and police undertook a mass hunt for the attacker. Widely publicized nationally, the Moonlight Murders became the subject of a lurid movie in 1977, *The Town that Dreaded Sundown.*[76]

Though these stories did not always involve teens—but often instead adulterous couples or even prostitutes[77]—they served to stigmatize the lovers' lane as a site of danger and depravity. What teen would not have second thoughts about an amorous hour "watching the submarine races" after reading accounts of robbers impersonating police officers on lovers' lanes?[78] Or after reading about a nineteen-year-old "psychoneurotic on leave from a mental institution" (1955) attacking a teen male and his thirteen-year-old girlfriend at a Los Angeles make-out spot, kidnapping the girl and ripping off her clothes?[79] Other stories were perhaps even more harrowing, like that of the "respectable" thirty-four-year-old veteran from Bowling Green, Ohio, who was jailed for repeatedly throwing acid in the eyes of high-school couples parked on a dark road, in an effort to sexually assault teen girls.[80] Often the stories referred to "pretty" or "attractive" female victims, and to the middle-class and youthful backgrounds of the perpetrators and their prey.[81] Others suggested that girls who habituated lovers' lanes later were seen appearing in "burlesque theaters."[82] Such cautionary tales made lovers' lanes seem scary to middle-class kids; and occasionally they were. Still, even if the oft-repeated accounts of worried adults were true, this hardly stopped teens from venturing to them.

Perhaps the most lurid of the panics over parking came from Shailer Lawton and Jules Archer, a Vermont doctor and a professor at a small college, in their book *Sexual Conduct of the Teenager* (1951). They quote a Massachusetts policeman saying, "Our biggest trouble with teenagers is in connection with parked cars." The cop noted that if his colleagues found parked teens "in any stage of undress," they arrested them for "disorderly conduct" and called their parents. Lawton and Archer fumed, "There isn't a city, town, or country area in the nation where teen-agers do not attempt to escape from adult supervision in parked cars for purposes of petting or sexual intercourse." Though police claimed that parked teens were in danger of rape and robbery in lovers' lanes, Lawton and Archer's main concern was that teens in the privacy of their cars were subject to "mounting sexual tension," and that in such unsupervised settings "most boys let their hands do the talking for them." Most teen sex, police told these authors, took place in dark vehicles in dark places: "Any protest the girl may feel inside is quickly softened by the environment and she realizes that she wouldn't be heard by anyone even if she felt desperate enough to scream."[83]

Automobile Sexuality: Codes and Gender Power

The dating culture, especially set in the teen's car, was fraught with ambiguity and stress. It involved inexperienced, emotionally volatile, but also shy and insecure teens playing distinct and often conflicting gender roles, and it often put the girl at a disadvantage. Shaping teen attitudes and behavior was advice from peers, parents, and the media, including warnings of the allure and dangers of lovers' lanes. Perhaps in a culture that increasingly expected expert personal advice (for childrearing, social manners, and personal success), it's no surprise that dating manuals were published for teens. It's hard to tell who read them. I suspect, by their contents and authorship, that most of the readers were female and middle-class. In any case, the manuals reveal both changing adult attitudes and the often perplexing dilemmas of youth in mid-century America.

Unlike the advice books directed toward youth of earlier generations, the dating manuals of Evelyn Duvall and the advice columns by Joan Beck or Sheila Daly were not overtly moralistic or religious. The advice book offered by the singer and evangelical Pat Boone warned that kissing for fun was "like playing with a beautiful candle in a roomful of dynamite";[84] still, he attempted to be understanding of teen dilemmas. And while these writers upheld traditional gender expectations, they focused on preparing teens for well-adjusted adulthood in loving marriages, with minimal stresses or emotional and sexual calamities. They even adapted a little with the times, becoming more tolerant of "petting with affection" by the 1960s.[85]

Duvall's 1950 manual offered a good summary of mainstream views of the time. She assured her young readers that "loving another is fine, and fun too," but that society now demanded far more responsibility from young couple. No longer were there chaperones or the eyes of gossipy neighbors to protect the young from themselves; "the automobile changed all that." Couples met outside the worlds of relatives and parents, and the car provided an "intimate privacy that invites love-making." Car dating required "considerable know-how as well as know-why."[86] Newspaper advice columns sometimes were even more cautionary, warning of the dangers of a steady male date who expected "special privileges," and of the temptation of the couple "going too far." These columns alerted young readers to the dangers of petting, warning that such activity would lead to a loss of reputation, eventually being shut out of the dating market and an invitation to the prom.[87]

All this placed burdens on the teen, but especially on the girl: "When you step into a car you are just as responsible as the [male] driver for what goes on." This included not only knowing that "speeding is murder," but the dangers of sexual tension. The trick was to take one's time and understand the process. This was easier said than done, because petting meant doing "what is sexually stimulating," and this "makes the couple ready for full sexual intercourse." While in marriage this was an "uninterrupted" process, Duvall noted, for the teen it was dangerous and the teen had to know how to stop.[88] Moreover, the same "physical involvement" applied whether the boy was just seeing how far he could go or was deeply in love. And once a certain stage had been reached, it became habitual, and then it would be difficult for the couple to turn back. Understanding and controlling this process was no easy task.[89]

Once again, for Duvall and other advisors that job fell mostly on the girl. This went back to old Victorian assumptions that the female was "more slowly aroused," as Duvall put it, and thus was more in control and more rational. As Beck added, "She bears most of the stigma of pregnancy." And, though boys should be on guard to realize that girls could be provocative without realizing it, most of the advice was directed toward the girl. The female was to slow the boy down without hurting his feelings. She might say, for example, "Oh, you're too much for me," while pushing him aside.[90] And of course it was the girl's responsibility to say no to parking.[91]

The male advantage, of course, had a lot to do with the fact that it was he who usually owned and drove the car and decided where to go. A Purdue survey in 1959 confirmed the advantage of males with cars: 78 percent of boys were convinced that "a car helps a boy to get dates." The car made the female subject to the male driver, and required her to display skill and finesse in controlling sexual contact.[92] Girls, as the writer Barbara Ehrenreich remembers from her teen years in the late 1950s, had to be "enforcers of purity . . . drawing the line of overeager boys. . . ." The girl who wanted to be popular had to be attractive and still have a reputation, and this meant that she had to be "crafty, cool and careful."[93]

Especially troublesome was the male-dominated space of the car. Historians have noted how the early automobile offered women opportunities for freedom from the groping and leering of men on trains and trams, and even a measure of mobile independence. Still, the auto soon became a man's machine, and its interior—as opposed to the porch swing of Victorian times, which was easily surveyed by parents—became a potential site of male sexual aggression. The legal scholar Carol Sanger claims that the association of the car with private domestic space has meant that courts often found that when a woman got into a man's car, she gave "a proxy for consent to sex." The private space of the home and car has, at least in the past, been a "place where battery and rape have been permissible" (as opposed to the street or other public places, where presumably women have not "volunteered" to engage in private relationships). This may explain why Robert and Helen Lynd, in their 1929 study of "Middletown," reported that teen girls who willingly rode in cars with boys sometimes were placed under court supervision. In 1947 the University of Michigan not only suspended a male student who had raped a female student in the back seat of a car, but also suspended the woman for conduct "not a credit to herself nor to the university." A rape conviction has required evidence of resistance, something difficult to prove about acts in a closed car; moreover, because the car seemed to signify consent to sex if the female climbed in freely, as late as the 1980s some courts still assumed that females who had just entered a car with a male were "asking for it."[94]

Still, there were restraints on male sexual advances. As recalled in Lane's oral histories from the steel towns of South Chicago and Calumet City, "double or triple dates were common because fewer people had cars," Still, this custom was preferred two-to-one over single-couple car dates in 1959, probably because the presence of another couple reduced sexual tension and male aggression. Double-dating provided witnesses to ward off gossip. And intercourse in the 1950s and '60s had special consequences beyond pregnancy. Any female who had sex with a boyfriend would be expected to marry him, "because it would be so hard to face another guy and not be a virgin."[95]

Besides relying on peer pressure to show constraint, parents also tried to fence in car sexuality. In a 1952 national survey of high-school students, 75 percent believed that their parents wanted to know "quite a lot" about the people they dated.[96] Fathers in Lane's study of teens in the 1950s and early '60s, especially those from traditional ethnic Italian families, attempted to impose curfews, demanding that their daughters be home by 10 p.m. One girl's parent grilled the boy about his grades, church attendance, and intentions, reminding him of a 9 p.m. curfew. Another girl reported that she had to park (and presumably neck) in her parents' driveway. "Mom would flash on and off the lights to signal me to come inside." A woman from Covina, California, who graduated from high school in 1964, recalled a rather strict upbringing: her parents did not allow her to date at night, definitely not to go to a drive-in with a boy; and they insisted that a brother or another couple accompany her on a daytime rendezvous with a boy. Mothers from her town accompanied groups of girls to community dances while the boys followed in their own cars.[97] At least some of the chaperone system had survived into the 1950s and early 1960s.

These cases were doubtless a bit extreme. As we have seen, by the 1950s going steady was common, and many couples began dating exclusively after just a few dates. Such pairs rode together, almost always in the guy's car, with the girl sitting conspicuously close to the driver on the car's bench-style front

seat. Physical contact was presumed. Moreover, despite curfews, Lane's interviews found that there were plenty of opportunities for escape from parental
prying: after summer dances sponsored by the "Y" or ethnic groups, carloads
of teens gathered around bonfires on the beaches of Lake Michigan (in a 1952
report, the parties included mixed "skinny dipping"). But most of the action
was in the car, which was required to "get around and, more important, make
out in," recalled a man in Lane's study. Even a steel mill that would light up
when the mill "tapped a heat" was an attractive site for viewing while sitting
close to the opposite sex in the dark. Police often ignored curfews and other
laws if the teens left their parking lights on. When officers announced on
loudspeakers at 11 p.m. that all under eighteen years of age were in violation
of the curfew, some parkers on Bobby Beach "would run like chickens," but
others called the cops' bluff and stayed.[98]

According to common belief, "scoring" quickly came to guys who picked
up girls from outside their own neighborhoods, who more often were "loose
as a goose" types, often poor loners, and less subject to local peer pressure.
Despite the braggadocio of a boy who claimed that he knew how to "strike fast
before the girl knew what hit her," and that he had mastered the "art" of how to
"flip open a bra with the snap of the finger," most boys demurred from pushing
girls they "respected." Usually the "decent" girl successfully resisted going "too
far," at least until she was well down the dating trail. Otherwise, few boys ever
got much past "second base" (fondling a breast). Referring to his girlfriend,
one teen male recalled that it "took a year eating burgers and going to movies to get in her pants." In large measure, the word of the advice books was
heeded. Neither the boy nor the girl wanted the girl to be "damaged goods."[99]

This pattern was, of course, not restricted to the upper Midwest focus of
Lane's study. Though interviewees were often vague about the details of their
parking experiences, a Latino born in 1948 into a working-class neighborhood
in San Antonio, Texas, is particularly suggestive. He recalled borrowing his
dad's station wagon and asking his dates if they wanted to "go over and watch
the planes land" at the airport. On a double date with his cousin he sat in the
backseat with his date, learning the arts of making out from his older cousin,
who was seated in front. Still, Hispanic parents lurked in the background,
prohibiting the practice of going steady, and expecting guys to marry by the
time they were twenty-five, soon after their military obligation.[100] The car was
liberating, but parents still called the shots.

The role of the car in initiating sexual contact extended to middle-class
neighborhoods. A male from my high-school class of 1964, who was well-
rooted in the "soc" or bourgeois culture of the time, recalled that he viewed
the driver's license as a permit to have sex. This made possible necking and

petting at parking areas, often after a dance or movie and before the girl was supposed to be back home. Spokane had a number of these sites, mostly located at lookout points above the town where the boy could invite the girl to see the "view." Activities varied depending on the "type" of girl ("fast" or "slow"), how long the couple had known each other, and whether there was a double date. Though these bourgeois fathers may have been more indirect than the working-class dads Lane recalled, they definitely drew the line on the issue of when their daughters had to be home.[101]

I was struck by the manner-of-factness, as well as the innocence, of many recollections of parking. An older man, born in 1937 in rural Washington state, noted that at Saturday night Grange dances, while girls and boys arrived separately by car, "some snuck out to the cars for a kiss or two." A rural boy from Wisconsin, born in 1958, remembered a typical weekend evening: "Pick up my girlfriend and park." And a still younger Oklahoman who was born in 1963 described an evening of cruising as a teen, racing the quarter mile north of town; "if we had a date, we might head to the woods for a little while," he recalled.[102] With the car, teen boys expected "a kiss or two," but it also often confined sexuality to foreplay. In fact, the car was as site as much of sexual constraint as of liberation.

This gradually changed, of course, as premarital and casual intercourse became more accepted in the late 1960s, and especially in the 1970s among college youth.[103] And this promiscuity certainly trickled down to high school. Even a lad who parked in the late 1980s in a small Oklahoma town could joke in an online interview: "Big back seat. Need I say more?? LOL!!" But, as we will note later, this shift seems to have been accompanied by a decline in making out in cars.[104]

The liberated spaces that American youths at mid-century carved out of their adult-controlled environments with their cars defined their coming of age in ways that broke sharply from the past. These spaces, the very public cruise route and the semiprivate lovers' lane, created opportunities to act out adult roles while also rejecting adult authority. Parents and the law struggled to understand and to hem in these spaces, tolerating cruises and offering empathetic advice to parkers while regulating the routes and demonizing lovers' lanes. Teens, especially boys, found freedom on their cruises, opportunities to express themselves and expand their peer group contacts, to compete in displaying and sometimes racing their cars, and even to learn the arts of sexuality. Despite its frequent disappointments, the cruise remained for many a positive memory and a subject of nostalgia later in life. Parking was more often a dream than a reality. It was an activity defined as much by constraint, anxiety (especially of the female), and awkwardness as by thrill, pleasure, and

satisfaction. In any case, parking shaped the emerging sexuality of several generations of American youth. Cruising and parking tell us a lot about growing
up with cars in the middle of the twentieth century. There is, however, another plane to explore: the impact of class and ethnicity on determining the
American teen car culture.

Greasers and Their Rods: Two Generations of Exclusion and Pride

When I was fourteen, a freshman in high school, and a member of the senior class of the baby boom, because of overcrowded schools I was obliged to ride a bus across Spokane (a city of about 170,000) from my lower-middle-class sector of town to the working-class quadrant, often called Hillyard. There I attended John Rogers High School, very different from the school closer to home that I would go back to in the tenth grade. Of students at Rogers, only 11 percent went to college in 1961 (compared to about 65 percent from the high school near my home). I was in a different world, and on the first day of class, toughs guarded the school doors demanding a dime in tribute to enter. I took metal and wood shop, mostly because my divorced mom thought I needed to learn some masculine skills. There I met white working-class greasers. We had little in common. But I got to know them more in band class, where I played in the drum section and had time to talk with fellow drummers while the band director was rehearsing with the more skilled clarinet section. A junior named Gary Freeman was the leading drummer . . . and also a hot-rodder. He was hardly the confused and angry James Dean from *Rebel without a Cause*, but rather exuded a quiet confidence and knowledgeable in the arts of custom-izing and powering up his late 1930s Ford. He and others spoke in an arcane slang with lots of words for "cool." Unlike the scary toughs guarding the doors or hanging out at the Pirate, the soda fountain across the street, Gary was tolerant of me, the nerdy outsider whose mom was an art teacher. In fact, he was protective. Later I heard that he had died in a crash. I never learned the details, but to me Gary thereafter seemed to represent the fading culture of the greaser—and I use the term without the pejorative connotations often associated with it. This was not because of his slicked-down hair or his black leather jacket (the common image of the greaser), but because of his craft and culture.

This was 1961, a year before the setting of George Lucas's nostalgic 1973 film *American Graffiti*. Lucas's characterization of the overaged greaser John Milner, with his '32 Ford, struck me as condescending. Milner was portrayed as a loser whose time had passed him by. No longer a teen, he should have moved on to adulthood and abandoned the cruise scene. Milner represented the end of the "greaser" era; in the movie we are told that he died in a car crash in 1964, just as my friend Gary did two years earlier. By the mid-1960s the hot-rodding greaser was giving way on the cruising trail to more middle-class types like *American Graffiti*'s Steven Bolander (played by Ron Howard, who also portrayed the clean-cut teen in the nostalgic TV series *Happy Days*). In the film, Bolander drove a 1958 Chevy Impala. He was hardly the working-class gearhead, but rather was the college-bound president of his class (though, in this coming-of-age story, he ended up staying home with his girlfriend and selling insurance, like Robert Young's character in *Father Knows Best*).[1] Bolander represented the aspiring middle-class kid. His car didn't have a souped-up engine, only moderate "decking." Howard's character reminded me of another kid I knew from the drum section from junior high through high school, the more middle-class school I returned to in the tenth grade. The son of a successful real estate salesman, he joined the social elite by high school; and when he was sixteen in 1963, his dad gave him his three-year-old Buick to drive his girl to the proms, school dances, and private parties. Unlike Steve Bolander in the movie, he didn't stay home, though he didn't go far. He became a successful businessman, and today he has four houses on the Washington coast. Cars and class seem to go together in youth as well as adulthood.

But the John Milners didn't all disappear in the mid-60s, nor did they all stick with their Deuce coupes. Earlier, some had abandoned the 1930s Fords, with their flathead V8 engines, for "lead sleds": Mercurys, mostly powered with overhead valve engines. A younger set, who came of age in the late '60s and '70s, moved on to the muscle cars that Detroit designed in imitation of the souped-up hot rods. The often-told story of how automakers introduced the muscle car perhaps represents the peak of greaser influence. Beginning in the early '60s, Detroit car designers went down to Woodward Avenue to watch and learn from the kids cruising in their stock cars with overpowered engines. In 1964, John DeLorean at GM adapted the kids' strategy to the Pontiac GTO, a 325-horsepower engine inserted into Pontiac's relatively small Tempest body.[2] Other muscle cars followed, like the Oldsmobile 442 (1964), the Plymouth Roadrunner (1968), and the Ford Torino (1968). Complementing this trend was the introduction of small, high-horsepower "pony" cars designed for young buyers—like the Ford Mustang (1964) along with the Plymouth Barracuda (1964), the Chevrolet Camaro (1966), and the Pontiac

Firebird and Trans Am (1967).[3] By 1970, competition between the Big Three car companies led to "factory hot rods" with 400-horsepower engines that appealed to the new generation of car-crazed youth.[4] Into the 1970s, the weekend cruise passed from one generation to the next at cruise sites throughout the country.[5] By the middle of that decade, gearheads were abandoning muscle cars for custom-painted vans or pickups. Some had citizen's band radios and powerful cassette-playing audio systems.

Another important variant on the 1970s gearhead was a more middle-class group of "hippie" youths who took great pride in keeping their aging VW "Beetles" working on the cheap. I had one such car (bought, when I lived in Milwaukee, with plywood over the rusty floor, apparently due to its having spent its youth on Buffalo's salted winter streets). Other youths, following the counterculture of the late 1960s, held onto old VW vans, some of which had peace signs painted on the front.[6] Despite change in vehicles, the ritual of customizing and cruising continued with the new generation.

Even in the 1980s—especially in smaller towns like Goshen, Indiana—a cruising tradition two generations old continued as the working-class youth with a hot car who maybe wasn't a big football star could still make it big on the cruise route.[7] An ethnography of a Chicago-area high school in the mid-1970s found thriving subcultures of "greasers." They seemed to "channel" the culture and customs of their 1950s predecessors. Though mostly nonviolent, they were not engaged in the school's extracurricular activities, nor did they attend school dances. Instead, these latter-day greasers were content to mill around auto shops, cruise, drink, and sometimes get into trouble with police on weekends. Though most of the greasers were white, some were black, and virtually all were working-class. Their identity remained centered on the car, of course, and many dreamed of owning customizing or repair shops after finishing high school.[8]

Notwithstanding this multigenerational story of the greaser, the image of John Milner as stuck in the 1950s has stuck with us. This is in part because the media have reinforced a stereotype and, through reruns, have perpetuated it. Despite the efforts of the NHRA and Robert Petersen's magazine empire to legitimize the hot rod (chapter 3), high-school greasers remained alternatively feared and pitied throughout their history. The film *Rebel without a Cause* (featuring James Dean as a middle-class teen hero with incompetent parents) introduced a violent image of youth as alienated thrill seekers without purpose.[9] This theme was repeatedly exploited in a "cycle" of hot rod movies that ran from 1956 to 1958, known as much for their garish publicity posters and titles as for their story lines. *Dragstrip Girl* suggested the powerful combination of unleashed speed and sex. The advertisement for the film screamed:

FIGURE 5.1. This movie poster reveals more about the stereotypes of adults (and some teens) regarding hot-rodders than about the actual content of the movie, which was in fact quite conventional and even bland. *Hot Rod Girl* (1957), American International Pictures.

"Car Crazy! Speed Crazy! Boy Crazy!" and featured an image of a greaser male embracing a reclined full-bosomed blonde female. *Hot Rod Girl* exploited adult anxieties about the raw sexuality of rock music, and featured out-of-control hot-rodders racing and playing "chicken." Later, *Hot Rod Hell* (1967) featured the A-list stars Dana Andrews and Jeanne Crain as a middle-class couple terrorized by a pair of dragsters even as their daughter is fascinated by the leader of the gang.[10] As the film historian Peter Stanfield notes, "The films and the advertising both depended on a schizophrenic conception of the teenager as not only a valued consumer but also a figure to be held in some dread."[11]

I would like to paint a rather different picture, perhaps more in tune with my memories of that year at John Rogers High School in 1960–61, but I think also more accurate. To reach a more nuanced and balanced understanding of the working-class greaser, we need to pause a moment to reconsider how he came of age with cars and high school. Cars gave these marginal youth an opportunity to define themselves apart from the prevailing society of the white middle class, even as members of that majority often pigeonholed them by their cars. By the time of the teen car, class distinctions were learned no longer primarily in the workplace, but also in high school and the surrounding extracurriculum. Owning and transforming a vehicle offered mostly white kids, from families lacking the money or culture for full participation in high school and college, a token of dignity, a check on the humiliations of the classroom and on the club and sports culture of high school that favored the white middle class. Through auto shop courses, part-time jobs in auto repair shops, and fathers passing down manual skills to sons, mostly white working-class youths developed a positive "greaser" culture of hot rods and cruising, thus compensating for what Richard Sennett and Jonathan Cobb have called the "hidden injuries of class," even as more affluent teachers and college-bound students looked down on them. The customized car offered a token of dignity to a group that had always been subordinate, but which in the mid-twentieth century was steadily losing ground.

The Greaser, High School, and Class

The greaser was a product of changes in the mostly white American working class that straddled several rising generations across the mid-twentieth century. He often came from small-town settings where the skills and pride of a manual craft culture still survived thanks to the mechanical features of the easy-to-modify passenger car. At the same time, those skills were not valued, especially in the setting of the American high school. This institution expanded to accommodate virtually every American teenager, with required attendance until age sixteen in most places. Nevertheless, the high school often retained its roots as a college preparatory institution with strong middle-class social and intellectual biases. Moreover, high schools as comprehensive institutions included students from different social and economic backgrounds, especially in towns where there was only one such school. This often produced subcultures of distinct peer groups. At the top stood the "preppies," sometimes also called "rahs" or "socs" (short for sociables, often members of shadowy social clubs), and below were the greasers (sometimes called "hitters"), along with intermediate groups. Whereas the socs were simultaneously conformist (adaptable to fashion dictates of the student elite) and aspiring (embracing adult-sponsored extracurriculum and driven to win good, if not stellar, report cards), greasers were often disengaged from school and rebellious against middle-class disparagement. They often faced an uncertain future of manual work under a boss. Although much greaser activity took place beyond the high school, their culture is incomprehensible without high school.

The high school was a relatively new and rapidly evolving institution in the 1930s when working-class youth car culture emerged. Although high schools originated in Boston in 1821, as late as 1901 they graduated only 6.1 percent of seventeen-year olds. Early high schools primarily prepared the middle class for college.[12] Working-class teens, especially boys, still were apprenticed or, more commonly, employed in menial jobs. However, high-school enrollment expanded dramatically in the following decades, with almost 29 percent of American teens graduating by 1930. High schools, however, were slow to expand beyond college preparatory courses: in 1928 only 13.5 percent of students took courses in industrial arts and 11 percent in bookkeeping, compared to 93 percent in English and 25 percent in algebra.[13] Still, high school was increasingly a part of the experience of most American youth. Most, including the children of manual laborers, attended for some time and were influenced by that experience, though many dropped out at the age of sixteen. High school then became a place where the social classes often mixed, and where class distinctions were learned.[14]

While curriculum was important, high school was also the setting for new peer groups that gathered outside the classroom. These groups set teens apart from their elders, teaching them how to be male or female and how to discover an ever-changing world of consumer goods and experiences. In particular, high-school peer groups shaped teen understanding of social class. The fact is that high school fundamentally transformed the transition from childhood to adulthood, no longer taking place at work under adult bosses, but at school, where same-aged students passed from year to year in distinctly marked classes (freshman to senior). All this made the peer group experience intense, rapidly changing, and ultimately unforgettable.

At the comprehensive high school, teens learned how to grow up from other teens, rather than from older workmates, bosses, or parents. Despite the authority of teachers and administration, the sheer numbers of students and their time free from class inevitably led to a peer culture that adults in high schools had difficulty controlling.[15] This culture first took form in an extracurriculum that had emerged from the 1880s. At first it was largely run by youth themselves, as sport and social clubs. Progressive educators tried to tame and control high-school peer culture by expanding the extracurriculum, in everything from sports and music groups to drama and French clubs, at least indirectly directed by teachers.[16] Inevitably, given the elite origins of high schools, these clubs often remained in the hands of students from wealthy families, and excluded many other students, including the greasers. In a late 1920s survey, only 3 of 145 club activities (e.g., industrial arts) related even generally to cars, even as auto shop classes began to appear in less exclusive institutions.[17]

As the historian Kevin Borg shows, public support for vocational education, including auto shop, grew out of student enthusiasm for car mechanics and support from the National Association of Manufacturers. This led to the Smith-Hughes Act (1917), which offered matching funds for state and local vocational education programs benefitting primarily white males. High-school shop courses followed, including a rare one-semester course in car maintenance. From the 1920s, a few schools offered full four-year vocational courses or cooperative work programs with local commercial garages. Inevitably, guidance officials channeled students who they assumed lacked math and science skills into auto shop courses, reserving electric shop for students with "higher" academic potential. As Borg notes, "In this context of truncated curricula, more or less coercive counseling, and educators' low expectations of auto shop students, it is not surprising that the auto shop became the preserve of working-class boys."[18] Auto shop sometimes built pride, but it also isolated working-class males from the upwardly mobile student body.

Moreover, during the Great Depression of the 1930s, when youth car culture took off, the numbers of teens in high school increased dramatically. Enrolment rose from 4.8 million to 7.1 million (from just over half of fourteen-to seventeen-year-olds to three-fourths). This growth came in part from the fact that working-class youth remained in school because of the job crisis. Still, this trend was part of a longer trajectory: By 1990, 93.7 percent of fourteen-to seventeen-year-olds attended high school. This trend, however, hardly democratized high school. Instead, by making the high school a comprehensive institution that admitted and even required the attendance of students from all backgrounds, secondary education became a mechanism to track students by social class (and race) toward or away from college and professional success. Once in high school, "poor and working-class students encountered deeply-held prejudices about their intellectual abilities," note the historians David Angus and Jeffrey Mirel.[19]

During the Depression, educators opposed expanding vocational education mostly because they were convinced that low-level students needed no more than general education and "occupational adjustment."[20] In effect, one of the principal purposes of high school was to separate those bound for "success" in the professions from those destined to dead-end jobs, and to do it on the basis of performance in academic courses and successful integration into the middle-class extracurriculum.[21] The greaser became the quintessential outsider.

These class biases of staff inevitably reinforced the social divisions within the peer groups of students based on the socioeconomic status of parents. Yet class was shaped by an emerging consumer culture of display and leisure unique to teens. As A.B. Hollingshead notes in his 1940–41 study of a small-town high school in Illinois, "Most high school boys and girls have a good understanding of the class system," even if that system was officially denied in schools and other institutions. Hollingshead found that students from each social class participated in sports clubs and teams, but few of the poor or working-class joined other clubs—a pattern found repeatedly in later studies. Class was expressed in and through manners and attitudes toward authority, but also in codes of and access to consumer goods—clothing and grooming, sites of recreation, and especially the quintessential consumer good, the car.[22]

Unfortunately, studies of high school peer cultures seldom say much about auto usage.[23] Yet, as we have seen in chapter 4, teens had driver's licenses (and, presumably, access to cars) in surprisingly large numbers : In a large national survey of high school students in 1960, 74 percent of students had driver's licenses by their senior year, 54 percent in their junior year, and even 17 percent in their sophomore year (when many were only fifteen years old).[24]

Still, class and regional differences in teen access were stark. James Coleman found, in a study of high schools at the end of the 1950s, that 82 percent of seniors in a small rural school owned cars, compared to only 42 percent from a wealthy suburban institution. Fifty-six percent of seniors from a rural high school claimed car customization as part of the "style of their group," compared with only 19 percent from the wealthy suburb. Small-town and rural teens often worked on their jalopies while children of the affluent and suburban kids often borrowed late-model cars from their parents.[25]

Nearly two decades earlier, Hollingshead had noted that popular girls and boys with well-to-do parents did not ride the bus to school; they arrived by private car:

> The new roadsters and coupes from the country are owned by the children of wealthy farmers, and no effort is made to offer rides to neighbors. . . . Most of those who come in the old cars and in groups carry lunches along with their books and eat lunch in the commons room in the basement of the high school. Those who come in the new cars eat lunch with relatives in town or go to a restaurant.[26]

In this highly stratified high-school peer culture that emerged by the 1940s, two groups stood out: an elite who saw themselves as adults in training, versus a shadow group of teens in rebellion; those destined for college and careers versus those who dropped out or barely finished high school; roughly, the socs versus the greasers.[27] These differences shaped teen attitudes toward and use of cars, creating distinct car subcultures. Simply put, the socs drove newer vehicles and seldom worked on their cars, while the greasers in high school often adopted a culture of customizing and displaying old cars. The socs took their cars to high-school dances and sporting events. The working-class students often hung out in garages or drove to soda shops or drive-ins. The middle-class teen employed the car to display status in imitation of "successful" adults, while the greaser used the car to rebel against those in charge. This pattern continued for decades.[28]

In some measure, greaser car culture became a refuge from the "hidden injuries of class" for working-class teens who were humiliated in the weeding-out system of high schools. But it had its positive side, as Richard Sennett and Jonathan Cobb show in their study of a Boston-area working-class neighborhood in the early 1970s. They discovered that these teens had often found a "counterculture of dignity" in their knowledge and skill in customizing or repairing cars. That culture was built on mechanical and driving skills and practices largely attained outside the classroom, and in extracurricular clubs that honored working-class craft attainments. Yet, as Sennett and Cobb also note, "boys who are good at car mechanics in school start to feel cut off from others, even though the possession of those skills might make them admired by their less-skilled peers outside of school."[29] They gained status in their own peer group, while being distained by the "socs." The car culture of the "greaser," with roots in the 1930s and 1940s, offered "losers" in the class-biased high school a space for self-expression, resistance, and competition even if that culture rarely led to moving up the social ladder. These mechanical attainments were a protest against a society that increasingly valued professional and entrepreneurial talent over the manual arts. The bourgeois youth in the Buick or Cadillac seldom could win a race against the greaser in the souped-up Deuce coupe. The greaser in *American Graffiti* may have been a "loser" whose culture had hardly prepared him for an adult world of bureaucracy, science-based technology—but he was a social type that did not go quietly into the ashcan of history.

Greaser Memories

The greaser culture is hard to document, in part because it is something of an outlaw and minority culture, subject to distortion by the media. Still, glimpses of it can be found in the memoirs of old hot-rodders—in magazines dedicated to their world, such as *Rod and Custom*, and in particular in interviews of contemporary car collectors. Most of these witnesses were born between 1925 and 1975.

An overriding impression from these sources is how young most were when they got bitten by the auto bug. Their earliest memories were often of playing with car miniature toys (like Matchbox, Japanese Friction, or Hot Wheels cars), reading car magazines, building and driving go-carts and mini-motor bikes, and learning from their fathers the makes and models of all the latest cars.[30] Some recall elders teaching them as small boys how to shift gears or, when they could reach them, how to use the pedals. Many learned to repair and rebuild cars long before they were old enough to drive. A man born in 1940 claimed that he already had owned "two or three cars" by the time he was fourteen and worked two jobs at fifteen (sometimes from 3 p.m. to 3 a.m.) "to make his cars go faster." Not much changed for a Long Islander born in 1952 who began a lifetime of engine and body work in the seventh grade, when he tuned up his teacher's cars.[31]

Gearheads not only came to automobiles early in life but usually worked to buy their own cars. Typical was a man from Harrisburg, Pennsylvania, born in 1957, who worked in a motorcycle shop as a teen to pay $800 for a 1966 Mustang coupe. A decade later, another gearhead from rural Missouri, born in 1968, bought a 1971 pickup with his brother for $350, earning his share of the money by pumping gas.[32] This was a world of men in garages and owner-operated service stations and body shops, where there was work for sixteen-year-old or even twelve-year-old boys. Often years before they could legally drive, boys mowed lawns, delivered newspapers, or even collected returnable beer and soda bottles to save money for that must-have car.[33]

Moreover, many growing up in rural areas during the 1950s found summer jobs on farms and ranches. A man born in 1937 from a tiny town in eastern Washington recalled shocking hay in the summer on a farm to buy a 1929 Ford Model A for seventy-five dollars. Later, a boomer from around Pittsfield, Massachusetts, born in 1946, worked all summer on a farm during his high school years in exchange for a 1953 Chrysler. A rural youth born in 1963, from Potlatch, Idaho, still bucked bales of hay in the late 1970s to buy a 1966 Ford pickup truck for hundred dollars, and even trapped and sold fur to fix up his string of cars and trucks. Some youths saved money by working on their cars in school auto shops. Others even used the machines and auto shops at military bases. A man from Wisconsin, born in 1946, who had enlisted in the navy in 1964, recalled a sign in his base shop: "Absolutely no work is to be done on non-naval projects before 1500 hours!" This was an obvious admission that sailors used shop equipment to repair or revamp their personal vehicles, at least after 3 p.m.[34]

As we have seen, these cars were cheap. Many were junkers. A man born in 1947 obtained his first car for thirty-five dollars, only to rebuild the engine and blow it up. A hot-rodder noted with pride that in 1956, at the age of about sixteen, he bought a '36 Ford with "lots of speed equipment" for one hundred dollars, emphasizing that it could beat a nearly new '55 Chevy in a race.[35] Whatever the price, an ethic of hard work and thrift was early entrenched in greasers. Many learned entrepreneurship when they bought, refinished, and sold a succession of cars. A California man born in 1937 made the point plain: "You didn't have a car if you didn't work."[36] Others from more affluent families had their parents buy them their cars, a fact not lost on the greasers. A Williamsport, Pennsylvania, man born in 1953 recalled that the rich kids "did not appreciate [their cars], so they would just beat them into the ground."[37]

Inevitably, many greasers closely followed the interests and even career patterns of their car-crazed elders. The father of an Orange County, California, man born in 1950 owned a car dealership and let his teen son store his "junkers" in the back of the lot (and later partnered with him in selling cars). Another teen graduating later from a northern Idaho high school in 1980 had a more working-class story. His dad, whose hobby was dirt-track racing, rebuilt engines and ran an auto junkyard. The son followed his dad, learning welding and small engines in high school and largely ignoring the rest of his classes.[38] A teen in the mid-1950s from Washington state, born in 1937, recalled with affection how his father and he had installed a V8 engine on a Model A roadster—a common occurrence in his small town, where most fathers had worked with farm or mining machinery. All the boys he knew in his early-'50s youth, except the single fatherless boy in town, had learned to work on cars. A late boomer from Oklahoma, born in 1963, also worked with his dad on a hot rod, installing an souped-up V8 flathead engine in his 1939 Ford, adding Crager SS rims, a tuck-roll interior, and even power steering before wrecking his pride and joy in college.[39]

Yet many who became gearheads had fathers who had no interest in cars, including some who didn't even own autos. These youth still relied on their elders. A man born in 1943 in rural Texas learned the fine art of rebuilding old cars from a man who owned a blacksmith shop but also dragged hot rods. Still another high-school graduate of 1959 picked up mechanical arts from an older neighbor while helping him restore a junker. The neighbor had four daughters but no sons, doubtless welcoming a surrogate son to bond with at a time when daughters weren't supposed to hang out in garages.[40] Much later, this changed. A woman born in 1983 recalled how, when she was seventeen, her sister's 1988 Pontiac Trans Am was passed down to her when she joined her dad in sanding and adding a racing strip.[41] The greasers' world was rich with personal attachments, which offered not only cross-generational bonding but very practical and personal skills.

While drawing personally on the manual skills of adults, greasers often were indifferent or hostile to the formal education of high school. A common story came from a 1960 high-school graduate from southeast Los Angeles. Though his parents demanded that he take Latin, he hated high school and never went to college. His father had a plaster business that he later took over, but his real interest was cars and their innards, beginning with a '32 Ford that he bought for seventy-five dollars and proudly took apart to see how it worked. Another teen from Baldwin Park, California, who went to high school in the mid-1950s, was eager to get out of school to work in a gas station "to make some money." The colorful car collector from Compton, born in 1945, whom we met in chapter 4, claimed that he "flunked out of high school" in 1962 after a teacher told him he would be a "drain on society." He got an apprenticeship as a tool-and-die maker, eventually earning good money.[42]

This pattern was widespread: greasers seldom seemed to be engaged in extracurricular activities, though some went out for sports. This was in part because their "hobby" continually required them to work on their cars or at jobs to purchase vehicles and parts. Certainly their lack of interest in school was partly due to an antipathy toward the abstract academic curriculum. Many who responded to my online interview admitted that their favorite subject in school was either auto shop or art, both of which are hands-on topics. They also often felt shunned by the popular middle-class students who dominated the extracurriculum. Though hardly a scientific sample, many from my survey avoided all organizations, clubs, and sports, preferring to hang out with their buddies at gas stations or garages. A Los Angeles man born in 1941 admitted to being middle-class but was a rebel, caring little for grades and hating high school. He noted that car club members "weren't cool" in his late-1950s high school. Another greaser, born in 1940, who grew up in San Diego, recalled transferring to a different high school "to be with my own kind" and to get away from a rival (middle-class) surfer group. A male from Potlatch, Idaho, born in 1963, admitted that he and his pals had been a small group, poorer than the others and "unpopular."[43]

Some old hot-rodders remembered learning from skilled and supportive teachers, including a Latino man who escaped the gangs of his neighborhood to teach auto shop in Anaheim in 1966 and later become a beloved elder in the hot-rod community.[44] Shop class was the favorite of a Marathon, Iowa,

FIGURE 5.2. This image from the *Los Angeles Times* (August 1, 1954), of hot-rodders holding an illegal street race in the San Fernando Valley in suburban Los Angeles, was accompanied by this caption: "Rod enthusiasts today, realizing such activities would put the sport back 10 years, impose strictest discipline not only on members who drag illegally, but on those who flout any laws of the road." Photograph by Dave Siddon. *Valley Times* Collection, Los Angeles Public Library. Used with permission.

man, born in 1950, who worked on his 1959 Chevy Impala there. A similar story was told by a male from Davis, California, born in 1963, who restored his 1968 Ford Mustang with help from his shop teacher.[45] But others hated their shop teachers, believing them to be poorly trained and ill-tempered. Of course, there were plenty of hot-rodders who went to college and didn't take shop courses in high school.[46]

But the rebellious spirit of the greaser often came out. In 1960, the Compton high school student described earlier was in a "car club" called the Quarter Rompers, which raised money by holding raffles for a color TV set (still rare at the time), the drawing of which was to take place in a parking lot at 2 a.m. There was no TV to win, and the club pocketed all the raffle money. In his "club" there were no formal rules: "We just looked at each other and pointed to the road, and there was a drag race." Another gearhead, born in 1954, proudly claimed that his teen years had been glorious: "The cars were the coolest, the chicks the bitchingest; the guys were bad-ass SOBs."[47]

And while the hot-rod culture was predominantly white, and remained so long after the civil rights movement of the 1960s, the love of fast and stylish cars was hardly absent in African American communities. However, as previously noted, black youth, especially in the cities, had less access to vehicles than did their white or Hispanic counterparts from rural or small-town America. It isn't surprising that merely a handful of middle-aged black men appear at car shows recalling their youth as hot-rodders. Their stories are very similar to those of white hot-rodders. An example was the sixty-three-year–old man I met at the York, Pennsylvania, street rod show in 2016 who, like many white males of his generation, had owned a 1960s muscle car and recalled street racing (but not cruising) on his way to high school in Baltimore. He had been introduced to cars and racing by an older cousin, born in 1946, who had a 1955 Chevy—a car that white males of the same vintage might well have owned. A fifty-one-year-old African-American man I met at the same show had started at sixteen with a 1970 Chevy Camaro, at that time an eleven-year-old car that he bought for two hundred dollars. He and his buddies—a group of three blacks, two Latinos, and three white guys—had hung out together in downtown Newark, Delaware, in the early 1980s. In 2016 they were still hanging out, "talking cars, drinking beer," and helping each other in their garages.[48] Though doubtless rare, this story suggests the appeal of a greaser culture that sometimes transcended race.

Greasers in a Changing World

The greaser culture was more than a boys-will-be-boys world of adapting to, while also resisting, the inevitable transition into the sobriety of adulthood. It was a community of shared enthusiasm for the car as both a symbol of youthful competence and achievement and a marker of maturity in boys wanting to be men. Suggestive of this is the Robert Petersen publication *Rod and Custom*. First published in 1953, *Rod and Custom* was supposed to bridge the gap between the hot-rod and customizing cultures, but from the beginning it tended to focus on a younger audience than did *Hot Rod Magazine*, which identified with the more mature returning veteran who could afford ever more expensive accessories. *Rod and Custom* was a "little pages" magazine printed on inexpensive paper in a pocket-sized format, ideal for a boy to carry. In fact, after the magazine shifted to a larger format in 1961, it published a letter from a schoolboy reader who complained that it no longer "fit into my schoolbook, and I won't be able to read your fine little magazine in class." Ads in *Rod and Custom* for Clearasil (a product used for clearing up pimples) and other youth-oriented products identified the audience.[49] Even more revealing was the magazine's shift, especially from 1959 to 1961 and again after 1966, toward go-carts (small-engine vehicles set close to the ground, appealing to boys because they required no drivers' licenses), scale-model cars (designed for assembly by boys as young as eight), and minibikes. These features and ads appealed to the pre-sixteen-year-old who was still too young to drive a hot rod but was eager to anticipate graduating to the real thing while playing with a toy model or a go-cart.[50] Intermittent stories and cartoons by Carl Kohler, reminiscent of the humor in other early teen or preteen magazines of the time like *Mad*, confirm this impression. One story told of a ten-year boy who, too young to drive a real car, begs his dad to buy him a go-cart as a consolation, only to find that his dad takes over and drives the go-cart himself.[51]

Yet *Rod and Custom* readers and editors resisted its becoming a youth magazine. Letters from readers frequently denounced the shift toward go-carts and model cars, forcing the magazine to return to an emphasis on rods and custom cars in 1961.[52] The author of a particularly revealing letter to the editor offered to write a feature on the impact of cars on high school life, especially dating, but the magazine editor replied simply, "No thanks."[53] And the jive talk of *Mad* was rare; Kohler's features were published for little more than a year. Neither the magazine nor its readers wanted to turn *Rod and Custom* into a magazine for kids or even teens. Yet there was also no attempt to drive away that age group. While *Hot Rod* and other car magazines (and their advertising) often featured images of sexy women along with custom cars and rods or auto parts, *Rod and Custom* avoided this appeal to the older male, especially after 1954.[54]

The magazine's identity remained tied in part to the boy who had not yet become a man, but who wanted to do so. Most striking was the utter lack of any reference to the age or occupations of featured customizers or racers. *Rod and Custom* clearly represented a "community" of males, from twelve-year-olds to men in their thirties, who shared an enthusiasm for the beauty, technology, and power of the modified automobile. For the older reader that culture dated from childhood, and for the teen it represented an entry into a world of men.

The greaser car culture was, like many hobbyist worlds,[55] conservative and cliquish but also innovative and radically individualistic. As we have seen, from the end of the war and through the 1950s, the Ford was favored. Also embraced were 1948–51 Mercurys, known as "lead sleds" because lead was sometimes used to customize and repair their metal bodies. In the 1950s the prevailing ethos was upgraded power with the overhead valve or Chrysler hemi engine. A "one-piece look," *Rod and Custom* advised in 1954, could be achieved by removing door handles, chrome, and even brand insignias, "frenching" lights with fiberglass and resin, and filling in joints and seams. All of this had roots in Harry Westergard's customizing shop in the late 1930s. By the 1950s, it was conservative.[56]

The hot rod was supposed to have a certain look. As one enthusiast wrote in *Rod and Custom* in 1967, "the appearance of a rod is, to a great extent, a timeless thing."[57] One of the functions of this magazine was to set boundaries, to mock the extreme and overly showy car (subtly challenging the extravagant modifications of people like Ed "Big Daddy" Roth and the trend in the early 1960s away from the "timeless" rod).[58]

Yet much honor was also paid to the innovator, especially in mixing components. *Rod and Custom* reported in 1957 that Johnny Neves had taken his brother's 1925 Chevrolet (cost: fifty-seven dollars in 1950), replaced the engine with a 1948 Mercury flathead, installed front and rear axles from a 1938 Ford, and added a 1938 gearbox. He went on to chop the cabin by three inches, and install black-and-white Naugahyde upholstery.[59] The ideal was often to buy a cheap body frame, like the 1930 Ford Model A roadster purchased for thirty-five dollars, and then to add expensive modifications.[60] Others went further, chroming the undercarriage or engine block and adding spinners to the hubcaps that looked "cool," even if this went against the "simplicity" theme. And paint jobs of up to thirty coats with stripes added to the spectacle. All this made the high and boxy pre-1948 car into a work of "art."[61] An editorial in *Rod and Custom* (1959) explained this ethos: "Something in the make-up of the average man . . . urges him to tinker with any piece of machinery unfortunate enough to fall into his hands. . . . The car is a lot more than just a way to get around. Car owners are always looking for some way to dress up, smooth out, and otherwise change the machinery they ride around in."[62]

All this could get expensive, and for those youths without dads who were willing or able to chip in, there were always shortcuts. Perhaps rather than installing new engines or upscale carburetors and manifolds, the teen hot-rodder could simply remove heavy "extras" like radiators and fenders, and drill holes in the body to get a bit more speed. And to get that distinct look without modifying the suspension, the kid could simply put a 220-pound sandbag in the trunk to lower the back end.[63] The point was always the individual modification, whatever the cost.

Hot rod magazines regularly touted the stories of supreme personal achievement, even if done on the cheap. The tinkerer who made tubing from junk (costing only $2.21) to link multiple carburetors to the engine was honored for his ingenuity as well as his frugality.[64] In one of the "funny stories" by Carl Kohler (1959), we read of how the girlfriend of "an average guy" wants to ride in a Triumph TR-3 owned by a wealthy man at a sport car rally, shaming her boyfriend who has only a souped-up 1955 Mercury. The hero's friend, "Dipstick," suggests that he build his own sports car from a go-cart. Not only does the hero win the girl back, but he leaves the rich guy with the Triumph "eating dust," yelling, "I bet you made this atrocity yourself"; to which the hero replies, "A finer compliment couldn't have been offered." In this seeming knockoff of Chuck Berry's classic rock song "Maybelline," in which an ordinary guy in a Deuce coupe beats a Cadillac carrying his unfaithful girlfriend, we learn that even a crude but handmade machine was superior to the rich kid's expensive toy.[65]

The individualism of the greaser's rod was expressed in still other ways. Especially common was the disdain for the corporate big-business world of Detroit. As early as 1948, *Hot Rod Magazine* noted how the 1948 Ford, "in accord with the California custom trend," was minimizing body ridges and chrome, even though the Detroit automaker was doing a bad job of it despite all their engineers and money.[66] The common story was that copycat auto execs were imitating the chopped hot rods with their low profiles in the 1950s, but just couldn't get the style and quality right. *Rod and Custom* mocked the 1953 crop of new cars for their poor paint jobs, loose suspensions, and underpowered engines. An editorial in 1959 reveled in this disdain of Detroit: "Every time the manufacturers take the trouble to make some function of a car automatic, the alert accessory makers announce a device to make something manual."[67]

For greasers, the vehicle was a special kind of consumer good. Although greaser's cars had become objects of fashion, their owners never saw the similarity with women's clothes or hats. The modified car seemed to be the one permissible consumer obsession for the young male.[68] For the greaser especially, the car was a man's product that defined male space, achievements, power, and value. Writing in 1980 of her adolescence on a Mississippi farm, Lydia Simmons noted, "Women rode in cars and otherwise didn't go near them." But teen boys saw cars as something that "engulfed them." The male youth lavished attention on his car as a "horse trainer groomed a champion," and before moving out of his parents' home he "had to have at least one tremendous wreck driving while drunk or flaunting [his] life as a daredevil and survive it. Otherwise one was not a man." She recalled how her brother had "grinned as he walked away from a car crash."[69] Women were occasionally draped over hot rods in photos of prized vehicles, and an early *Hot Rod Magazine* feature, "Parts with Appeal," pictured starlets in swimsuits along with auto accessories. In 1951 the magazine even sponsored a "Cheesecake Derby" in which "girls" competed in their own jalopy race at an unmanly fifty to sixty miles per hour. There were also the inevitable "woman driver" jokes: "Does she know much about cars? No, she thinks you cool the engine by stripping the gears."[70]

FIGURE 5.3. Members of the Ancients Car Club from suburban Los Angeles, aged from fifteen to eighteen (1963). Dressed in classic "greaser" fashion, they are late aficionados of this tradition. Photograph by Gordon Dean. *Valley Times* Collection, Los Angeles Public Library. Used with permission.

The hot rod was a male fashion and a focused way for boys to express their manhood. As Amy Best puts it in a later context, boys' work on cars expressed their masculinity, while girls' efforts to transform their bodies expressed their femininity. "Both converge in these car spaces [as in cruising], where boys' cars are presented for display much in the same way as girls' bodies are, that is, for boys to see."[71]

Throughout my conversations with old greasers and hot-rodders, I often found an understandable desire to tell me about all the details of their restorations and modifications; how they turned a mangled piece of rusted junk into a vehicular beauty; how they advanced from one car to the next, sometimes in a series of smart purchases and sales, sometimes after wrecking several cars in succession—often with detailed recollections of when it happened and how much it all cost. Yet occasionally, some of them would wax just a little philosophical about the attraction to wheels. A high-school graduate, born in 1968 and brought up south of Kansas City, Missouri, recalled the thrill of working on his first car, a 1971 pickup truck: his effort gave "the vehicle a 'soul' sort of, otherwise, it's just a tool that spent hours on an assembly line like pop's vision of a car. After modification, it's a mechanical object one can sort of have a relationship with as an extension of yourself, part of who you are, not the original designer or assembly line worker."[72]

Hot Rodders versus Restorationists: A Contrast in Culture and Class

Of course, not all American teens who grew up with cars were hot-rodding greasers. There were also those often more affluent kids who borrowed their fathers' cars or were even given late-model cars as teens to show off and drive to high-school dances and sporting events, and, of course, to use for "parking." But few of these youths raced or customized. Often their first interest in cars came from an encounter with the commercial world rather than from a workshop or garage. A collector of antique cars born in 1936, from eastern Washington, made a scrapbook of car ads when he was in elementary school. A boomer from southwest Missouri born in 1947 recalled the thrill of waiting for local car dealers to tear off the brown butcher paper on their display windows when the new models of 1958 and 1959 were "unveiled."[73] These people learned about cars not in garages, but in auto showrooms. Sometimes they grew up to be restorationists rather than hot-rodders.

Often the cars that this group first remembered were very different from the favored models of hot-rodders. A man born in 1951 in Elkton, Maryland, who later obtained a graduate degree, wrote that his first car was a 1956 Chevrolet station wagon. While he later owned a Model A, he never got it running, nor did he race or belong to a car club. Instead, he was fascinated with older luxury cars and their history. A car enthusiast born in 1936 in Conestoga, Pennsylvania, remembered that his first car had been a 1937 Chrysler Imperial, though he had longed for a 1942 Lincoln Continental Cabriolet and a 1940 Chrysler Town and Country convertible. He identified with luxury cars rather than vehicular power and speed. As a teen in the 1950s, he had rejected the modifications of the hot-rodders. Even though greasers would have dismissed him for his preppy interest in the camera and drama club in high school and his love of French and Latin classes, as a teen he drove to the Jersey shore and went to the drive-in to try to get the girls to join him. He was no goody two-shoes. Another man, from rural West Virginia, remembered with fondness his first car, a 1966 Renault Caravelle—a French sports car that was a hand-me-down from his sister. He was active in his church choir and went cruising with a gender-mixed group, with no interest in sex.[74]

Later in life some of these men joined groups like the Antique Automobile Clubs of America (AACA), devoted less to the souped-up Deuce coupe or its descendants than to Chrysler Imperials and Packards from the late 1930s, Chevy Corvettes from the mid-1950s, or even foreign sports cars like the Triumph and Sunbeam in the 1960s—each of which at different times was a distinct marker of status and class. These lovers of antique automobiles were attracted to the beauty and, later, the authenticity of the "original" car, not to speed or personal modifications. The difference between these youth cultures was partially regional: the non-rodders were more likely to be from the East, centered originally in Pennsylvania where the ACCA began (see chapter 7). And certainly some of the difference was a matter of personal taste and temperament. But most of all, the difference was one between middle- and working-class culture.

My conversations with three elder leaders of the AACA, each about eighty years old in 2015 and with Pennsylvanian roots, make these observations more concrete: first, their initial encounters with cars shared experiences with the hot-rodders. Like the greasers, they were machine-oriented from early childhood. The first member, who later became president of the AACA, recalled how when he was between sixteen and nineteen years old he filled a neighbor's barn with twenty-six old cars given him by locals. These neighbors knew they could have gotten only ten or twelve dollars in trade for each car, and they believed this youth would "preserve them." And this became his lifetime obsession—to guard automotive heritage. Growing up in the 1940s, he and other future devotees to antique car restoration were entranced by the parade of cars, especially the distinct styling of American cars from the 1930s through the 1960s. They grew up fixated not on the flathead Fords, or on any Fords for that matter, but on the ascendant GM or Chrysler models, often relatively new cars costing far more than the junkers that the hot-rodders began with.

Another AACA elder came from a Plymouth family, but abandoned this loyalty when the Plymouth introduced a boxy—to him, stodgy—model in 1949. At age fourteen he was converted not to Ford speedwagons but to Pontiacs, which he talked his dad into buying new. In high school, he owned in rapid succession a 1937 Chrysler Imperial, a 1948 Chrysler convertible, and even a 1947 Pontiac station wagon, all of which a hot-rodder would have disdained. The latter car cost $795 when he bought it with help from his dad. Despite his rapidly evolving taste, he never modified any car. His best friend had a new 1951 Hudson Hornet (a mid-priced car), and he could list the specific years and models of all the cars owned by his high-school friends, each boy being identifiable on the road by his vehicle. Each of his friends was loyal to a particular car company—mostly GM but also Chrysler, and definitely not Ford, still the tribal home of the hot-rodders. Instead of chopping and channeling his cars, from the age of sixteen this AACA member learned the art of "detailing" from a high-school teacher—polishing exteriors, cleaning interiors, and adding touches like whitewall tires. From these years he later recalled that modifications in a car's engine or body "drove him crazy." His idea was to make the car better by making it more original. From childhood he collected car sales literature that served him well in his restorationist interest, and from childhood he gathered old car ads that he put in scrapbooks.[75]

A third AACA leader, about the same age as the other two and likewise a Pennsylvanian, came from a small rural town where his father had been a mainline Protestant clergyman and his mother an artistic homemaker. Though precociously mechanical, in contrast to his parents, he was indulged by them. Rather than sending him to a liberal-arts college, they enrolled him in a trade school, where he learned the skills and discipline necessary for success. In his twenties he found a niche in distributing parts for the Sunbeam, a British sports car that appealed to a very select audience. His youthful taste in cars was similar to that of the other AACA members—late-model Hudsons and Pontiacs—and he, too, moved rapidly from car to car, buying his first Sunbeam, a 1963 model, in 1964.[76]

All these biographies suggest a more conservative, certainly more middle-class teen car culture: sharing a fascination with the machine, but not one with competitive racing or with modifications for style or speed, or a disdain of Detroit engineers. This nongreaser group was attracted to a wide range of cars as part of the diversity of American consumer culture. Ultimately they were obsessed with authenticity and purity. Although members of this group did eventually restore their cars, as teens they were interested in high-end, fashionable cars, not beaters or junkers. They did not buy thirty-five-dollar jalopies with money earned pumping gas; they purchased vehicles that often cost a thousand dollars or more, bought with personal savings, on the installment plan, or with money given by or borrowed from their parents.

This difference may have often been rooted in class distinction, but it was expressed in a contrasting personal encounter with the car. For the rodder, the car represented a craft relationship and an expression of independence and power; for the largely middle-class teen who later collected and restored antique cars, the car was an expression of personal taste, status, and pride in the quality and uniqueness of the individual vehicle.

The Fate of John Milner and Other Hot-Rodders

As Matthew Ides notes, the greaser's world emerged out of a particularly fortuitous period when the individualism of the white male was often rewarded with success. This may have been especially true in Southern California. While there was some evidence of blacks and Latinos in the early car clubs, especially in the multiracial near suburbs of East Los Angeles, by the mid-1950s the hot-rod culture had moved to the more distant all-white suburbs of Glendale, Pomona, and Pasadena, and had become almost all white. And in these growing towns, adult hot-rodders easily found manufacturing jobs and opportunities for auto-based small businesses (e.g., service stations, car dealerships, repair shops, or custom and speed shops). Others inherited or founded plastering, electrical, or other building contracting businesses. Evidence that some greasers grew up affluent or at least moved up is sketchy and anecdotal, but suggestive. Two leaders of the Cal-Rods (discussed in chapter 3) turned their mechanical skills and entrepreneurial savvy and hard work into successful businesses: one was first a worker, but then became an owner of an auto-parts business in Baldwin Park, and another became a manufacturer of plastic novelties and toys. Other hot-rodders simply grew up to become well-paid machinists or truckers; today they live comfortably on pensions and savings, and are rich enough to buy and customize the now costly cars of their youth. Gearheads from South Chicago or Detroit in the 1950s and '60s often could afford carefree teenage years with an easy transition to adulthood in steel mills or auto plants in a time when the wages were higher than those of schoolteachers. It was no different in the many small and rural communities throughout the country where the hot-rod culture prospered. Staff at Peterson's car magazines understood that their audience was primarily white, male, and upwardly mobile; and thus they neglected nonwhite, down-market hobbyists.

This produced a curious mix of rebellion and conformity; of working-class pride, but also middle-class aspiration; of separation from the stodgy world of dads, but also a desire to learn the skills and accomplishments of those who were old hands. As we saw in chapter 3, some car clubs, which may have started rebellious and engaged in "pranks," eventually "grew up" into being respectable affiliates of the NHRA, engaged in charity. While the car may have remained central to the identity of their members, as they matured, hot-rod clubs evolved into social clubs, with their members as interested in meeting females at dances as in tooling around in their manly vehicles. As we will see, much later in the twentieth century these same clubs (or their successors) became homes for the respectable, middle-aged, nostalgic collector of old cars (chapter 8).[77]

Like other youth-based groups, greaser communities were ephemeral even as they often strove to create and sustain a "timeless" tradition. Not only did the clubs break up with the members' inevitable transition to adulthood (military service, marriage, and occupational divergences), but the enthusiasm of one cohort faded with the rise of the next in a succession of fads. Inevitably, the young broke with the no longer young, and this rupture was facilitated by the very nature of the car as a consumer good: it changed continuously. While the romance with the Model T and its successor, the Model A, survived into the 1950s and beyond, along with a postwar obsession with the Deuce coupe and its family of Ford V8s,[78] by the mid-1950s a younger generation of youths were beginning to lust after high-compression modern vehicles of the dominant line of cars after World War II: those of General Motors. Typical was *Rod and Custom*'s 1957 feature on a Seattle customizer who had taken a 1949 Chevy and added Cadillac fenders, an Oldsmobile top, a 303-cubic-inch Olds V8 engine, and a Cadillac stick-shift box.[79] Lynn Wineland, editor of *Rod and Custom*, noted in 1958 a change in his readers' attitude. No longer were they interested mostly in the old cars of the pre-1948 period; they now wanted to customize new 1958 Chevys.[80]

Inevitably, older gearheads lamented this trend. One complained that the Deuce coupe no longer appeared "around schools, drive-ins or just cruising down the street." Instead, "glittering car shows" displayed exotically customized modern cars; and, in a quest for the trophy, a new generation asked only, "How can I be 'kookyer' than the others in my class" of cars in shows. Traditionalists complained about the influence of George Barras, with his introduction of "plastics, painted windshields, swivel seats, and other gimmicks." In 1961, when *Rod and Custom* was featuring the wild car designs of Ed "Big Daddy" Roth, like his "Beatnik Bandit,"[81] one irate reader wrote that hot-rodders needed to return to the "honest design" of the old chopped and channeled "beauties" like the Ford coupes and Mercury lead sleds.[82] Yet in 1967 Tex Smith of *Rod and Custom* chided hot-rodders who wouldn't go beyond the Deuce or the "T," insisting that rodding was about innovation and an "honest inquiry into all things mechanical," and that without willingness to change, rodding was "about as exciting as playing spin the bottle with an old maid."[83] Petersen's magazines continued to introduce new car concepts and try to win readers to change (promoting customized pickups in 1959, vans in 1970, and even low riders in 1974).[84] But it was hard for some, as they grew up and grew old, to give up the "timeless" hot rod. This was no different from the attitude of Elvis Presley fans who had once been daring teenagers screaming for the "king" in the mid-1950s, but who after 1968 adored the bejeweled Elvis in Las Vegas, resisting and resenting the new young and their enthusiasm for the Beatles and later rockers.

Greaser car culture was a distinct product of a particular time and often place, born of both opportunity and exclusion. It was a period when used cars were cheap and manual skills still counted, giving mostly working-class white boys a vibrant peer culture in which to compete, shine, and grow into manhood. Yet that culture emerged from a setting, high school and its surrounding society, where these same youths were also often rejected for what they didn't have: new cars and the expensive clothes of the preppies, and the recognition of many high-school teachers who honored academic rather than mechanical achievement. Their mocking of the sports car and of the "brass" at the Detroit car companies was only the tip of the iceberg of their resentment. Yet, like other manifestations of American working-class life, greaser car culture often led to dreams of entrepreneurship and movement into at least the basement of the mansion of middle-class respectability. For others, the hot rod still offered a self-contained world of pride and accomplishment, separated not only from adult "socs," but from others in the car movement—including Latino low riders, our next topic.

Low, Slow, and Latino

At a neighborhood car show in suburban Covina, California—amid the fifty or so hot rods, muscle cars, and antiques, beside each of which stood a white man or couple often well past sixty—I met a middle-aged Mexican American man. He was proudly displaying a red and white 1963 Chevrolet Impala, top-of-the-line, perfectly preserved, but with an open trunk full of polished hydraulic machinery. Nothing speaks more about the range and the division of American car culture than the striking contrast between this lowrider and the white world of the hot rod—vehicles reflecting a common enthusiasm, but largely apart.[1]

In mid-twentieth-century America, where the used car was relatively cheap, readily available, and often economically necessary, the car was both a gateway to the mainstream and a marker of distinction for many who were excluded from privilege. This vehicular opportunity extended not only to white working-class youths, but also to minorities. While African American youths surely owned automobiles and sometimes participated in the customizing culture, the fact that many of them grew up in inner cities where cars were less prevalent for either white or black youth meant that black teens had less opportunity to identify with the car. Rather, we find a parallel but distinct car culture in Latino communities in the suburbanized and small town worlds of California and the Southwest, built around the lowrider and several generations of Latino youth and their elders.

From the late 1940s, youths of Mexican heritage began cruising down the main streets of Southern Californian towns in their used Chevrolets, a legacy of "zoot-suit"–wearing youths of Mexican backgrounds, against which resentful whites rioted during World War II. In the 1960s and 1970s, the lowrider tradition grew in East Los Angeles and the East Bay area of Northern California, as well as in parts of New Mexico and Texas. These customized full-size cars, with their low profiles and slow cruising speed, stood in sharp contrast to the high and fast hot rods of the "greasers." These stylized vehicles inevitably were the target of white officials in the 1980s, even as they symbolized Latino expressiveness and rebellion.

Low Rider Stories

Though they had arisen near each other, sharing similar identities of growing up with the car, the greasers and the Latino low riders adapted very different automotive traditions. This came from their contrasting social and cultural backgrounds, but also from the fact that low riders as a minority often attempted to differentiate themselves from the hot-rodders and their aesthetic.

The Latino lowriding culture has attracted attention among anthropologists and journalists since it burst on the scene in the Southwest during the 1970s. The anthropologist Brenda Bright identifies the culture as simultaneously "bad" and respectable, "mean and clean," defiantly countercultural but also deeply rooted in family life. The low rider's world entwined the mass culture of the modern American vehicle with elements harking back to Mexican life. In this sense the lowrider materialized a "deterritorialized" culture that was no longer located in Mexico, but which perpetuated Mexican values and customs. In contrast to the high (if sometimes chopped and often channeled) profile of the pre-1948 hot rod, usually a Ford, and frequently modified to go fast, the Latino lowrider was low and slow, altered not for speed but for style and heritage, and was often a late-model GM car. This was about more than being different from the white hot-rodders. With small, wide wheels and dazzling paint jobs (up to eighteen coats), the lowrider achieved a distinct look: instead of rejecting the 1950s trend of long, low, and rounded vehicles (promoted by GM design chief Harley Earl), the low rider exaggerated that look with his car. Rather than boasting about the engine's power and successes at the drag strip, the low rider took pride in the car's mere appearance on the road, going slow on the cruise to dominate the procession and force others to take notice of the car's customized beauty. As Mario Ruelas recalled about cruising as a youth in East Los Angeles during the 1960s, lowriders "were so slow, but that is what everybody used to go for, just to be seen on the street with a lot of cars and people in the business parking lots and all that. It was like a car show on wheels."[2]

Yet the lowrider had its own heritage, mystique, and perhaps legends that not only set it apart from the hot rod but also gave it a distinct ethos. While the lowrider culture was similarly part of a distinctly male world, beginning with an "adolescent concern with style, personal identity, and mechanical skills," it was often also situated in a world of family and "gifting, tinkering, and bartering within kinship and friendship networks."[3] Latinos relied on used and junked cars, often within families, handed down from grandfathers or uncles, sometimes passing through a number of hands as they were repaired and customized as family projects. Exemplary were the Ruelas brothers— Ernie, Fernando, Julio, and Oscar—born in Tijuana, who settled in South Los Angeles in 1956. Their mother was a single parent, and their uncle Tinker became a substitute father. He introduced the brothers to wheels, first buying them go-carts as preteens, then taking them to scrapyards to buy and modify bikes and scooters with lowriding modifications. "We started doing the car thing when we were very young," noted the second brother Fernando in 2007. "At 11, 12, 13, we basically owned our own cars already. Back then you could buy a car for $15." In 1962 the boys founded the Dukes, a long-lasting lowrider club, when Julio was just eighteen and Fernando was only twelve. Out of the Dukes grew a famous lowrider custom shop. The club became part of an extended family tradition passed down to the sons of the brothers, sometimes providing activity and focus to keep the teen offspring "off the streets" and out of neighborhood gangs. The brothers' sons began with pull wagons and pedal cars, and the Dukes integrated preteens into the club with their bicycle lowriders in 1977. As teens, the sons climbed on the minitruck craze in the late 1980s, but as adults they returned to the lowrider tradition of their dads, remembering the car shows of their childhood. The Dukes established a number of chapters, and after the death of Fernando in 2010, his sons inherited the shop and club.[4]

My encounters with Latino car enthusiasts tended to confirm this familial and community pattern. Least like the story of the Ruelas family is that of a Mexican American, Jorge, born in 1948, from West San Antonio, a poor and predominately Latino/a neighborhood, who grew up before the lowrider movement had fully developed. Jorge recalled that when he was a child, cheap 1930s and 1940s cars were available, especially to veterans with a little money who had acquired knowledge of the youth car culture from their military experience outside the community. By the 1960s, older Latino youth led the way, adopting the hot-rod techniques of glasspack and cutout mufflers, exotic paint jobs, and even more powerful hemi engines. After marriage, however, this ended and a new generation of customizers would take over.

All this sounds similar to the story of the Anglo hot-rodders. Yet there were differences. Some Latino youths shared cars. And in this case, the youth's car was a focal point of community. In the early 1960s Jorge, along with other boys nearby, gathered regularly at Freddy's driveway to watch him work on his 1940 Ford. Freddy, a high-school dropout at seventeen, had made good by

FIGURE 6.1. Four Hispanic youths parked at a Pup 'n' Taco parking lot, two of whom are polishing their cars before cruising the streets of East Los Angeles (April 15, 1979). Photograph by Dean Musgrove. *Herald Examiner* Collection, Los Angeles Public Library. Used with permission.

enlisting in the navy, returning to the neighborhood when released. Freddy always welcomed the neighborhood boys, teaching them about car restoration and giving them rides. Jorge accompanied him to junkyards to get parts, learning the art of searching for bargains and negotiating with dealers. Latino/a parents of the local boys approved of their learning from Freddy. He offered an appropriate male space.[5] The car culture passed from older to younger people—often, but not necessarily, through the family.

Perhaps even more typical was my meeting with younger Latinos who had grown up in the 1970s and '80s and had participated in the lowriding movement. In 2016 I talked with a man, born in 1961, at a car show where he displayed his early 1960s Cadillac and showed me the under-the-car chrome and hydraulics. A member of the Lifestyle Car Club since 1979, he recalled that he had bought his first car, a $250 Ford, at fifteen. But, like other Los Angeles Latinos, he reserved his true love for GM cars, especially Chevys built between 1958 and 1977, when their trunks were large enough to accommodate hydraulics. He learned the fine points of lowriding "from his Hispanic culture"—in his case, high-school friends rather than family members. In the late '70s he, like so many others from his community, cruised Whittier Boulevard, especially the section in East Los Angeles. Still, family always came first. He recalled having to sell his prized 1964 Chevy four-door, a classy lowrider, for twenty thousand dollars in 1999 when he was in his late twenties, in order to help buy a house. While this low rider may have been atypical—being a college graduate born not in East Los Angeles but in the "Valley" north of the city in Glendale—another Latino at the same show, born in 1964, fit the common pattern. As a teen he worked on 1963 and '64 Chevys with his brother, installing parts, especially engines, obtained from junkyards. Lacking cash, he often traded cars with others. The first car he owned by himself was a 1965 Chevy he received from his mother when he was sixteen years old. He soon replaced it with a better 1965 Chevy sold to him by his girlfriend's father (later his father-in-law) for a nominal fifty dollars—with, however, the engine removed. Of course, he and his buddies found another junked engine to build a classic lowrider. He bought a junked hot-rod pickup in 1990 (a time when those small trucks were popular) and, over the years, gradually restored it. He was proud to note that he did so with the assistance of his then young daughter, promising to share it with her when she was old enough to drive (which he did). He, too, was part of a broader Latino car culture, and recalled riding with buddies in the back of a pickup on Whittier Boulevard during the summer of 1979, when the authorities closed it down.[6] On my Internet interview site, a Latino from Denver told a similar story, though he was a generation younger, having been born in 1980. He reported how he had been introduced to lowriders by his dad, who had founded the Sophisticated Lows car club in the early '80s, and with whom he had painted and customized lowriders in the family garage when he was a teen. Again, the lowrider tradition passed across the generations.[7]

Lowrider Origins and Styles

The origin of the lowrider is somewhat complex, even obscure. Most commentators trace it to the barrio of East Los Angeles in the mid-1940s, where automobile transportation was essential despite the residents' poverty. Already the preferred used car was the Chevrolet, beginning with the 1939 Deluxe model; usually these were four-door family models, in contrast to the preferred two-door of the hot-rodder. Later, a few low riders favored the 1949–51 Mercury, which was easily customizable. These cars were often called "bombs," and they preceded the modern lowrider. Adaptations included special hubcaps, grilles, and bumpers, many of which were found at junkyards. For the status-conscious, a special addition was dual Appleton spotlights. Some customizers made their own parts, and a few navy veterans painted their cars with navy-gray primer. Jobs, available after 1950 in car and other assembly plants, gave Mexican-American youths training in paint and bodywork. Especially noteworthy were modifications to create a low profile. While Anglo hot-rodders sometimes mocked Mexican-American cars for their shot suspensions, which were common in old cars in Hispanics' price range, these car owners turned this "fault" into a virtue, sometimes cutting the suspension coils to further lower the car especially in back (rather than raking the car in front, as was the white hot-rod custom). Mexican Americans also mounted small tires to lower the car (and because they were cheaper than high-profile hot rod tires). Some low riders put sandbags in the trunk.[8]

Certainly, the most distinct feature of the lowrider was the substitution of the standard suspension system with a set of hydraulic lifts that were powered by batteries in the trunk and operated from switches under the dashboard. This machinery allowed the car to sit very low to the ground and then be raised, sometimes suddenly, to produce a "jumping" effect. Curiously, this innovation seems to have been the result of a 1958 rule in the California Vehicle Code that required all vehicle bodies to be no lower than the bottom rim of the wheels—an obvious challenge to customized Mexican-American vehicles that sometimes scraped uneven roads. In 1959 Ron Aguirre, a Southern California customizer, refitted the hydraulics from the bomb doors on junked World War II planes onto his heavily modified Corvette. This technique was soon adapted for lowriders, making it possible for a driver to raise the car

FIGURE 6.2. The hydraulics in the trunk of a Cadillac lowrider, owned by a proud middle-aged Hispanic (June 16, 2016). Church of God Car Show, Covina, California. Author's collection.

body to avoid scraping and, at the sight of a cop, to beat getting a ticket. Later, aftermarket manufacturers sold these hydraulic systems. Still later, air bags mounted between the wheels and frame did the same job, though many low riders preferred the old hydraulics. In the 1960s, the ability to "hop" (by raising the front with lifts, then releasing the pressure to bounce) became part of the competitive lowrider culture, and was often featured in car shows.[9]

Customizing the interior became just as important. Lowrider historians date this tradition back to the hot-rod designs of Harry Westergard in the late 1930s, and note how his student George Barris passed on this craft to an early Latino car club, the Thunderbolts, in the late 1950s. Yet lowrider custom interiors contrasted sharply with the hot-rod cult; instead of rolled and tucked vinyl, the Latino ideal was crushed velvet upholstery, even swivel seats, and chainlink steering wheels. Rather than one or two colors, by the 1960s, the emerging lowrider cult ideally had multicolored paint jobs with many layers of lacquer, and even hand-painted pictures evoking Latino religious or folk-culture themes.[10]

This distinctly Mexican aesthetic may have links with the pachucos of the 1940s, or with their offspring who spoke a hybrid "Spanglish" slang called caló. Male pachucos wore zoot suits—oversized midlength suit coats and high-waisted, baggy peg leg trousers—with spongy shoes and sometimes watch chains, flat hats with feathers, and hair coiffed in shiny pompadours. The females dressed in black blouses and pants or short black skirts with mesh stockings. This look was hardly new to mid-1940s Hispanics. The zoot suit, which may have originated in Harlem in the early 1930s, was adopted at various times by Italian, Filipino, and even Japanese immigrants and their offspring. When Mexican-American youth, dressed in their flamboyant zoot suits, ventured outside the barrio, whites and especially local police were enflamed. This led to the famous Zoot Suit Riots of June 3–13, 1943. A fight between zoot-suited Mexican Americans and seven white sailors sparked a week of whites beating pachucos, violent encounters that often culminated in the arrest of the Mexican-Americans by white police. This event and the clothes and cars of the pachucos were later memorialized by *Lowrider Magazine* in the late 1970s and 80s with feature stories and photo displays of pachucos dressed in zoot suits. This association of the low rider with the heritage of the zoot suiter lent the lowrider movement legitimacy, and made it a bridge across several generations of ethnic pride. Like hot-rodders, low riders were rebellious, but less against their elders than against Anglo society. And the racial profiling that these Latino youth experienced when "driving while brown," a common expression, was shared across several generations. Low riders were sometimes called "cholos," a term with roots in the nineteenth century, associated with bandits and later with new immigrants and gangs. By the 1970s, cholos were dressed in the distinct uniform of khakis, sleeveless white T-shirts, bandannas, and tattoos. Proud in their "vida loca" as rebellious youth, the cholos also made it easy for outsiders to link the low riders to crime and gang violence.[11]

Yet the lowrider had still deeper roots. Lowrider expert Paige Penland claims that the communal character of this distinct car culture dates back to the 1920s, when poor Mexican immigrants formed mutual aid societies for sickness and death insurance. Along with forming social clubs, they sometimes bought group cars by pooling their meager resources.[12] Other writers have stressed that the emphasis on display and the slow cruise have roots in the Mexican tradition of promenading around the town square or zócalo, and even that the appeal of hydraulic "jumping" is associated with Mexican festive horse shows that featured stylized equestrian hopping. Instead of dressing up and walking through the zócalo to attract and flirt with young single females, they drove their dolled-up cars, low and slow, to show off to the females along the route. Others claim that the lowrider tradition can be dated back to the Moors in eighth-century Spain who decorated their horses with silver saddles; sometimes even draping them in roses—a decorative tradition that was adopted by the Spanish and later brought to Mexico, and which then transferred quite naturally to cars.[13]

Cruising Whittier Boulevard predated the modern lowriders, and attracted Mexican-American youths throughout Southern California by the early 1960s. Whittier was a street where Latinos could meet Anglos or blacks with little conflict, and where cruising was a "Chicano alternative to Disneyland," according to R. Rodriguez in 1984. It was a tradition for a Latino I met when he was a teen in 1956. And it wasn't restricted to Southern California. Chicanos from San Antonio cruised Commerce Street in the 1960s. At that time, only men rode in cars, and females stood on the street to admire the scene—a legacy of a prewar tradition in which mothers kept strict control over their daughters and their contact with men in public.[14]

The lowrider culture was distinct in many ways: it was all about display rather than racing, and it had complex Mexican origins, shaped by discrimination and misunderstanding by an Anglo majority. It was a product more often of family and community relations than of high-school peer culture. Yet it shared with the white hot-rodders and customizers the influence of club life and media.

Lowriding Clubs and Their Clashes

Like the mostly Anglo hot-rod clubs, low rider organizations sometimes had roots in neighborhoods and high schools. Moreover, early predominantly Latino clubs were not always ethnically segregated. The Dukes of Los Angeles, for example, when they first appeared in 1962, included African-American members from Watts and Compton. The club even organized dances with black car clubs like the Professionals and the Imperials, and even with white groups like the Igniters and the Drifters. To a degree, this reflected the multiethnic character of East Los Angeles neighborhoods in the 1950s and early 1960s. Later, the area became more homogenously Latino/a when whites migrated to outer suburbs. In 2003 Jose Martinez, from the Klique Club, recalled how white hot-rodders on Van Nuys Boulevard welcomed low riders in the 1960s. The cruise then was "full of everything: blacks, whites, Mexicans, bikini girls on roller skates, bands, six lanes of cruising. It was really nice." In 1964 clubs like the Imperials not only cruised Whittier Boulevard, but organized parties with white clubs from Long Beach.[15] This may have been exaggerated, but in any case it did not last.

While these clubs didn't have an "adult" body like the NHRA to organize and oversee them, low rider clubs attempted to put on a respectable face, eschewing the image and behavior of gangs. Though members of the Dukes had been part of the 38th Street Gang, the Ruelas brothers started this low rider club in 1962 as an alternative to gang life, and in their cruising expeditions on Whittier Boulevard they saw themselves as part of the Chicano pride movement. Other clubs also considered themselves to be antidotes to the gangs boys often got into before they were old enough to drive, and believed that the Latino car culture helped to forge stronger ties with family. Latino clubs often outlawed drinking and drug use at shows and on cruises. Some members of the Groupe Car Club, organized in 1973, had been gang members but broke from it. Car clubbers "didn't want to fight any more; they just wanted to work on their cars," as member of a Santa Ana club noted. They were "home-owning, job-holding, respectable citizens." Fernando Ruelas from the Dukes joined the Imperials and the Groupe to form the West Coast Association of Lowriders in 1978. Among their activities were a "Christmas Toys for Kids" car show, benefits for the United Farm Workers, and even programs for prisoners.[16]

But police and white cruisers did not always distinguish between gangs and low rider clubs. The low riders' insistence on driving at slow speeds (sometimes as slow as five miles per hour) and the striking differences between their custom cars and those of whites certainly annoyed whites and drew the attention of police. Early in 1980 in San Francisco's Mission District, unorganized whites in their "high" cars hurled insults at "low" members of the Browns Car Club on the cruise. A leading member of the Browns claimed that the group sought cooperation with other cruisers and police. Still, his mustard-gold 1973 Impala—with its high-powered boom box blasting out the club song "We Are Family," its chain-covered steering wheel, it interior ceiling covered in symbols and signatures of club members, and its the hydraulic lifts—seemed to provoke negative reactions from Anglo cruisers: some even tossed trash into its windows. Many low riders retreated to the south end of town, where they lived. And police looked for these low-slung vehicles, scraping the road with their undercarriages, to single out for citations. Moreover, many Latino car clubs were ephemeral, perhaps even more so than hot-rod clubs. This made difficult any quest for stability, mature leadership, and respectability.[17]

Lowriding had very different meanings in the Anglo and Latino communities. White bias against Hispanics in low-profile cars dated from the late 1940s. However, the actual use of the term "lowrider," according to Penland, originated in Los Angeles soon after the Watts protests of 1965, when cruisers rode low in the front seat—often with seats removed, sometimes, in the view of unfriendly witnesses, to avoid the scrutiny of police. As a result, the term took on a derogatory or unsavory meaning from the beginning, especially when used by police and white cruisers.

Yet within the lowriding community, this auto styling carried communal and cross-generational meanings. Low riders turned the ritualized route of the cruise into promenades of family and friends celebrating weddings, anniversaries, or quinceañeras. And the younger brothers of cruisers anticipated and imitated their elders by bending the front forks of the bicycles to make them low. Still, despite efforts of club leaders to eliminate gang violence, clashes periodically broke out between club members.[18]

Moreover, fueling the mistrust of Anglo authorities was the fact that by the late 1960s, the low rider had become a "symbol of Chicano resistance to assimilation," and a challenge to the "outside interests" that owned most of the businesses along the predominantly Latino/a cruise route of Whittier Boulevard in East Los Angeles. The Chicano movement emerged in 1962 with the founding of the National Farmworkers Association in Southern California and, as a Mexican-American expression of a wider civil rights and ethnic identity movement, it was a major influence into the mid-1970s. A Chicano rally on July 3, 1968, on Whittier against police harassment of low riders led to a riot, with bricks thrown at amassed police amid three days of violence. Despite the protests of club leaders who claimed that the emerging Chicano movement was nonviolent, the clubs were blamed for the disturbances, and the cruise route was blocked for months. A loose coalition of clubs formed to reduce fights between members. While Whittier was reopened late in 1969 for cruising, a march on the avenue, on August 29, 1970, against the Vietnam War led to another confrontation with police and the deaths of three protesters. The cruise route was once again shut down. Many of the clubs soon disintegrated. Cruising continued in the 1970s, moving to Elysian Park, Hollywood Boulevard, and Crenshaw Boulevard. Fights between clubs returned.[19]

These tensions came to a head once again in the summer of 1979, especially on an unincorporated one-mile strip of Whittier east of the Long Beach Freeway. Long a site of Latino mating games, an account by a *Los Angeles Times* reporter captures a perhaps common Anglo perception of the Whittier Boulevard cruise:

> By 3 am, they've come down to make the scene. . . . Displaying their "bad rides," the gents listen to disco tapes in their newly lacquered sedans, juiced with hydraulic lifts and bordered by meticulous chrome side piping. Cruising in the opposite direction, there is a carload of gigging young chicanas, chomping on gum, brushing their hair and rhythmically bobbing as they sing along with the hit blaring from the radio: "Ma-ma-ma-my Sharona." . . . They deposit their empty beer bottles on the double yellow road divider as they hit a red light in an innocuous display of what they call *la vida loca*.[20]

While some Anglo onlookers might have been amused by this spectacle, police claimed that the teenage ritual had gone "sour" with the appearance of gangs on the Whittier route, often clashing after 4 a.m. These confrontations had led to the deaths of sixteen youths on Whittier in the previous eighteen months. The violent reputation of low riders had been fueled by the demonstrations and mass arrests that followed the premier in March 1979 of *Boulevard Nights*, an exploitation movie that featured cruise life on Whittier.[21] Moreover, cholos, dressed in their uniforms of khakis, white T-shirts, and headbands, mixed with peaceable low riders who were merely seeking contact with the opposite sex. It's no surprise that a one-mile strip of Whittier was closed to cruisers on March 23, and even less unexpected that one low rider asked a reporter, "How come they don't close Van Nuys Boulevard? Why in East LA? It's 'cause they're white people there, what else?" Jo Garcia, a Los Angeles cop, summed up the common view among whites: The low riders were mostly nice kids, "but sooner or later, wherever you find low riders, you find that gangs start showing up, too."[22]

Inevitably, the low riders moved to new sites like Hollywood Boulevard.[23] Particularly notable was the shift toward San Fernando Road north of Los Angeles. An officer opined: "If you had some flashy [Anglo middle-class] sixteen-year old girl out here, some of these gang members would have her for an hors d'oeuvre."[24] Similarly, in San Diego's National City district, Highland Avenue became a site of lowrider cruising in September 1979. A cop reported: "Generally a carload of males and a carload of females will cruise side-by-side. . . . Someone will get upset with being held up and a fight will break out."[25]

In an effort to avoid gangs and police pressure, low rider clubs organized car shows as a substitute for cruising. Some clubs even obtained permits to park in vacant lots, though they still complained that the police harassed them and drove them away. By the mid-1980s, many clubs had disappeared, even as contact between black and Latino cruisers led to the association of rap music with low riding.[26] This story was repeated in places like Santa Fe, New Mexico, and San Jose, California.[27]

Identity and Commercialization: *Lowrider Magazine* and the Aesthetics of Latino Car Culture

The contradiction between rebellion and respectability came together in lowrider media, especially *Lowrider Magazine*. And with it inevitably appeared commercialism, echoing trends in Petersen's hot-rod periodical empire and its impact on youth car culture. The magazine was launched in 1977 by San

Jose City College students Larry Gonzalez, Sonny Madrid, and David Nuñez, who had obtained student government funds to publish a Chicano magazine. From the beginning, *Lowrider Magazine* focused on car culture. Like Petersen's magazines, *Lowrider* financed itself with ads for car accessories. For most of its first year, the magazine was hand-distributed locally. At first, its use of barrio slang offended more conservative Mexicanos. But the magazine won an audience after November 1979, when it began featuring cover photos of Latino women in bikinis standing beside lowriders. Despite its initial success, the magazine ceased publication in December 1985. It was revived in June 1988 and was moved to Fullerton, a suburb of Los Angeles. More successful in the 1990s, it reached a monthly circulation of twenty thousand. Perhaps inevitably, it was purchased in 1997 by McMullen Argus, a prominent publisher of car magazines, raising its circulation to forty thousand by 2014 and in the process becoming still more commercial and less ethnic. In 1999 the editor of *Lowrider Magazine* claimed that 40 percent of its readers were Anglo, in contrast to the 90-percent Hispanic readership of thirteen years earlier.[28]

At first, especially, *Lowrider Magazine* embraced the identity politics of La Raza, and sometimes reported on police clashes with low riders. But even at the beginning, the magazine did not emphasize political news, but rather promoted identification with La Raza and Azteca while featuring the cultural heritage of the low rider. In March 1979, for example, an issue included old photos, solicited from readers, of 1940s and early-1950s Mexican-American youths, often clad in zoot suits, with their low-profile "bombs." Other issues focused on the drive-in and oldies music scenes from the 1950s. These articles reminded readers of the assertiveness of the postwar generation, linking it to the later Chicano movement.[29] This emphasis was also a way to convince young readers not only to embrace a cross-generational ethnic identity, but also to reject gang culture. As thirteen-year-old Angel Ortiz, a lowrider enthusiast, wrote in a letter to the magazine in 1991, "Instead of killing off the Raza, kill off all that bullshit with gangs and drugs."[30]

Although decidedly a male magazine, the early issues of *Lowrider Magazine* attempted to address the wider audience of girls and women. The September 1981 issue included an advice column from a "wise aunt." The "aunt's" counsel concerned a wide variety of issues, from loneliness and dating problems to teen pregnancy and domestic violence. The message was usually conservative, warning girls against casual sex and advising females how to get and keep a man.[31] Especially in the early 1990s, before being bought out, *Lowrider Magazine* appealed to young readers with articles on youth football, and even the regular features "Love Hurts," about the difficulties of young romance, and "Love Lines," messages of romantic interest between shy teens. Still, the appeal

FIGURE 6.3. A lowrider with a stylish paint and trim job. Used by permission of Robert Genat.

to youth went beyond the personal. Letters from readers were expressions of teen pride in a heritage identified with the lowrider tradition.[32]

The central theme of the magazine, however, was always the cars, which were often lovingly described. A customized 1959 Chevy painted in candy forest and hunter green, with a velour and mohair interior, was featured on the cover of the December 1988 issue. No detail was ignored, including its long and low trunk, into which pump and cylinders were stored for the car's hydraulics. *Lowrider Magazine* regularly sponsored car shows, and featured tips about customization.[33]

The lowrider was the canvas upon which customizer displayed his artistry, but it was also a commercialized product onto which much bling was added. From the beginning the magazine was a commercial enterprise, with local and then national ads from companies offering lowrider accessories. By the early 1980s, *Lowrider Magazine* had won the sponsorship of Schlitz beer; but that changed in 1988, when the magazine featured the "Budweiser Lowrider of the Year." Later it included ads from El Pachuco, a retailer of used and new zoot suits.[34] And by 2005 the magazine had partnered with fashion company, Del Rio, to sell young women's clothing, an extension of a "lowrider" clothing line for men introduced in 2002.[35]

Of course, a big part of the sales effort was to drape "hot" female models over those equally sexy lowrider cars. In the early 1980s, when feminist protest against such exploitation was reaching the Latino/a community, a debate ensued about whether featuring young women in suggestive poses on *Lowrider*

Magazine covers was appropriate. The magazine's staff justified it by claiming that these women represented the best of community womanhood and helped to make the magazine commercially viable.[36] Sex sold, and low riders seldom challenged traditional patriarchal attitudes. In 1974, young women from East Los Angeles organized a low rider club called the Lady Bugs, but it soon disappeared. Most clubs would not let women join, relegating them instead to "service" roles. Even lowrider-themed cable shows in the late 1990s continued to link female allurement and the car: for example, *Livin' the Low Life* was hosted by Vida Guerra, a sexually attractive Latina with little knowledge of cars.[37] Gender equality was not a part of the lowrider movement, and this made a commercialized objectification of women inevitable; but then, neither was there much room for women with wrenches among the white greasers.

The low rider's focus on commercial accessories sometimes led to personal extravagance. One low rider proudly told a reporter in 1979 that he had bought his car for thirty dollars but customized it for three thousand, explaining: "You have to treat [your car] better than your girl." Fred Rael of Espanola, New Mexico, who was in his forties in 1999, admitted: "[I] stopped going to college so I could fix up my cars." Low riders often took special care to get the "right" whitewall tires and hubcaps; and the plush and colorful interiors put the tuck-and-rolled upholstery of the classic rod to shame.[38]

But how do we understand this aesthetic priority, especially when such luxury put great strain on the finances of working-class Latino customizers? A common argument is that all this was part of Hispanic culture, a festival mentality that compensated for daily hardship and penury with unbounded extravagance in that one special object of personal display: the car. When one is poor and ethnic, an effective strategy to enjoy and display luxury is to focus limited resources—and in the United States, where the automobile was king, what could be better than to save and spend on a car.

Though expressed in the symbols of traditional Mexican culture, lowriding is not simply an affirmation of La Raza. Rather, the lowrider is part of an alluring consumer culture. This second explanation of lowrider elegance began with the preference for American cars, especially those made by the dominant American company, GM. Noteworthy also is the bias toward the Impala, the luxury model of the entry-level Chevrolet, or even the preference for the more upscale Buick Riviera. These choices affirmed Latino/a membership in American consumer culture.

A third explanation, advanced by the Norwegian social anthropologist Martin Høyem, draws on the notion that these vehicles display an "outlaw myth." The lowriders' owners did not adopt the bourgeois dress and manner of the Anglos who had first possessed these once luxury vehicles. Rather, they often embraced the cholo language and style, sporting shaved heads with "wife beater" tank tops and khaki pants, and a working-class style that even echoed prison garb while still connoting an air of defiance.[39] Drawing on Octavio Paz's explanation of the Mexican-American zoot suiter in the late 1940s, Høyem argues that while the low rider separates himself from the dominant society, he "also pays homage to the society he is attempting to deny." This is a common working-class pattern, in line with Thorstein Veblen's observation that consumers down the status ladder emulate the standards of those who are higher. But, in addition, this quest often leads to exaggeration that both admires and mocks.[40]

Finally, the lowrider was more than an expression of sardonic fealty to the American car status system and consumer culture. It was also a means of attracting the admiration of women, even though the car itself was is considered to be a man's space. While a Latina teen received a quinceañera, an often extravagant party, on her fifteenth birthday, her teenage brother sometimes got a car instead. The lowrider was the quintessential car for the "playboy"—an allure to attract females, rather than a way to show off power to other men, as was the case with the hot rod. This difference is perhaps revealed in the contrast between hot-rod pop songs: the Beach Boys' "409," "Shut Down," "Little Deuce Coupe," and "GTO" are tunes praising the uniqueness or power of cars. Even Chuck Berry's "Maybelline" was more about rivalry between a Deuce coupe and a Cadillac than about Maybelline herself. By contrast, lowrider music focuses on dancing and romance. In fact, favored lowrider songs have been slow ballads, rhythm and blues, doo–wop, and harmony soul from the 1950s and '60s. The tempo of these songs fit the slow procession of the Latino cruise. But the music itself is revealing; it originated in the postwar generation of Mexican Americans who had abandoned the ranchero and mariachi music of their parents for songs that embraced the commercial culture of the United States. Interestingly, however, this emerging group favored not white country music or Tin Pan alley songs, but African-American rhythm and blues. As late as 2011, collectors of these old songs, who were called "souleros," played the B-sides of old 45-rpm records from the 1950s and '60s at soulero balls, perpetuating a multigenerational tradition.[41]

The lowrider represented a striking mixture of heritage paired with commercialism, of familial loyalties coupled with defiant individualism, and of appeals to traditional romantic values along with cheesecake. It was an exhibition of extravagance in the lives of young men who did not have much opportunity for such display. That excess was expressed in the code of consumerism even as it seemed to challenge that code. Most of all, while affirming masculine prerogatives as did the greaser, the mostly male low rider sought less the thrill of competitive speed and power than the admiration of his community and of the opposite sex.

Generational Challenges

The 1970s and 1980s may have been the heyday of the lowriders. But these cars continued to encounter the old problem of rejection by the outside community, and the continued identification of this car culture with youth gangs lingered. Despite a sixteen-year tradition of successful local lowrider car clubs, Santa Clara county in California banned car shows in 1993, apparently because of concern about the cruising that spilled out of the showgrounds. The growing association of the lowrider with gangsta rap didn't help. Local authorities sometimes billed the shows for extra police costs relating to the cruising that took place in nearby streets after the shows closed, and organizers even dropped the term "lowrider" from their names in the hope of saving their shows. In the 1990s, redevelopment officials attempted to clear Santa Clara Avenue of low riders, while often tolerating Anglo cruisers from the suburbs of San Jose.[42]

As was the case with the greasers, lowriding was also challenged by generational change. Despite proud claims of the hobby being a family and community culture, by the mid-1980s there were already signs of divergence when younger Latino/as appeared in the cruising procession with minitrucks and late-model Japanese cars. In 1986 a thirty-seven-year-old low rider from San Diego and longtime member of the Latin Lowriders Club told a reporter that he might try to get his thirteen-year-old son interested in lowriders, but admitted, "He'd probably want one of them trucks." After the appearance of a new hydraulic design in 1989 that made Asian and European cars more adaptable to lowriding, a rising generation of Latinos was quick to adapt to Volkswagens, Toyota Celica Supras, and even Corvettes. These vehicles were less likely to be targeted by police—and, innovative and representative of a rising generation, they were more "cool." In the 1990s, though, the traditionalists held on with their twenty-year-old long and low Monte Carlos and Coupe de Villes. But things had changed. A veteran lowrider from El Rito, New Mexico, uttered a common complaint: "Kids buy a new truck, lower it, put some rims on it, and that's it." No longer appealing to the young were the lowriders of the past: those old one–of–a–kind beauties that might be modified every few years, often as the projects of brothers or friends, perhaps embossed with portraits of relatives who had passed on, or with classic religious themes.[43]

Like the white working-class teen's hot rod, the young Latino's lowrider was an expression of the frustrations of exclusion, but also an affirmation of identity and achievement. The white hot-rodder and the Hispanic low rider were the products of two related but distinct traumas. For the hot-rodder, there were the frustrations of being betwixt childhood and adulthood, but also the "hidden injuries of class" in high-school peer culture that rejected their values and accomplishments. For the low rider, there were the pains of ethnic discrimination in a predominately Anglo culture that saw their heritage as alien and often criminal. The car was a mode of often satisfying escape from those frustrations—offering an alternative world in which to measure success and status, and to provide an affirmative community.

These two car cultures, however, provided only partial solutions. The hot rods and lowriders sometimes only further isolated their riders, reducing their opportunities for moving up in a competitive bourgeois society based on academic achievement, access to capital, credentials, and contacts. At the same time, these car cultures did not foster a clear alternative to the one that prevailed in society. In fact, the drivers were compromised by commercialism, and by their own ambiguity about rejecting or joining the mainstream.

Yet, as part of a wider youth car culture, the teenaged white greaser and Latino low rider both motored their way into adulthood and found meanings in the transition. This unique American experience was, however, challenged from the 1970s as its quintessential expression—the cruise—was attacked by adult authorities who had tolerated it for at least thirty years. This, we will see, was the beginning of the decline of growing up with cars.

Last Stand of the Cruiser

The American teen car culture reached its peak in the 1960s and early 1970s with the era of the muscle car, cheap gas, and well-paying factory jobs that awaited high-school graduates. Greasers were still kings of the road while Mexican-American youths in their lowriding, slow-moving late-model Chevys were parading down Whittier Avenue and elsewhere. This story, at least the white part of it, is romanticized in George Lucas's film *American Graffiti* (1973), which celebrates the end of a presumed golden age of the cruise in the early 1960s. Nevertheless, the cruise culture went on, only to begin its decline in the mid-1970s with the high fuel costs of the oil crisis of 1973 and 1979, and the subsequent downturn in the American manufacturing economy, especially the American auto industry.

But there was more. A little-recognized trend was that law enforcement was beginning to crack down on cruising, and on kids and their cars intruding on public (especially commercial) space. Years of periodic and intensifying police restrictions resulted by the end of the 1980s in the eclipse of cruising in large population centers and many small towns. This story was part of the decline of the white, largely working-class greaser. The last stand of the cruiser is also about the clash of race and age: an assault on the Latino low rider, and a reversal of the surprisingly permissive attitude of adults toward autonomous youth.

Cruising had long threatened the adult community and especially commercial space, interfering with shoppers along the car route and often driving paying customers away from business zones. Yet, through the 1950s and 1960s, adult authorities had tolerated this incursion, seeking to contain it and usually recognizing it as a rite of passage not all that different from their own "sowing of wild oats." By the end of the 1960s, however, authorities in Detroit were beginning to clamp down on kids for hanging out in drive-ins and commercial lots, and, of course, for racing. The same occurred in the Los Angeles area, where police and local authorities feared the appearance of cruisers from outside their neighborhoods, who were often perceived as gang members, especially if they were black or Latino.

But the police crackdowns were stepped up in Los Angeles from the mid-1970s—for example, on Van Nuys Boulevard in northwest Los Angeles, and especially in Latino sections of Whittier Boulevard in the east Los Angeles suburbs. Battles between cruisers and police led to citywide and countywide cruising bans in the late 1980s. This challenged the rights of youth to automobility on public roads (and doubtless also on lovers' lanes).[1]

So what accounts for this change in the late 1970s? Battles over contested leisure and commercial spaces have been common in history, as in the struggles over public access to royal forests or town squares for festivals in early modern Europe, but these conflicts were between social classes, rather than across generations. There have been other "moral panics" against rambunctious youth in the past, most recently efforts from the 1930s to restrict their access to movies, toy guns, and comic books. Underlying these assaults were the introduction of new and, to elders, unfamiliar commercial products that appealed to youth and seemed mighty suspicious, even dangerous, to adults.[2] Panicked parental assaults on teen crowds at early rock concerts—especially over the "dangers" of race mixing—occurred in the mid-1950s.[3]

But this attack on cruising was different. It was not centered on the vulnerable child and the threat of a commercial popular culture, as were many moral panics of the past; rather, it challenged the freedom and mobility of youth that for many decades had been conceded by adults as part of the transition to adulthood. Challenging this right was to deny the sixteen-year-old full membership into the "republic of drivers." To attack the cruise was to delegitimize a marker of maturity at a time when American society was lowering the bar of entry into adulthood, as in the constitutional amendment that gave eighteen-year-olds the right to vote in 1971. Given the history of American permissiveness toward young drivers, this was a sharp and puzzling break from the past.

The war on cruising reveals a new chapter in generational conflict and mistrust. Why it occurred at this time is not obvious. The era of the sharpest generational conflict in the twentieth century was the 1960s, as adults "freaked out" over the drugs, sex, and rock 'n' roll of youth as well as the political radicalism of young people in opposition to the Vietnam War and racial discrimination. But all this had abated by the late 1970s and '80s, when the cruise was widely suppressed. The war on cruising probably says more about adults and a reduced tolerance for "disorder" than about youth. Still, as we shall see, the cruise did seem to change in the late 1970s with signs of racial conflict and crime. Just as important, the authorities had difficulty in suppressing the cruise, having to deal with repeated "resurrections" of the practice. All this suggests not only the persistence of teen car cultural traditions, but the need of youth for spaces for expressions of sexuality and individual pride.

Early Signs: Complaints and Costs

Memoirs identify the decline of cruising on Detroit's Woodward Avenue with the rise of gas and car prices, and with the beginning of the shift to foreign cars and the loss of factory jobs in Detroit. But economic pressures on cruisers only partially explain the trend. Commercial interests also were increasingly threatened by youths interfering with shoppers along the cruising route, often driving paying customers away from business zones and especially from fast food joints. And business eventually prevailed over the kids. But neither change came quickly.[4]

Reports in the *Washington Post* early in 1980, for example, painted a picture of a high school ritual that was fading due to increased gas prices and rising car costs. A youth still committed to the old car culture with his 1968 Camaro muscle car complained that his high school parking lot in Fairfax County, Virginia, was full of little more than compacts, doubtless many of which were borrowed from parents.[5] Also in 1980, lowriders in the Washington area still gathered at a local shopping center parking lot for evening races, but there was a price: one teen admitted to having to work two jobs to feed the 365 horses in his Camaro. In desperation, he was forced to drive his mom's Volkswagen Rabbit, complaining, "If I was born ten years earlier, things would be a lot easier." A teen in the small city of Allentown, Pennsylvania, shared this lament, noting that it cost twenty to forty dollars per weekend to keep up with the cruising ritual.[6]

The cruise was slowly dying by the 1970s and the early 1980s, but it was not simply a victim of gas or vehicle prices. The cruise was repressed. By the middle of the 1960s, the authorities were already clamping down on kids for looping through drive-ins without stopping, parking in commercial lots, and of course for racing. As early as 1963, business owners in Royal Oak, Michigan, an affluent Detroit suburb along Woodward Avenue, complained that teen loitering in drive-in parking lots discouraged family patronage. In response to this pressure, police ticketed teens for loud mufflers and traffic violations. Moreover, a new ordinance imposed fines for driving through parking lots without stopping for food, and required drive-ins to post barriers and guards to discourage cruisers.[7] By 1968, some popular drive-ins along Woodward

Avenue and elsewhere were charging entrance fees that were redeemable upon purchases.[8] That year, instances of teen gang muggings and fights led to further crackdowns on Woodward, and in 1970, police imposed a temporary curfew on teens on the Royal Oak section of the route.[9]

Yet it took a long time for the cruise to crumble. In 1977 the police chief of Livermore, California, in the Bay Area, felt it necessary to call a "cruising summit" of area police to discuss "our mutual problems with cruising and large youth gatherings on the streets and at parties." Still, he insisted that he had "no intention of doing away with cruising by teenagers." Instead, his goal was "to eliminate the vandalism and traffic violations that often accompany this innocent pastime."[10]

So what turned the officials from regulating drive-in and cruising crowds to banning the cruise altogether? The best explanation can be found in the records of Los Angeles. The key was a change in how authorities perceived automotive teens: increasingly police saw them as aliens, outsiders. For a generation, cruising had taken place on the main thoroughfares of dozens of Los Angeles suburbs. For the most part the cruisers stayed in their own neighborhoods, and thus interlopers were easy to identify and control.[11] But by the end of the 1960s, the neighborhood cruise tradition was breaking down as cruisers could and often did congregate in favored regional routes often far from their home turf. Thanks in part to the extensive network of freeways, they could gather and disperse quickly across the region. In many cases this made cruisers appear more threatening to locals and to the police; and the "problem" of the mixing of "good kids" (local, largely white) with the "troublemakers" and gangs (especially those who were Hispanic and African-American) became an obsession of the authorities.

In the summer of 1968, police swept Whittier Avenue, especially in East Los Angeles, to arrest drug offenders and stem gang violence. In the 1960s, reports of cruising bands of teenagers harassing customers at widely dispersed shopping centers appeared sporadically in the press. Especially notable were accounts of violence between carloads of warring gangs, and racially charged incidents: Five carloads of Pasadena cruisers into South Los Angeles (white kids in a black neighborhood) were reported to have tossed a gasoline-filled bottle into a car.[12] Yet, despite the rise of racial conflict in the 1960s (the Watts disturbances in August 1965, most notably) and signs of clashes when mobile youth from one ethnic group crossed into the "territory" of another, the cruise survived the 1960s. This would change by the mid-1970s as the cruising crowds became alien, leading to a decade of sporadic skirmishes between cops and kids.

Containing the Cruise: Los Angeles, 1974–90

A flash point of conflict between local police and youth over "cruise nights" culminated on Van Nuys Boulevard in northwest Los Angeles in the spring of 1974, when police banned parking along the boulevard from 9 p.m. to midnight, citing the energy crisis and vandalism. Youth car club members complained that local officials refused to respond to requests for alternative gathering sites like public parks or parking lots. A few months later in July, Bellflower, a municipality south of Hollywood, put the brakes on cruising on its main boulevard as kids from around Los Angeles, many no doubt refugees from the Van Nuys cruise, clogged the street, disrupting commercial traffic. Police made sweeps on busy nights, enforced curfew laws, and ticketed cars parked on the street after 9:30 p.m. to discourage cruising. Finally, in August of 1974, local officials made the boulevard a one-way street going north to ease the flow of "legitimate" traffic from the freeway to shopping centers, but thereby also discouraging youth from riding up and down the boulevard to meet cars full of members of the opposite sex. A sheriff claimed that many cruisers were "girls 12 to 14 . . . cruising . . . after curfew."[13] Be that as it may, this was no longer the manageable parade of local kids who were known by and sometimes even related to the patrol officers.

Trouble on Van Nuys continued the next year as ten to fifteen thousand youths from as far away as San Diego converged on the boulevard on the first Wednesday in July. Many may have been enticed by disc jockeys who had spread the word of the revival of the "ancient" tradition of cruise night. While police had maintained a low profile for many weeks, the crowds along Van Nuys had gradually returned to their unmanageable levels. Kids protested the fact that police harassed them with curfew violations, and the cruising tradition even won some cross-generational support: "One angry father, whose son received a ticket, referred to the operation in 'scatological terms,'" according to a reporter, and complained that "adults don't get tickets for loitering. They just arrest the kids."[14]

Similarly, a cruiser's rights group formed in 1976 in response to a crackdown on Whittier Boulevard, a long artery that extended from central Los Angeles to East Los Angeles and on into the suburbs of Whittier, Montebello, and Pico Rivera. As we have seen, this street had long been a center of cruising by minorities, especially Latinos. One member noted, "You wait to grow up to be old enough to cruise Whittier Boulevard," and complained that increased ticketing for broken taillights, public and underage drinking, and curfew violations was mere harassment. Cruisers insisted that police blamed the many for the troublemaking of the few. But even local adults objected when police attempted to barricade portions of the street to drive off the kids, because it disrupted their businesses or access to their homes. Individual cops admitted to reporters that the tradition was hard to break up, and many were content with merely keeping it under control.[15] The crackdown was hardly a simple affair of repressing lawlessness; it provoked opposition.

By August 1979, however, police began to step up their efforts to actually eradicate cruising. This change cannot be explained by any single factor, but an early and important issue was white anxiety over the "invasion" of their suburbs by Latino low riders from East Los Angeles. While the section of Whittier Boulevard that went through a Latino neighborhood was closed in March 1979 (see chapter 6), later that summer, police from white neighborhoods further east got state authorities to close their portion of Whittier Boulevard Friday, Saturday, and Sunday at 9:30 p.m. as cruisers moved east from Los Angeles. Moreover, police reported that gangs from as far away as San Diego were responsible for a wave of assaults. The police claimed that their goal was not to stop cruising, but to stop crime. Still, teen cruisers interviewed about the closure saw police action as a joke. The point of the rite was simple: "You look for a girl. You look for a guy. You get a phone number. You go out tomorrow night." A Latino cruiser thought the problem was with the "cholos" gangs, not the majority; but another youth admitted that cruising was "just a tradition gone out of control."[16]

Partially in response to the closure of Whittier, during the second weekend of September 1979 carloads of male and female Chicanos gathered on Highland Avenue, which ran through Hollywood far to the west of Whittier. This led to fights and the arrest of 170 youths, many for underage drinking and curfew violations. And, as noted in chapter 6, in November a new mecca for cruisers appeared on San Fernando Road north of Los Angeles, drawing cars from East Los Angeles as well as Long Beach. Further out, in the Orange County suburb of Santa Ana, the city council authorized police to use "all resources" to reduce cruising—perhaps an attempts to preserve the upscale image of the town and to keep the Latinos and blacks out.[17]

But the crackdown went much further than a targeting of nonwhites. It was an attack on what police perceived as a mounting threat of a new and alien generation of youth. The next summer, on June 25, 1980, police closed down a one-and-a-half-mile section of Van Nuys Boulevard after 9 p.m. following complaints that youth were heaving firecrackers from their car windows. The larger problem was that the number of cruisers, by one count fifteen thousand, was so great that the cost of policing the street, requiring at least 150 police, was prohibitive compared to that of the fifteen police required simply to close

FIGURE 7.1. Whittier Boulevard in Los Angeles, barricaded to prevent cruising (September 2, 1979). From "Barriers Make Boulevard Night an Empty One." Photograph by Rick Meyer. Coll 1429, box 1093, neg folder #290475r, *Los Angeles Times* Photographic Archives (Collection 1429). UCLA Library Special Collections, Charles E. Young Research Library, UCLA.

it. One policeman at the blockade, who had cruised the same street himself in 1960 while he was in high school, rationalized the crackdown saying: "This is a different generation with a different outlook. They don't have the discipline we had. I was afraid of officers, saw them as unapproachable." He blamed the brazen disrespect of authority and increased vandalism of youth in 1980 on single-parent homes and sexual permissiveness. A local city councilman, Armani Bernard, praised the closure, demanding that it continue until "the habit is broken." Yet, despite meetings with car clubs, letters sent to the parents of offenders, and enforcement of trespassing ordinances, the decade-long struggle of the police with cruising continued. As one reporter noted, "How do you reduce in weeks what has been accumulating for 25 years? How to regain the calmer nights of 1960 against the drugs and hostility toward police of 1980?" Another officer opined: "It's like shoveling sand against the tide."[18]

Not unexpectedly, in response to the route shutdown, in July 1980 the kids shifted quickly to a new site, Reseda Boulevard, six miles further northwest, in a move fueled by announcements from citizen's band radios and disc jockeys. The police responded just as quickly, ticketing cars parked in private lots and, after shooing kids from the sidewalks, citing cruisers for vehicle violations. A female crew manager at a Van Nuys Arby's drive-in restaurant declared the blockade a farce. Business at her store was down; more to the point, she declared: "I used to cruise when I was fourteen years old. That was seventeen years ago. It was rougher then and worse than it is now. The kids are gonna do it and they need a place to go." In the mobile society of Los Angeles, such a gathering place for like-minded people seemed to be essential, and oldsters, remembering their youth, often supported the kids. Still, on July 9, the police closed down Reseda. But, as another cruiser boasted, "Sepulveda's next after this. There's dozens of streets. As long as word gets around."[19]

And of course it did. Automobility made it easy for the cruisers to shift to other routes. This led to a sort of "Whac-a-Mole" game of beating down one cruise site only to see another emerge. As soon as February 1981, officials from Montebello closed a two-and-a-half-mile section of Whittier Boulevard running through their town on Saturday nights. Even so, a week later the cruise traffic on Hollywood Boulevard increased 25 percent.[20]

In fact, a very similar standoff occurred on Hollywood Boulevard a few months later, in July 1981, with the noted prominence of lowriders, and police concern about the infiltration of gang members among the ten thousand cruising cars. But cracking down on petty violators was so time- consuming, and the police so outnumbered, that officers usually only issued warnings to underage beer drinkers and the like.[21]

A more cost-effective solution was adopted by the Los Angeles City Council, in August of 1981, allowing the blockade of Hollywood Boulevard between Gower Street and La Brea Avenue, through the heart of the tourist district. Facilitating local efforts to crack down on cruising, the state legislature passed a law in 1982 explicitly sanctioning these efforts to close cruise streets, when driving "for purposes of socializing and assembling interferes with the conduct of businesses, wastes precious energy resources, impedes the progress of general traffic and emergency vehicles, and promotes the generation of local concentrations of air pollution and undesirable noise levels." Such a declaration appealed to adults of various political stripes. The state ceded the particulars to local authorities.[22]

Of course, these efforts didn't stop the cruisers from coming back to Van Nuys or Whittier after police removed the blockades. Mass arrests occurred in July 1982 on Van Nuys, and in September 1984 on Whittier.[23] Hot-rodders and lowriders tried to establish new routes. From August 1984 through March 1985, up to eight thousand youths in cars besieged Elysian Park, north of Dodger Stadium. Despite police raids and arrests after the park closed at 10:30 p.m. on weekends, cruisers kept coming, cutting the locks on the gates to the park, frightening elderly residents with their drinking and parking in private driveways. The head of a local residence association admitted in March 1985, "They are more of a show-off crowd than an angry crowd," but veteran police officer John Jergensen insisted, "You just can't let cruisers get established." He spoke of them as if they were an infestation of insects. Of course, in the eyes of many local residents, they were.[24]

Soon the authorities tried a new approach. In May 1985, the county set up checkpoints to stop cruisers from repeatedly circling another stretch of Whittier in East Los Angeles, ending the parade in three weeks. In January 1986, back on Whittier Boulevard, the city council of Pico Rivera followed suit by authorizing police to set up random checkpoints, effectively banning cruising by stopping cars that passed the same spot twice in four hours. In August 1986, the same tactic was used on Balboa Boulevard in the affluent town of Newport Beach, south of Los Angeles, after sixteen- to twenty-five-year-olds turned their traffic jam "into a mass party, car-hopping in groups to socialize." The police upped the ante by prohibiting cars from passing a "checkpoint" more than two times in three hours. That October, the Los Angeles City Council unanimously passed an ordinance allowing police to ticket cruisers for tying up traffic in any area that the Police Department designated as being congested by cruisers.[25]

The police sought this flexibility in their gorilla war with the cruisers, and in 1988 law enforcement introduced computers to aid in the "clocking" of cars by recording their license plate numbers as they crossed checkpoints, nabbing the cars and their occupants with a warning after two turns, and ticketing them after the third. Very few of the cars ever passed the checkpoint a third time. In order to accommodate citizens with business on the targeted streets, police were given discretion. One cop noted that if a driver was "not wearing tank tops, shorts, and tennis shoes," that person was not targeted as a cruiser.[26]

Playing a kind of guerilla war with the cops, the cruisers held on to their tradition as long as possible.[27] But 1990 seemed to signal the end of Southern Californian cruising. Hawthorne, California, a suburb famous in the 1960s as the hometown of the Beach Boys and their songs about cruising and hot-rodding, had remained a cruise site for locals throughout the 1980s. Local police were reluctant to crack down on the kids, nostalgically recalling how they themselves had cruised down the main drag and hung out at the old A&W root beer stand when they were young. But by 1990, things had changed. Hundreds of cruisers from Whittier and San Fernando Valley descended on Hawthorne, on the instigation of the Rollerz Only Car and Truck Club, whose members reportedly passed out ten thousand flyers denoting Hawthorne Boulevard as their new go-to cruise site. Gang shooting on the route led to extra police assigned to "drive cruisers out of town." A police sergeant, Robert Cooper, noted: "The city just can't let it go on and let all those folks who like to shoot up the town come in and have target practice."[28]

FIGURE 7.2. Cruising teens standing behind their muscle car are arrested at a cruise site on Hollywood Boulevard (January 25, 1981). Coll 1429, box 1231, neg folder # 293940 27a. *Los Angeles Times* Photographic Archives (Collection 1429). UCLA Library Special Collections, Charles E. Young Research Library, UCLA.

That same year, Modesto, California, the setting of *American Graffiti*, introduced a checkpoint system on McHenry Avenue, then the popular cruising site. In March 1990, curfews at 10 p.m. for fifteen-year-olds and 11 p.m. for six-teen- and seventeen-year- olds were also enforced. The crackdown was a response to a flood of out-of-town cruisers drawn to the mystique of *American Graffiti* and driven from cruise sites in their own towns. Many residents, fearful of gangs, claimed to "feel like prisoners in [their] own homes on weekend nights." By 1990, Modesto was no longer the small town Lucas remembered. The population had grown from about 30,000 to 160,000. The police and the cruisers no longer knew one another. Still, bowing to tradition, the city continued to tolerate "Graffiti Night," a fifteen-year-old event held on the Saturday after high school graduation, that attracted up to eighty thousand cruisers on a well-regulated five-mile strip. The difference was that the participants were mostly adults, and the event celebrated distant memories of youth rather than the thrill of liberation from childhood and the promise of new adventures.[29] As result of the crackdown, McHenry Street on Saturday night was quiet the following spring, free of "troublemakers" and courting kids.[30]

While cruising reappeared periodically in the 1990s on Hollywood Boulevard, on Colorado Boulevard in Pasadena, and on Whittier Boulevard in Pico Rivera, especially when patrols were relaxed, quick enforcement and rising fines deterred cruisers.[31] Yet it took sixteen years of repeated confrontation, from 1974 to 1990, for law enforcement finally to quell cruising. In fact, it would not die until many years later in many small towns and suburbs throughout the nation.

The Surprising Persistence of the Cruise

Despite the Southern California crackdown and, as we shall see, much imitation of it elsewhere, the tradition survived. Even in outlying Los Angeles suburbs, especially on Oxnard's Saviers Road, cruising was tolerated as late as 1991. Despite sporadic reports of vandalism, gang fighting, and the appearance of lowriders and minitrucks blaring rap music from customized stereos, Oxnard police believed that the Los Angeles ban was unnecessary. They only asked for noise abatement and curfew enforcement. The city council agreed, and the next year it reauthorized this thirty-year-old tradition of cruising on a one-mile stretch of Saviers. But in September 1992, the council finally banned the cruise, citing increased gang violence and instituting the checkpoint system.[32]

Many other sites shared this reluctance to embrace the solution of Los Angeles, often believing that their neighborhood kids weren't really a problem. A common solution was to channel cruisers into alternative routes that were less disruptive of business (as in Laurel, Mississippi, in 1988 and in Princeton, West Virginia, in 1987),[33] or to designate a parking lot for the socializing of cruisers (as in Cedar Rapids, Iowa, in 1991 or in Columbus, Indiana, in 1993).[34] In 1989 Hutchinson, Kansas, considered opening a teen center, but local youths were skeptical and an appropriate site for rent couldn't be found.[35] Most of these alternatives came from small relatively homogenous towns, far from ethnic gangs. Even a good-sized city like Madison, Wisconsin, tried in the 1990s to "manage" cruisers by channeling them away from residential areas, hiring more police, and posting more "no stopping" signs and even notices that suggested alternatives to cruising.[36] But Madison was an especially liberal city. Another novel solution adopted by the small town of Big Stone Gap, Virginia, in 1993 was to abandon its policy of strict enforcement of noise and traffic rules to dampen cruising. Instead, this town offered prizes for customized vehicles and encouraged businesses to stay open for the patronage of cruisers, many of whom came from surrounding towns. As a newspaper report summed it up, "If you can't beat 'em, make money off of them."[37]

Whatever the local situation, containing the cruise was often problematic and motives were full of ambiguity. Many communities were divided between those who saw cruising as fine, often because they had indulged in it as teens, and those who feared that the cruise had changed from *American Graffiti* to

Boyz n the Hood, as was reported from Anderson, Indiana, in July 1993.[38] And police were sometimes hesitant to enforce the law. Some felt that they were caught between the demands of adults and the disdain of the kids. A Yakima, Washington, cop admitted in 1994 that he had cruised "an hour or two" as a teen and would enforce a new curb on "tooling" the town "very judiciously."[39] Periodically, politicians and advocates of civil liberties challenged cruise prohibitions, as, for example, in the 1990 class action suit of Jerome Buting against four Wisconsin towns with anticruising ordinances.[40]

The authorities also found it hard to enforce controls, especially on routes that were long and suburban instead of short and downtown. The experience in Galveston, Texas, in the summer of 1982 seems to have been common outside large metropolitan areas: When police cracked down on cruisers, parents complained about the thousand-dollar bail, and police retreated to issuing warnings. Inevitably, the cruising returned. In September 1985, though police claimed that almost all of the teens had beer, made easy by the right of nineteen-year-olds to purchase alcohol at the time, the police found it hard to enforce the law.[41] Near Hempstead on Long Island, New York, the tradition of teen cruising died hard. In June 1987, lower gas prices and an improved economy brought out kids, often from affluent families, with high-powered Buick Grand Nationals and late-model Thunderbirds.[42]

Even in the 1990s and beyond, cruising continued. Bans were often sporadically enforced, and were resisted by teens, sometimes by parents, and even by merchants. In the conservative town of Joplin, Missouri, in 1992, cruisers confronted police after checkpoints were established, honking as they drove past the police department in support of a repeal of the ban.[43] While businesses sometimes sought crackdowns, as in Portland, Oregon, in 1999, police let up when merchants subsequently complained of a loss of weekend business.[44] Local officials sometimes recognized that cruisers were local, and doubtless their own or their friends' children, and that the panic elsewhere simply didn't apply to them: As one Santa Fe city councilor noted in 1994, "You can't take [the cruise] away from them." And as late as 1998, the *Greensboro News Record* of North Carolina could report, "It's stronger than ever."[45]

Yet public authorities saw the cruising tradition as a threat, and gradually repressed it throughout the country. From the early 1980s, even relatively small cities like Lancaster, Pennsylvania, were closing down cruising routes.[46] Even if not provoked by outsiders or fears of gang violence, the confrontations so familiar in the Los Angeles area in the 1980s were duplicated across the land. For example, in August 1985 the shore road of the resort town of Virginia Beach was clogged with slow-moving cruisers, estimated at 165,000 on one weekend and likened to "killer bees swarming all over," many with stereos blaring. Some rode in jacked-up four-wheel-drive trucks, both noisy and intimidating, upsetting hotel keepers who were trying to keep their paying guests happy. But with a police force of only forty (double the force of the previous year), and recognizing that some of the cruisers were children of local people, some of whom had beach condos, one exasperated police officer told a young man, "If you want to pick up a girl, fine . . . as long as you do it at a red light."[47] This was a tough job for law enforcement.

Inevitably, perhaps, the checkpoint system of Los Angeles was quickly adopted across the country. In 1986, the summer after it was introduced in California, the city council in Newark, Delaware, prohibited passing a checkpoint three times on weekend evenings, punishable by a one-hundred-dollar fine or ninety days in jail. That same year, Georgia passed a statewide authorization of the checkpoint, and many towns from Pennsylvania and North Carolina to Minnesota and Washington adopted the same system, or blocked off cruise routes and enforced laws against curfew, loitering, and other offenses.[48] Florida spring-break cruisers faced barricaded beach roads.[49]

The decline of the cruise turned out to be a ragged affair. Bans came to Fargo, North Dakota; Milwaukee, Wisconsin; and Yakima, Washington in 1994.[50] But the custom was still practiced in Saint Louis, Salt Lake City, and Tucson, Arizona at the end of the 1990s. There was even a revival of the cruise in Southern Californian towns like Santa Ana and Pasadena, and surprisingly also on Sunset Strip in Hollywood, when police let down their guard in the late 1990s.[51] It was only in March 2009 that police in Tuscaloosa, Alabama, called for a curfew to stop local cruising.[52]

Still, as the police wore down cruisers and as militant cruisers grew up and gave up, the dwindling crowds made the cruise much less interesting to the kids. Old cruise routes, especially after discouragement by the police, often were abandoned: downtown routes lost their appeal as the bright lights moved to the suburbs, and "cruising" on foot in shopping malls no longer attracted youths over fifteen.[53]

These battles over contested spaces are common in history, but the struggle over youth cruising took on a distinctly modern, largely American cast. The sites of contention were no longer town squares, village greens, local forests, or meadows where the poor sought places of recreation or sustenance. They were ribbons and blocks of blacktop where powerful, fast-moving machines housed contenders for control of lanes and parking spots. And the competitors for this space were new, too: they were not local villagers or poor farmers seeking a temporary respite from toil in a boisterous festival, or landless laborers hunting for meat and fighting the local lord or gentry; they were children coming of age, claiming adult status and challenging maturity by turning serious money-making spaces into sites of play. This represented something really new: the rise not just of a new generation to challenge the old, but of children at the cusp of adulthood, with new fully developed bodies and not yet mature personalities, at the wheels of powerful machines.

In this light the question might be: Why was cruising tolerated at all? The fact that automobiles were plentiful in America, cheap enough for teens to possess, especially outside large cities, and legal for them to operate at the surprisingly early age of sixteen explains a lot. The cars were relatively easy to operate, thanks to modern technology. American parents had long accepted and even embraced the middle teen's right to operate these machines, and tolerated the extraordinary mobility the cars gave them. There is no better example of the freedom granted to American teens than sixteen-year-olds, often with much younger passengers, driving fifty miles or more in 1990 to parade themselves and their powerful vehicles on McHenry Street in Modesto, California.

The still difficult question is: Why was the cruise tolerated as long as it was, and why was it so difficult to eradicate? Part of the answer is simply that the legal and administrative difficulties in quashing such an entrenched activity—especially in Southern California, where local jurisdictions and the freeway system made it easy for auto-mobile teens and youth to move from one police authority to another. By the 1970s, cruising had become a tradition that successive cohorts of kids expected as their "coming out party." As we have shown, public opinion often favored the cruisers. Adults often fondly remembered their own teen experience parading in their cars, and identified with the current crop of cruisers. Even police were sometimes reluctant to go after the kids. After all, many had grown up in the towns they now policed, and had once cruised the streets they now patrolled.

Yet by the mid-1970s, law enforcement was beginning to act. In Southern California (and doubtless elsewhere) "friendly" neighborhood cruises were being invaded by gangs and racial outsiders. When police closed one strip of road, youths quickly drove to another, making the problem of the "other" greater, often in numbers that the local cops simply could not handle. Local merchants had long been discontent. But with the increasing traffic of cruisers, few of whom were customers, on main streets where business was already suffering from the spread of shopping malls, that unhappiness grew. In perhaps a vain attempt to save central business districts, local business leaders demanded action. But the attack on the cruise went well beyond all this. The obvious conclusion is that by the 1980s, American adults simply were no longer as tolerant of youth as they had once been, especially when cruisers intruded on adult space.

Despite the cruisers' often extraordinary resistance, the even more persistent labors of the authorities largely ended their tradition. This did not finish off posturing in cars, or even racing. Rather, as we shall see in the next chapter, the cruise took new forms: —nostalgic displays of the cars of elders' fond memories, and a new wave of youthful car enthusiasm in the "fast and furious" generation.

The Slow and Nostalgic versus the Fast and the Furious

By the mid-1970s, the American teen car culture was already in decline. With inflation raging and job opportunities declining, American youths found it harder to purchase and run American cars. The American automobile industry saw a parallel downturn with the "Japanese invasion" of Toyota, Nissan, and Honda, as Japan began to outproduce America car makers in 1980 and the US share of world auto production fell to 30 percent in 1981.[1] Adult authorities and society were also growing far less tolerant of ceding time and space to cruising kids.

Curiously, it was about at this time that a nostalgic wave for past teen car culture swept the country. Mostly middle-aged white men sought to recapture their youth in a tangible symbol of that youth: what else but a car? The most obvious setting for this was in car clubs and old car shows, where mostly suburban men in their forties and early fifties gathered to share memories of the 1950s and early 1960s, showing off and sharing, as they had as youths, their cool cars and stories. At the height of the crackdown on cruising in Los Angeles in 1981, these middle-aged car lovers formed cruising clubs in Anaheim. But in fact the gathering of old hot-rod enthusiasts had been going on since 1970 and even earlier with the founding of the National Street Rod Association. Things had changed from when these men first got the car bug: they no longer raced or cruised the main drag ostensibly to hook up with girls. Instead, they often clustered around drive-ins for orderly, family-friendly nights of "cruising," with plenty of showing off and "bench racing" (reminiscing about road contests of one's youth) as middle-aged men and often couples reminisced about a long-lost youth. Divided by age, the older enthusiasts held on to the romance of pre-1948 street rods, a younger group "finned up" with 1950s Chevys or even the garish 1959 Plymouth, and the youngest proudly displayed their 1960s muscle cars, each group following the fad of their distinct teen years. Despite this panoply of styles and age, nearly all these old cars collected in the 1970s and later were American-made at a time when imports were winning new car consumers. For the next quarter century, street-rod clubs, shows, and cruises (which were really parades) grew across the country as thousands shared memories of their youths constructed around cars. Of course, these nostalgiacs did not reconstruct their youth, but remembered it through the filter of time and change. The cruise was bowdlerized in nostalgia, but its hold on the no longer young was a powerful testament to the significance of youth and its vehicles across the lives of many Americans.

About the same time, something very different was happening in the world of many of the currently young. In the decades after 1980, while their elders reminisced about the glory days of American automobility, a portion of youth embraced imports, especially the sporty Japanese vehicles that were flooding the United States. Many of these youths came from nonwhite families, reflecting the changing racial and ethnic composition of the rising American generation. This group was often inspired by a new generation of car-oriented action-adventure movies—notably *The Fast and the Furious* (2001),with its Los Angeles–based street racing that featured Japanese cars and a multiethnic cast. While less prominent than earlier teen car culture, the shift to Japanese racers marked a generational divide between young and "old" teenagers. The latter group held on to their gas-guzzling muscle cars and their disdain for the Japanese "rice burners" owned by their younger counterparts. At the same time, a few of the young channeled the teen years of earlier generations in an embrace of vintage rods and even campy rat rods. This chapter will explore this changing landscape of car culture since 1970.

The Origins of the Street-Rodder

Already by the mid-1950s, hot rodding was in decline. The stripped-down and souped-up 1930s Fords and even the lead sleds of the late 1940s were no longer competitive in races with high- performance Detroit stock cars; and soon the finned GM vehicles with their stock high-compression overhead-cam engines and more modern look challenged the Deuce coupes at the cruise scene. Inevitably perhaps, the out-of-style became the nostalgic. As early as 1957, a small group in their late twenties—led by Dick Scritchfield, who had been a hot rodder since 1944, when he was fourteen, and later became a speed shop owner) formed the LA Roadster Club, dedicated to preserving the heritage of the early-1930s open-car roadster. No longer interested in racing and with families to raise, the LA Roadsters cruised to points of interest in the Los Angeles area, for family picnics.

The Roadsters were a pioneer street-rod club, as opposed to hot-rod clubs that raced. They were featured in *Hot Rod Magazine*, and the club survives today as a major player. But the movement really took off only in the mid-1960s, with groups like the Early Times Car Club of southern California, specializing in *closed* cars from the '30s. Its members were not all older men recalling a romantic youth. In fact, Early Times was founded by the brothers Tom and Bill Booth in their father's garage. As teens, the Booth brothers abhorred the expense and packaged power of the muscle cars that drew other youths of the 1960s. Instead, they embraced the world of early-1930s sedans and coupes. Sharing their name with a popular whiskey brand, the club cultivated a more daring image than the Roadsters but still maintained strict standards for membership, requiring proven skill with the welding torch and, for much of its history, insisting on the purity of pre-1948 cars with clamshell fenders. A member recalled in 2014 that club members treated Plymouths and Studebakers as "foreign cars," and mostly favored the "classic" Ford. Still operating after fifty years, the club membership has aged, with members in their seventies, often retired business and professional men who once perhaps were greasers.[2]

Other street-rod groups appeared in Wisconsin, Nashville, and San Francisco at the same time, all rejecting the "excesses" of the "funny cars" of Ed Roth, the elaborate customizations of George Barris, and—unsurprisingly, considering their middle-aged Anglo membership—the lowriders. They gloried in the resurrection of drivable pre-1948 cars. The dash was on for recovering "vintage tin" in junkyards, in the hope of recovering an innocent or golden age of automobility. Still, old car clubs feared that state and local authorities would ban these antiques from the road. Therefore, they promoted "safe and sane" shows and rallies far away from the old haunts of hot rods of the past. The Roadster Roundup, founded in 1965, met in the small town of Visalia in the San Joaquin Valley of California, with sponsorship from local motels, the Junior Chamber of Commerce, and Elks. Many of these clubs, like other hobbyist groups, were exclusive (accepting only members who successfully restored pre-1934 Fords, for example) and remained small and sometimes ephemeral.[3] This nostalgic turn paralleled a very similar quest for a lost youth in the resurrection of early rock music with groups like Sha Na Na, and the return of Elvis Presley to the limelight of Las Vegas in 1969.[4]

These street-rod clubs largely replaced the old racing clubs. In 1970, Tex Smith of *Rod and Custom* estimated that the number of traditional hot-rod clubs had dropped to five thousand "at most," compared to their peak of perhaps thirty thousand; and most of the survivors had evolved into social clubs. At the same time, drag races had become commercialized, reducing the need for clubs to organize them. The new generation of clubs was composed of "settled family men," many of whom had been in the old hot-rod groups as teens and youths. While the old clubs had usually lasted only three to five years, breaking up when members left for the military, college, or marriage, the new organizations were more stable, with core memberships of successful men who now had money to play with. And these street rodders were far more socially acceptable. As Smith saw it, by 1970 a fenderless 1929 Model A had become "cute," no longer a threat to Western civilization: "Time, and man's penchant for antiquity, has worked in hot rodding's favor."[5]

After the NHRA declined to sponsor the street-rod clubs as a subset in their organization, the editors of *Rod and Custom*, along with a number of street-rod clubs from California, Minnesota, Tennessee, and even New York, joined to organize the first Street Rod Nationals in Peoria, Illinois, in August 1970. This led directly to the National Street Rod Association (NSRA). The latter event was open to all driveable pre-1948 cars, though Fords predominated. Billed as a family event, it was attended by six hundred people. This first national meeting of street rodders was militantly noncommercial and casual, with many attendees camping. Activities included the "show 'n' shine" display of prized vehicles, which included prizes for the best three-window vehicle and even for the best non-Ford car (such were rare among street rodders). In contrast to the professionalized hot-rod shows, this one stressed the ordinary guy with an understanding wife who gave him the time and access to the household budget for his hobby. The next year, *Hot Rod Magazine* joined in to sponsor a second meeting of street rods (called the Street Rod Nationals) in Memphis, recognizing the "good ol' days' attitude of the sport" of street rodding. This event was also a down-home affair, complete with a dance, a river cruise, and even buses for those wives who wanted to go to shopping. There was a turtle race and even a greased pig contest, all to recall the wholesomeness of an "early fair," in sharp contrast to the rebellious tone of 1950s clubs. The Memphis meeting of street rodders was twice the size of the first gathering in Peoria. The Street Rod Nationals became an annual event that soon had to be divided into eight regional meetings. Inevitably, these events became more commercialized, promoted not only by the old magazines, like *Hot Rod* in November 1974, but also by new ones, like *Street Rodder* in 1971.[6]

Ever responsive to the hobbyist market, new hot-rod parts manufacturers, like the Deuce Factory and Total Performance, appeared by the mid-1970s to take up the slack in the decline of junked parts. Street-rodders generally wanted cars that they could drive and repair and even be comfortable in, add-

FIGURE 8.1. Typical street rod show, National Street Rod Association, York, Pennsylvania (June 2016). Author's photo collection.

ing plush bucket seats without embarrassment, and installing cassette players in the 1980s to play old Chuck Berry songs. By the 1990s, as Albert Drake notes in his memoir, "a guy from a dental lab" would buy a '31 Ford coupe and equip it with a 350-horsepower engine with a Turbo 400, hoping to see the value go up.[7]

And by the 1980s, despite resistance from old-timers, cars manufactured after 1948 were admitted to some street-rod events. In 1982, Jerry and Elden Titus organized a customs meet in Wichita for later models, called Lead East; and in 1987, the ex-NSRA official Gary Meadors broke away from the NSRA to found the Good Guys Rod and Custom Association, for street rods built as recently as 1986. Meadors's organization attracted a younger crowd, reaching 64,000 members by 2016, with twenty-four commercial shows a year. Others also appeared, including the Old Farts Car Club, the Over the Hill Gang, the West Coast Customs, and Hot Rods Unlimited, just to mention some of the larger clubs centered in Southern California (though clubs blossomed across the country). Some clubs, like the Over the Hill Gang, were exclusively male; others, like the Old Farts, took pride in their lack of bureaucracy and budget.[8]

A still greater divide separated the street-rodders from the antique car collectors, reflecting the long-lasting class difference in teen car culture that separated greasers from preppies (chapter 5). This distinction is seldom acknowledged in interviews with club members; in fact, street-rodders and antique collectors often claim to respect and appreciate each other's contributions. Still, the origins and development of the Antique Automobile Club of America (AACA) suggests a path quite different from that of the street rodders. The AACA has roots not in California, but at an auto show sponsored by a Philadelphia car dealer during the Great Depression in 1931, who hoped that the publicity would attract customers. Two participants decided to form a permanent club of antique auto owners and, in 1937, began publishing a newsletter for members. Rather than originating in the culture of the high-school greaser, the AACA was part of the petit bourgeois world of small-town shopkeepers, insurance salesmen, and even local bankers, and small manufac-turers. Membership was similar to the Kiwanis, Elks, and other the fraternal clubs that had flourished since the mid-nineteenth century. Their enthusiasm may have had its roots in youth (as seen in chapter 5), but not in the rebellious world of the working-class hot-rodder. By 1947 the AACA had formalized rules of competition, dividing old cars into eleven classes to distribute awards, which were a big part of the club's activities. Membership in the AACA was only 850 in 1948, and it grew to about 50,000 by 1985. But since then, the AACA notes, its "growth has remained steady," perhaps reflecting the aging of the hobbyists and the rise of independent clubs.[9] Unlike the street-rodders with their customized vehicles, antique car enthusiasts have as their primary goal "preserving a piece of history in its original form," and judges at their shows deduct points for having the "interior redone or having a part wrong."[10] These differences reflect contrasting childhood memories, as in many cases the tension between the greasers and socs has survived into old age.

Cruise-ins and Bench Racers

This nostalgic impulse,[11] be it for rods or antiques, went much further than car clubs and meets. By the 1980s it also took the form of "cruise-ins" at local drive-ins and similar venues. At these small, familiar places, often themselves sites of romantic memory, mostly middle-aged men with their sometimes indulgent wives gathered to reminisce about their fun-filled days of teenage cruising. Ironically, perhaps, during the height of the January 1981 crackdown on youth cruising in the Los Angeles area, such a group met at an A&W drive-in restaurant in Anaheim to reminisce about their cruising days in the 1950s and 60s. Dave Gibson, a forty-two-year old chiropractor, posted a news-paper ad for old-car enthusiasts over the age of thirty-five who were interested in cruising "like we did in the '50s." He was surprised to see more than fifty cars show up. This was the beginning of the Orange County Cruise Associ-ation (a loose affiliation of local car clubs); the Orange County Cruise Night was then held the first Friday of every month.[12]

Despite the term "cruise," (often called cruise-in), this event had little in common with the hooking-up or racing of the old teen cruise nights. Instead, it was an orderly, family-friendly evening of showing off vintage cars and "bench racing," as the middle-aged men swapped stories. The events usually prohibited alcohol, loud radios, pets, wheel spinning, "burn outs," and often cars made after 1970.[13] At the same time, this nostalgia for a 1950s youth could be experienced vicariously. Another "cruiser," then a twenty-nine-year-old firefighter, bragged that he had seen *American Graffiti* thirteen times and wished he had been a teenager in those golden years of cruising. Car shows continue to be peppered with young enthusiasts who "channeled" a youth that was not their own. And their elders still wanted to share their memories with the next generation. In a 1991 newspaper interview, a forty-four-year-old mother of two from suburban Los Angeles who had met her husband cruising happily asserted: "I have to bring my kids and show them what happened in my day. I know they'd love it." Inevitably, this expectation led to disappointment. Even if both parents and kids loved cars, their affection was usually for different vehicles that came from different youths.[14]

By 1984, the cruise-in world of Southern California had broadened from nostalgia for the hot rods of the 1930s and '40s and even the Chevys of the 1950s to include the Mustangs and muscle cars from the 1960s. That summer, men in their early forties congregated in a parking lot on Balboa Avenue in south Los Angeles to show off their '65 Mustangs, CT Chevelles, Super Sports, GTOs, Camaros, and Chargers, all cars of a newer generation commemorating their youth.[15]

Ironically—even hypocritically—a merchant's group on Van Nuys Boulevard in May 1986 sponsored a "classic car parade," despite the fact that five years earlier, merchants on that same street had pressured officials into banning teen cruising. These businessmen hadn't changed their minds about the teens, of course. Entry applications for the parade required a picture of each car, and an official admitted that only one car was rejected: "It was some gang type [car]. We recognized the Chevy right away." This was an obvious reference to a contemporary lowrider, the latest edition of the young rebel's vehicle. Despite the fact that the lowrider was a descendent of the Deuce coupe that some of the organizers might have owned in the 1950s, the organizers harbored no comradely feeling across generations—or race.[16]

By 1984, with its 1,200 members (most from "thirty or forty" local clubs), the Orange County Cruise Association was too big for drive-ins alone. On Labor Day, the association held a car show at the Orange County Fairgrounds, with Budweiser beer sponsoring. The meeting welcomed everything from 1950s Cadillacs to rusting Ramblers. And not only did the police embrace this gathering, but they contributed more than their share of off-duty participants. At the 1991 gathering a boomer gleefully noted, "The cops were always after us when we were kids. Now the cops are the kids, and they give us a lot of respect." At the same time, in order to keep out the low riders and other "lowlife," the association didn't announce the location of the "cruise" until couple of days before the event. These middle-aged guys had long forgotten any of their youthful lawlessness. A forty-one-year-old insisted that he was no James Dean, no rebel without a cause. His cause was his street rod. Another offered a more philosophical perspective: "The cars are the magic symbol of how things were in the 1950s and the things you did in high school. . . . . [The street rod] represents the things you wanted to do then and couldn't afford to do."[17] The Orange County Cruise was a way of not just returning to a lost youth, but of fulfilling the dreams of that youth.

These gatherings proliferated in the 1990s. The Route 66 Rendezvous through San Bernardino, California, was a tribute to the transcontinental highway made famous in the 1950s by a popular car-themed TV show. In 1995 it attracted 190,000 visitors to "Show-n-Shine" events and parades.[18] Another spectacular old car show was August Nights, organized by Reno, Nevada, tourist officials seeking a crowd during the seasonal lull in the gambling business. By 2013 it was so popular that Reno's nostalgic car scene extended from May 22 to October 5 as various casinos, car parts stores, and restaurants took turns holding cruise-ins.[19] Surely one of the largest nostalgic cruise events occurs in the last weekend of August along Detroit's Woodward Avenue. As we have seen, this north-south route on Detroit's eastern edge was the site of teen cruising from the 1950s, which declined only in the 1970s as it did elsewhere. But the tradition was revived in 1995 as the Woodward Dream Cruise, a weekend event that shared little with the cruising culture of past teens, except for the cars. At first it was a fundraiser in one neighborhood, but very quickly most of the towns along Woodward got involved, as did numerous corporate sponsors, especially Chevrolet. By 2004 an estimated forty thousand vintage vehicles entertained 1.5 million car lovers.[20]

Old car gatherings also have been held in small towns throughout the country, especially since the 1990s. Doubtless trading on the aura of its hometown boy, Elvis Presley, Tupelo, Mississippi, sponsored the Blue Suede Cruise starting in 2003, combining the usual car show with vintage rock bands.[21] Other such events have been often held weekly in warm weather at convenient drive-in eateries, which make their parking lots available in hopes of increasing business, or in conjunction with small-town or suburban festivals.[22] Many have been old family-owned drive-ins: Be Bop Burgers in Santa Barbara, California; Disilfink Drive-In in Gettysburg, Pennsylvania; Carmichael's in Long

FIGURE 8.2. Nostalgic spectators at the Woodward Dream Cruise, Detroit. Used by permission of Robert Genat.

Island, New York; and Mickey's in East Harford, Connecticut. Officials from sites as diverse as Tacoma, Washington; Keene, New Hampshire; and Decatur, Illinois have hosted vintage car events, as has Petaluma, California, a town where some of *American Graffiti* was filmed in 1972. Cruise-ins offered raffles, collected for local charities, and even held contests, such as one for the highest beehive hairdo on a woman.[23] The rules hadn't changed by 2016, nor had the sites: drive-ins, county fairgrounds, and even firehouses, with registration fees usually donated to some local charity.[24]

Cruise night groups often separated into distinct castes, reflecting the age and social background of their members. For example, in the summer of 2003 a subdued gathering of thoroughly restored hot rods and mid-1950s classics was held at a middle-class restaurant in the largely white northwestern section of Milwaukee while a racier working-class event took place at a Near South Side eatery where Latinos showed off their lowriders and blasted rap and salsa music from car speakers and boom boxes.[25]

Lovers of the gas guzzlers of the 1960s and early 1970s were thrilled to return to the days before "the EPA throttled authoritative performance and before the FDA made us feel guilty about eating a cheeseburger," as street-rod memoirist Robert Genat wrote.[26] A middle-aged street-rodder from rural Wisconsin, born in 1958, summed up the appeal of these events: "I have burnt out on the muscle car thing and rebuilt a Model A hot rod. Going back to the roots of where it started. I have joined a club where I'm the oldest in the club. This is my church, as we all worship the automobile. Power has become less important, and just looking cool getting there is the goal."[27]

Street-Rod People

It is difficult to construct a simple profile of the "typical" street-rodder and "bench cruiser" today. But interviews with a range of them suggest some patterns. Many, especially the more active ones, seem to have been car-clubbers as teens, returning to the hot rod after raising families, accumulating resources, retiring, and perhaps abandoning other motor hobbies of their early adult lives (speedboats, sports cars, etc.). Many, of course, strive to find the dream car of their youth. As one collector from Orange County noted: "You can tell when they were in high school by their dream car." Even so, for many, buying that car today has become impossible, with the cost of restored hot rods climbing to $200,000, and even the once plentiful Chevys of the mid-1950s selling for $50,000 or more (almost all requiring cash payment). Street-rodding has become a hobby of the well-off (probably a minority of ex-greasers) who can afford these prices, even though a point of great pride for many street rodders is to have kept the same dream car for decades since their youth. In 2016 a Cal-Rod member born in 1956 was delighted to show me his Model A with a 1955 Oldsmobile engine and a dragster "scoop" air intake on the hood, which in one form or another he had owned since his teen years. He admitted that he was lucky to have graduated from high school, though a successful concrete contracting business enabled him to keep up with the rising costs of hot-rodding.[28]

For some, at least, the street rod represents an age gone by, an America that has been superseded by "diversity." Not surprisingly, on the rare occasion when politics was mentioned at the LA Roadster show in June 2016, a group of male street-rodders told me that they were part of the "silent majority"—a curious referral to President Richard Nixon's appeal to the white middle class who opposed anti–Vietnam War protesters and civil rights activities. One member of the group said he was "tired of all the b.s.," and, though a registered Democrat, said he couldn't remember when he last voted for candidate from that party. Then Republican presidential nominee Donald Trump may have said some "ridiculous things," he said, but he "has it together." Another man in the group complained that the "Democrats take all the political jobs," like the teachers who "get to be millionaires" in retirement. These men all claimed that, in contrast to the teachers, they had "worked hard," often in physically demanding construction or manufacturing jobs, even though one admitted that he was "lucky" to have come to maturity in the late 1950s and early '60s, benefitting from the boom in Southern California at that time.[29]

There was often a great sense of tradition among street-rodders. The historian Robert Post, reporting on a car show at the Oakland Museum of California Technology and Culture in 1998, notes a fifty-year continuity that made these displays "celebratory exhibits." They demonstrated an extraordinary dedication to detail and skill, essentially a conservative impulse.[30] Even in a study of middle-aged women owners of muscle cars at Michigan in the early 2010s, few challenged the often very macho world of the muscle car enthusiasts. Instead, these women embraced the world of muscle cars out of memory of a mechanical father's or brother's Pontiac GTO in the 1960s, or as a means of solidifying a relationship with a "muscled" husband or boyfriend. Even the occasional single women who owned muscle cars did so to fulfill a personal dream dating from youth, not as a challenge to men. The car show world was, for them as for the men, a family event—an opportunity to engage in community charity and uphold a tradition.[31]

The dominating emotion of street-rodders was nostalgia and the deeply conservative values that often accompanied it. In interviews, cruise-nighters recalled how radical rock music was when they were young, and how their parents hated their heroes: Elvis Presley and, even more, Jerry Lee Lewis, with his raw brand of music. But they also recalled how innocent the 1950s and early '60s had been. What a contrast between the cynicism of present-day rap or hip hop and the 1957 hit song "Wake Up Little Susie," about a couple who fell asleep at a drive-in movie and feared that their "reputations" would be "shot."[32] As in so much nostalgia, the elder cruisers had forgotten or romanticized their old rebelliousness. And they often did not see their own experience in the youth of today.

Still, despite this basic adherence to the past, a lot had changed for these old street-rodders since they were teen hot-rodders. Obviously, fewer could do the mechanical work; some admitted to "writing big checks" for others to do it. And, while many clubs were very narrowly focused on ancient roadsters or early Corvettes, or even on Edsels and Studebakers from the 1950s, and often were beset with rules (like those giving preferred parking spots to senior members), there was also a trend toward greater informality, with less organizational hierarchy.[33] These old teenagers had loosened up.

Perhaps the most striking trend was the increased role of women. Not only did women join the club leadership instead of just running the charities and preparing the picnics, but females even appeared with their own rods (though sometimes as widows who had inherited their deceased husbands' passion or cars). Part of this, I think, is a result of a big change between the male's teen years of male bonding (noted in chapter 4)—when females, as a man born in 1937 recalled, were "just dates"—and his years of patient compromise and interaction with a wife in marriage, which brought women into the hobby. A common story is the longevity of the street-rod marriage, especially for those who wedded young in the 1950s and early '60s. A veteran of the LA Roadsters since 1967 joked about how he had bought and sold perhaps five hundred cars since getting married, but had kept his wife happy by splitting the profits, which she used to nicely furnish their home.[34] Penny Pichett, a hot-rod widow born in 1946, had had no interest in cars as a teen, beyond pleasing her hot-rodding boyfriend, hoping he would outgrow his obsession. She ended up marrying him and building a diner business by catering to hot-rodders. She and her husband founded the West Coast Kustoms Club in 1981. She bonded with the other club wives and did charity work, but later ran the club after her husband's death, maintaining it as a major player in the world of street rods.[35]

Perhaps inevitably, some clubs tried to maintain a "serious" male car-cruising tone by excluding women or, when they were present, continuing to treat them as helpmeets. Yet this was not always the case. The Cal-Rods, which in the 1950s had had a girls' auxiliary (the Cal-Rodettes, discussed in chapter 3), were resurrected in 1999 by Don Scurti, its original founder, and Vic Cunnyngham, but no longer separated the sexes. Not only did women now serve in leadership roles, but some, even including single women, participated at events with their own street rods. In 2016 the club had about three hundred members, perhaps only a third of whom were from Baldwin Park, where the club began in the 1950s. The club offered car cruises, but also a revival of the old spring picnics, poker runs, charity events, Christmas dinner dances, and even 1950s sock hops at the old high school.[36] The years had dissolved some of gender divisions of the old Cal-Rods, but they had also turned it into a social club loosely built on a memory of youth.

The nostalgic trend was not restricted to old hot-rodders. Low riders who had participated in large car clubs like the Elite and Dukes Car Clubs in the 1960s and 1970s revitalized those clubs in the 1990s. The brothers Mario Jr. and Albert De Alba, sons of the veteran lowrider Mario Senior, who had founded the Elites, took over that club in 1991. The De Alba brothers insisted that members of the club not be in street gangs. As Albert put it, "We want pure positive, more family oriented, grown-up people." The revived Elite organized car shows and picnics, much as did other nostalgic car clubs. But they were not a same-age peer group, as were the street-rod clubs. With members from nineteen to fifty-four years of age in 1999, the club continued the cross-generational tradition of the Hispanic community. Similarly, the Ruelas brothers, who had been key players in the Dukes, moved to the suburbs of Whittier and La Habra as they aged and continued the club, passing the tradition down to their sons.[37] A fifty-five-year-old low rider I met at a street-rod show in June 2016 with his 1963 Chevy happily remarked that, while his Latino art form had long been rejected at street rod shows, his heritage had recently been recognized by the prestigious indoor Grand National Roadster Show in Los Angeles. He also took delight in the fact that Whittier Boulevard, closed by the mid-1970s because of Hispanic gang activity, had recently been reopened once a month for nostalgic low riders and admiring youths.[38] Though predominantly an expression of white male nostalgic peer bonding, that longing to reconnect with the cars of youth reached into the Latino community and was even embraced by some women.

Fast and Furious: Youth's Answer to Nostalgia

By the 1990s, while middle-aged car lovers huddled into their generational tribes, some American youth found their own, very different car culture. The new kids on the block were attracted to the very vehicles that frustrated their elders: the "rice burners," those small but sporty, mostly Japanese cars with their buzzing rather than roaring engines, which symbolized the decline of the American automobile and of a generation's bygone youth. And many of these cars were new or nearly so.

Underlying all this was the simple fact of increased affluence and the accompanying increase in multicar families. The percentage of US households with two or more cars rose from 30 to 60 percent between 1969 and 1997. By the 1990s, well-off parents were willing to buy their teen offspring new or at least late-model used cars, in part to ease stress in the harried lives of families in which both parents held jobs. In the flush years of relaxed consumer financing before the 2008 recession, dealers were eager to sell cars to young drivers.[39] Amy Best's striking ethnography of latter-day cruising in San Jose (ca. 2003) notes how the lowriders and minitrucks of Latino youth no longer prowled the main drag. They had been replaced by SUVs, Mercedeses, and Lexuses—parental cars driven by a more affluent group of teens from the outer suburbs. Police seem to have selectively enforced anticruising laws to eliminate the annoying lowriders, with their loud music, from a district under redevelopment.[40]

This shift toward imports by the 1990s was natural, given the eclipse of the American car industry and the success of Japanese and carmakers in overcoming their older image as producers of cheap, underpowered economy vehicles. Despite emitting a buzz rather than a roar, Asian sports vehicles were now "rice burners" only to the older generation brought up on muscle cars.

And both Japanese and European companies challenged the old marketing ideal of GM's Alfred P. Sloan: that buyers would work their way up the ladder of success with a progression of car brands, reaching the pinnacle with a Cadillac only if they were very successful. Import companies introduced youth-oriented status vehicles, like the Lexus or the BMW, for those no longer willing to wait until middle age for luxury.[41]

But the generational shift in car aesthetics was about more than an embrace of the foreign car and a rejection of the old American model. It encompassed new ideas about tinkering, sometimes led not by native whites but by immigrant children. This movement was started around 1992 by Asian American youths in California, gradually expanding to Hispanics in the Southwest, and to African Americans and whites in the East.

The pioneers began with hand-me-down Honda Civics, often received from their parents, which like the Model Ts of their predecessors were plentiful and cheap. Many of these cars cost less than five thousand dollers in 2003, and often had well over one hundred thousand miles on their odometers. Though the Civic was hardly an obvious candidate for speedware, any more than the "T" had been sixty years earlier, with new kinds of tinkering (now called "tuning" or "tricking out"), this new generation of hot-rodders could make one go from zero to sixty miles per hour in five seconds. Gone was the old stress on multiple carburetors; instead, the new generation of enthusiasts hacked the car's computer to modify the fuel injectors; and instead of installing overhead-valve kits on flathead engines, they added turbochargers and special exhaust systems to increase the flow of air and fuel. The new generation sometimes worked long hours in fast-food joints and minimum-wage janitor jobs to earn the cash to buy adjustable struts and sway bars. Rather than "frenching" a car's body, they installed spoilers and sideskirts, sometimes along with LED lights in florescent or blue and 130-decibel stereos, perhaps in unconscious imitation of low riders. The club was quickly joined by owners of other imported cars including low-end BMWs, Volkswagen Jettas and Golfs, and even domestic vehicles like the Ford Focus, the Dodge Neon, and the Chevrolet Cavalier—all, like the Honda Civic, relatively cheap and small, sometimes sporty, and easy to accessorize. The technology and look had changed; but in the end, the new generation of customizers shared with the older hot-rodders a quest for speed and style.[42]

The trailblazing role of Asian American youth is especially revealing. In a 2004 ethnographic study of Asian Americans in race car crews, Soo Ah Kwon found youths from families of middle-class, often professional Asian immigrants who arrived after 1965 (when discrimination against Asian immigrants was eliminated). From the late 1980s, these car enthusiasts avidly read Japanese

FIGURE 8.3. Two members of the Penn State Car Club working on a late-model tuner car, a Mazda Miata (April 2017). Photograph by Jimmy Daehnke. Used by permission of the photographer.

car magazines, defying the American identity of older hot-rodders. Lacking access to the drag strips, they often raced illegally, but by the mid-1990s many had joined import-only shows and races. The race car teams that Kwon studied all had quasi-Japanese names, such as Rocketsu or Team Hokori. These Asian Americans pointedly rejected Korean cars like Hyundai, which they considered inferior, as well as "Bondo cars," which were modified with cheap body kits. Instead, they added fifteen or even forty thousand dollars worth of power and customizations to their cars. Clearly, these were not the children of mechanics or laborers as many hot-rodders had been; they often came from "pretty well-off families." Some received substantial sums of money from their parents for getting good grades in school.

Yet they also resisted the "demasculinized image" of Asians common in Anglo society. They did so by imitating the hypersexual hip-hop "gangsta" look of some African-Americans by wearing baggy jeans and puffy jackets, all to counter the "model minority" image of the "nerdy" Asian. Young Asian-American women sometimes appeared in midriff-baring T-shirts and tight jeans, draping themselves over the cars for photo shoots in a fashion reminiscent of some of the images of Latinas at lowrider shows.[43]

This "tuner" car culture spread well beyond the Asian Americans of California. In striking contrast to the street-rodders, in a 2003 survey, only 42 percent of these young car enthusiasts were white and 28 percent were Asians, with the rest African-American and Hispanic; 74 percent were between eighteen and twenty-five years of age, and 20 percent were women. The Specialty

Equipment Market Association claimed that sales of custom and power accessories jumped from $295 million in 1997 to $2.3 billion in 2002. This money mostly went for new shop-installed import–tuning equipment. Again, an industry survey in 2000 found that the new customizers came from households earning $57,000 and that most lived with their parents, saving money often while working to soup up cars. This was part of a modern trend: the young male who deferred marriage and commitment for a long period of freedom and personal consumption.[44] Still, the old tradition of teens doing their own customizing survived, if in new forms. For example, in 2006, a group of high school students from Glens Falls, New York, installed in their cars not tachometers, but PlayStation 2 video game consoles, interior glow and exterior "underglow" lighting, and even nitrous oxide injection kits for extra boosts of power.[45]

And power, as always, remained a large part of the youth car scene. Strikingly reminiscent of the street racing of 1940s adolescents, a now mixed-race gathering of youths tested and competed their mostly imported tricked-up rides in places like Ontario, California. While the old haunts of the early hotrodders had long been too heavily clogged with traffic jams and police, Ontario in 2001 was a Los Angeles exurb more than forty miles east of the city; and the new kids raced on streets lined with warehouses and factories, largely empty late in the evenings and relatively unpatrolled for traffic. In June 2001 at about 11 p.m. each evening, some three to five hundred cars, each often with three or four youths inside, gathered in empty streets: some to watch and others to race. At midnight, pairs of cars would pulled out, one after another, to form a "conga line." A youth standing in the middle of a street would raise his arms to signal the first two cars in the line to start a quarter-mile drag race, to be followed by the next two more cars and so on. As these races drew their attention, police would use a helicopter and thirteen cars to break them up, arresting perpetrators, imposing fines, impounding vehicles, and suspending licenses. Still, young lookouts armed with cell phones would warn the race participants of incoming cops, enabling most of them to avoid punishment. Slight variations of this ritual took place in suburban Seattle, in the California cities of Fresno, Sacramento, and San Diego, and elsewhere. Youths in cars met in large industrial parking lots to form lines; then they cruised down quiet roads, occasionally stopping their processions to start a race.[46]

As in the 1950s, the police responded not just by more law enforcement, but by sponsoring speed contests at Los Angeles drag strips for this new generation. In the spring of 2003, youths with their souped-up Hondas took pride in beating large but underpowered Ford Victoria police cars in "top the cop" races at the Infineon Raceway in the San Francisco area. Even earlier, in 1995, again reminiscent of the early-1950s efforts of Wally Parks and the NHRA, the National Import Racing Association was formed with corporate sponsorship to legitimize competition between imports and to remove it from the public streets.[47]

Again, as it had done with exploitation hot rod movies like *Hot Rod Gang* (1958) and *Drag Strip Girl* (1957), Hollywood tried to pick up on the new racing trend. Universal Studios led the way with a remake of the 1955 car chase movie by famed exploitation film maker Roger Corman, *The Fast and the Furious*. Rob Cohen, a veteran of street racing himself, was the director of the new version released in 2001, claiming in a newspaper interview that street racing had once again become the "heartbeat culture of fashion, music, style." Universal invested $39 million, hoping for a summer hit. Despite a multiracial cast, the cars were definitely Asian, starring a Toyota Supra with a nitrous-oxide injection button on the steering wheel and flames coming from the exhaust pipe, along with an equally cool Mitsubishi Eclipse and Mazda RX7.[48]

The plot, standard for action films, involved two teams of racers. One was led by Dominic Toretto (played by Vin Diesel), a truck hijacker, whose gang was infiltrated by Brian O'Conner (Paul Walker), a cop who fell for his sister. The other team was led by Johnny Tran, whom O'Conner incorrectly targeted as the hijacker before reluctantly realizing that Toretto was the real culprit. O'Conner eventually revealed his identity to Toretto and his sister when he intervened as Toretto's team planned to hijack an armed truck. Meanwhile, Tran goaded Jesse, from Toretto's group, into a race for possession of each other's car. Refusing to pay up when he lost the race, Jesse was murdered by Tran's gang. The cop and Toretto chased and dispatched the killers. After a final drag race, O'Conner, the cop let Toretto escape to Mexico.

The new version of *The Fast and The Furious* dispensed with the thin overcoat of moral righteousness formerly required of action films. Instead, it was about male bonding, and ultimately about the new Japanese cars and street-racing culture. Notably, the producer hired experts and veterans from the National Import Racing Association as advisers. As always, the kids (40 percent of the audience was Latino) went to see the movie for the cars and the hip-hop music track. It earned $145 million in theaters and another $51 million in home video sales. Having noted the Latino crowds that the first *The Fast and The Furious* had attracted, the producers set the remake in Miami. Ultimately, there were six sequels by 2016 and more on the way, attracting not only ethnic American youths but an international audience, including young Chinese, with settings around the world (including Japan in *Tokyo Drift*).[49]

Reviewers of the first version of *The Fast and the Furious* saw mainly an exploitation of the rapper culture: its language, its music, and especially its touting of conspicuous consumption.[50] But the success of *The Fast and the Furious* series (especially the early sequels) depended on its being set in a new, exciting world of tricked-out imports driven by multiracial groups of urban youth. Because it was inspired by import street racing, the first movie convinced Los Angeles area police that they needed to patrol theaters that were showing the film to stop copycat racing by enthusiastic viewers.[51]

The age of the fast and furious led to an upsurge in the sale of neon and body kits, especially for the sporty Honda Civic Si. This "factory hot rod" was designed to be cheap and customizable for youth, and was a sharp break from the nondescript Civic of years past. An ad for this model in 2002 featured sixty-five Los Angeles youth with "their rides done up with flashy paint jobs, turbocharged engines and specialized lights."[52] Yet, just two years later, the *Wall Street Journal* reported that the Honda Civic was losing its appeal as a "tuner" car, challenged by new youth-oriented vehicles like Subaru's WRX and especially Toyota's Scion xB, introduced the previous year as a cheap version of the Honda Element and the BMW Mini. The Scion was a boxy vehicle designed for the Japanese (thus the characteristic Japanese domestic market, or JDM, look) with a fixed fourteen-thousand-dollar price tag for relatively easy purchase by young buyers presumably open to all things Japanese. After all, this was the generation brought up on Sailor Moon and Power Rangers, who disdained the American minivans they had so recently been obliged to ride in with their soccer moms. The Scion had "factory customization," with big wheels and even options for graphics in the paint job. It looked like no Toyota that their parents had owned. Toyota tried to make it into a lifestyle brand, with a short-lived magazine and even a fashion line. But the company hoped that moms and dads who had driven and trusted the Toyota brand would buy the Scion for their slightly rebellious offspring.[53] Import luxury brands, including BMW, Mercedes-Benz, and Lexus, also introduced relatively low-priced entry-level models for young buyers. And naturally, the declining voice of the American car industry wanted to be heard by this rising generation of youth. In 2001, following earlier efforts to soup up its revived Mustang and F-150 pickups with engine and suspension upgrades, Ford introduced the sporty Focus, promoting it as a "global hot rod."[54]

This effort to win youthful consumers was not always a success. The Scion never met expectations, and was discontinued in 2016. Tastes changed rapidly, and marketers recognized that the young were increasingly hard to please and equally hard to reach.[55] Mindful of this, carmakers consciously adapted to presumed youthful interests. Metallic color options, rubber floor mats for easy cleaning (to deal with sand at the beach, perhaps), electric outlets on the console for computer chargers, and other gadgets became common features.

By 2003, the Honda Element was promoted as a "dorm room on wheels," equipped early with a plug-in for MP3 players. And Toyota promoted its Echo as an ideal new starter car for youth.[56]

Yet the bigger problem was that the young were less easy to reach with traditional advertising in magazines and network and cable TV. Carmakers tapped into the new media and digital culture to reach the rising generation. At the May 2003 Los Angeles Auto show, Mitsubishi showed clips from the sequel 2 *Fast 2 Furious* that featured the Lancer Evolution, a 271-horsepower sports sedan that sold for twenty-nine thousand dollars. It's hard to imagine that teens and youth would really be in the market for such an expensive car, but the aim of Mitsubishi's advertising was partly to create aspiration. Moreover, Mitsubishi showrooms also featured lower-priced models with ads that featured the band the Barenaked Ladies and offering zero down and no monthly payments for a year to lure first-time buyers. Product placement in movies was an old promotional tool, so it's no surprise that Mitsubishi made sure to have its Evolution model included in the *Fast and Furious* series. Ads for the Scion in 2005 still ran on TV (though late at night and on cable, presumably to attract youth), and they featured computer graphics and even advice on how to accessorize the car.[57]

Most innovative were the efforts of automobile companies to get their new models featured in video games. Marketers realized, of course, that youths, especially males, played video games long after childhood; they estimated that forty million Americans were at the controls in 2005.[58] Some companies offered "advergaming": online games to introduce the young to their new models. The 2006 Subaru Impreza was featured in the game Showdown, giving players a "real feel" for driving these cars. Mitsubishi "partnered" with PlayStation in the game Gran Turismo 4. PlayStation not only featured Mitsubishi vehicles in its games, but gave the carmaker its database of game registrants.[59] Cars, of course, were also the focus of violent video games like Grand Theft Auto. The first version promised that a player who "play[ed] it right" would "move up in the crime family, graduating to drug dealer, kidnapper, and drive-by shooter." Another such game was Carmageddon, in which the play involved running down pedestrians. Such games, noted Jason Hall of Monolith Productions, appealed to "adolescent humor," and were ways "to vent steam."[60]

The less acknowledged goal of placing cars in video games was to expose the young, even players still too young to drive, to new models. Players of Gran Turismo might be only kids, but "even twelve-year-old game players get interested in the car, talk about it with friends and aspire to buy it," noted Wesley Brown, marketing analyst at Nextrend. No longer did the car bug come from watching a big brother or uncle rebuild a beater; now it came from driving autos virtually in a game. Associating the new models with rap videos and action movies, merchandisers believed, would build brand identification before the kids lost interest in these edgy markers of youth culture.[61]

The "fast and furious" generation, those coming of age in the mid-1990s and beyond, surely had abandoned the old "American" car culture of the LA Roadsters, or of the muscle-car enthusiasts who had disdained "rice rockets." In some ways this was inevitable, as the available pool of customizable cars shifted to imports. The new generation of "tuners" had to have more money to get into the game than their forbears had needed: after all, even used cars increased dramatically in price in the 1990s, partially because they were driveable at higher mileages than the old beaters had been. Yet the new kids had a lot more in common with the old than was sometimes recognized by either group.

An interesting illustration of this point is an online forum for young car enthusiasts called Stanceworks.com, founded in 2009 out of a body shop in Costa Mesa, California. Taking a rather philosophical point of view, Stanceworks insists that vehicles are "blank canvases" that demand the creativity of customization. The site features a wide range of this expressiveness on everything from hot rods to JDMs, including the boxy Scion XB and the slant-lipped Subaru. Mike Burroughs's story of his discovery and transformation of a 1928 Ford Model A pickup offers a striking example. The truck, which he found on Craigslist, was and remains rusty and covered in dirt, suggesting to him the "yellow powdery silt from the El Mirage dry lake bed," a heritage of the manly generation of racing in the 1930s. Yet Burroughs insists that his vehicle is more than a recovered junker; he has added "too much underneath the rough exterior that is new." His most important addition is a modern BMW engine, a touch that makes the Model A "his" hot rod. While "channeling" earlier generations who grew up with cars, Burroughs has still made his own personal contribution to hot rod culture through a modern youth embrace of the import.[62]

Youth versus Youth

The clash between youthful rebellion and nostalgia for youth continues to the present in successive cohorts of auto enthusiasts. Car identities have long been shaped by generational shifts: muscle-car aficionados share a memory of growing up in the late 1960s and early 1970s, when American-made, rear-wheel drive, midsized vehicles equipped with overpowered gas-guzzling engines were all the rage before the oil crisis of 1973 and the Asian conquest of the American car market. For many in that generation, Hondas and Toyotas

became an affront to the memory of their youth, even as Japanese cars became the preferred vehicles of the young—and, as it turns out, of much of the
American car-driving public.[63]

But car culture across the generations sometimes worked in more subtle
ways. Consider the retro-hot-rod and more extreme rat-rod movements
that emerged in the late 1990s. These were enthusiasms that attracted some
youth of that decade, the same generation that also embraced import tuners.
Curiously, these movements were a reaction to relatively well-off fifty- and
sixty-year-olds of the time who no longer worked on their favorite cars, and
who instead bought already-restored rods, sometimes with fiberglass bodies
and high-end crate engines. Recently, this impulse has taken the form of the
"restomod," a vehicle still in the form and look of the "classic" hot rod, but
equipped with modern technology.[64] Derisively labeling these beauties "trailer
queens" for their showiness, cost, and lack of utility, retro hot-rodders shared
with their forbearers of the late 1950s and early '60s a distaste for the cost of
the show cars and for the commercialization of drag-racing culture. To some
degree, this movement was the latest gasp of an increasingly marginalized
skill culture—often working-class and rural, at least in origin—against the
inevitable commercialization of the hobby and the rise of the moneyed owner.
While some retro hot-rodders were older (sometimes in noted father-and-
son teams of restorers),[65] what is especially notable is that some were white
youths protesting the betrayal of the traditions of past white youths as well as
rejecting the high-tech import cars of their peers. In fact, this movement stood
against the "fast-and-furious" crowd, many of whom were not only nonwhite
but were affluent enough to buy foreign factory hot rods. Often too young
to identify with the muscle-car enthusiasts, yet hostile to both the "trailer
queens" and the "rice rockets," members of this revived traditional hot-rod
movement sought communion with the hot rods and culture of an earlier era:
the 1950s generation with its fascination for 1932 to 1940 Fords.

Leaders of this retro hot-rod movement included Kirk Jones and Jay Ward.
In September 1997 they organized a car show they called Billetproof, in reference to a rejection of fancy accessories associated with the company Billet
Specialties. Jones and Ward attracted twenty-six "traditional '50s and '60s-
style Lead Sleds and Roadsters" to the parking lot of a bowling alley in the
Bay Area town of Albany, California. Graduates of design and art schools,
both organizers had grown up with car customization, and had much more in
common with the traditional hot-rod youths than with the fast-and-furious
crowd. Throughout high school, Jones had spent his Friday nights dragging
for money in cheap street racers, and later had built nostalgic rods painted in
primer that stuck out at car shows dominated by pricey "billet" cars. Jay Ward

had a similar background. His father was a drag racer, introducing him to the delights of the traditional self-built hot rod. The Billetproof shows became a brand, with a series of six shows and drag races across the country by 2016. It was sold in 2007 to the Sacramento hot-rodder Alan Galbraith.[66]

The retro hot-rod movement was embraced by some established shows, like the Goodguys Rod and Custom Association, as well as by a number of magazines, like *Ol' Skool Rodz*, *Hot Rod Deluxe*, *Garage*, and *Traditional Rod & Kustom*. Inevitably, cable TV began to feature reality shows built around the retro hot-rodder, such as the Discovery Channel's *Monster Garage* in 2002, and *American Hot Rod* in 2004. Many members of this faction rejected reproduction bodies, Billet wheels (especially chrome-plated instead of painted steel wheels), and LED taillights. Some magazines featured retro clothing (the Dickies brand, for example) and of course rockabilly music. While the Billetproof show claimed that it wasn't trying to relive the past, and had participants ranging in age from sixteen to eighty, many, as hot-rod commentator Jack DeWitt notes, were young rodders "invested in a past, not their own, which is preferable to the present."[67]

A more radical version of this young person's rejection of trailer queens was the rat rod, equally inspired by the hot-rod culture of the 1950s but modeled after "crude imperfect homemade rods, perpetually unfinished and largely despised within the original hot rodding community." Reminiscent of the earliest hot rods that raced on the Southern California dry lakes, rat rods featured old engines that sometimes needed coaxing to run, primer without finishing paint, and often comical add-ons. The taste of rat-rod enthusiasts partially reflects their lack of funds to buy aftermarket reproduction parts. Like their predecessors from the 1930s, '40s, and '50s, they depended on junkyard parts, and couldn't have paid much attention to "authenticity" even if they had wanted to. And they didn't. Some rat-rodders cultivated retro music (even swing from the 1940s, though mostly 1950s rockabilly), but many sported edgy demeanor, tattoos, and wild hairdos. Influential was the humor and attitude of 50s and 60s customizer Ed "Big Daddy" Roth, famous for his vehicles that looked, and nearly were, impossible to drive. As a group, rat-rodders celebrated the shocking and delighted in the crude, strange, and raw. The look was bound to jar even the street-rodder: in one case, combining a Farmall tractor front end with wrenches for door handles, street signs for a floor, 1964 Ford Thunderbird seats, and a gear shifter in the form of a hand grenade. At a NSRA event in 2016 I saw a rat rod "promenade" down the road between street-rodders and their cars. The driver told me all the particulars: it was based on a 1948 Nash body but was powered by a 1941 Buick straight-8 engine; it sported headlights from a 1912 Buick, and featured as a front grille

FIGURE 8.4. A rat rod, and skeptical street-rod viewers (June 2016). National Association of Street Rods, York, Pennsylvania. Author's photo collection.

the air intake from the jet engine of a P47 airplane from the 1940s. This rat rod had taken him three years to build. Bystanders were curious, but the three men I talked with agreed that it looked ridiculous and that they "wouldn't be caught dead in it." Even the tough hot-rodder from Compton I met at the LA Roadster show insisted that rat rods were "cheap." A real hot rod, he said, did not include "saw blades or chain sprockets." Proud of his authentic Ford Model A, he dismissed rat-rodders: "They don't care . . . don't do any research." Most traditional hot-rodders, young and old, shared this disdain for rat-rodders. And I'm certain that the rat -odders don't give a tinker's damn.[68]

Still, some from the retro hot-rod crowd joined the rat-rodders in a shared uniform: blue jeans or black pants (from Dickies) with rolled-up cuffs, white or black T-shirts, and black work shoes for men; and black sheath skirts or vintage dresses, and even Bettie Page bangs and high heels, for women. Tattoos of presumed 1950s themes were common, including traditional sailor's anchors, and even pinups. Music had also to be just so: Gene Vincent, Eddie Cochran, and Elvis Presley from the mid-1950s, but not the Las Vegas version of Elvis from after 1969. Rat-rodders identified with the bad boys of the '50s, and with the movies that featured them, such as *Hot Rod Gang and High School Confidential*—not with *American Graffiti*, with its condescending image of the hot-rodder. At the heart of these movements was a rejection of their peers in the tuner culture of the Hondas and Subaru Impresas and the digital culture of the video gamers. As DeWitt notes, this culture of the retro and rat rod often was illusory: a rejection of the present and its material culture for a celebration of the 1950s by people who had never lived in the 1950s. For them, that culture was a romantic image, not a memory (a curious feature of many forms of commercialized nostalgia culture).[69] Furthermore, this "invented tradition" was often inaccurate: the embrace of tattoos and the making of Bettie Page (a star of "nudie-cutie" magazines and "blue" movies in the '50s) into an icon are strange, considering that neither was associated with the real 1950s hot-rod culture. Most of all, the retro- and rat-rodders, like their predecessors, were fighting against an inevitable tide of commercialization: merchandisers soon were selling them "vintage engine parts" and "old-looking, freshly built rusty bodies."[70]

The Slow and Nostalgic, the Fast and the Young

The contrast between the car cultures of the once-young and currently young in this chapter tells us a lot about the ephemerality of modern stuff, especially the mobile kind. It also informs us about aging in a culture that values youth and its memories, and about the struggles of the young to find a fresh identity in a car culture dominated by the past. This story seems to lead us to the end of the road, the eclipse of generations of Americans growing up with cars. Visiting old car shows in the second decade of the twenty-first century, where the old celebrate the accomplishments of their own youth, I see an obvious decline. I was struck by the empty fields at the 2016 NSRA Show in York, Pennsylvania. Attendants at the front gate estimated that participation had dropped by half in five years. The graying of the crowd was confirmed by a prominent concession that offered powered chairs for the disabled. Organizers have recognized this trend for some time. Though, from its founding, the NSRA had rejected all cars made after 1948, it adopted a new rule in 2010: admitting vehicles thirty years old or older. By 2016, this new rule allowed car model years as recent as 1986. Yet in 2016, I saw few cars that dated even from the 1950s. Tailfins were still rare. Other shows, of course, have had more success attracting younger collectors with youthful memories of muscle cars and even imports. Even the Grand National Roadster Show, long the champion of roadsters and of two-door chopped and channeled rods, now welcomes lowriders with hydraulics. The "old farts" claim to welcome Latino cars and even rice rockets, but few of those cars come to their shows.[71]

Some collectors I met in Los Angeles in 2016 admitted to admiring "tuner cars." Youths today spend thousands on Hondas and Toyotas in the same way that members of the older generation once looked for the hundred-dollar car, noted a member of the LA Roadsters from Sacramento. Neither generation was particular, he said. The "key [was] the modification" and the personal pride that went into it. Oldsters, he insisted, were too obsessed with particular cars, and not with the craft and accomplishment of vehicular transformation. A Cal-Rod member from the class of 1956 admitted that he and his peers "were really blessed" with access to cheap beaters that could be modified and souped up. Lots of old timers like him, he said, "forget where we came from." Hot-rodders from his day drove the equivalent of today's rat rods: junkers that they made into beauties, or at least into expressions of their work, skill, and personalities. He even noted that he gives rat-rodders old parts to help them build their works of mobile art, just as older men did for him decades ago. Another street-rodder from Columbus, Ohio, born in 1946, pointed out that vintage rods have simply become too expensive for many beginners. Inevitably, as the younger enthusiasts replace his generation, new types of less expensive cars will fill the shows, representing younger memories, including the Volkswagen minivans of the 1960s and the vans with custom murals from the 1970s. Inevitably this means that nostalgic oldsters will have to welcome the customized but rusty 1959 Chevy sedan with a couple of Hispanic brothers in the front seat.[72]

Yet how likely is such a blending of generations? At car shows I saw, interspersed with the greybeards, the occasional teen with an interest in cars that long preceded his own upbringing.[73] More common, though, is resentment and pessimism regarding the "next generation." Even the Hispanic hot-rodder born in 1941 whom I met in 2016 complained that the guys driving Honda hot rods really didn't know cars. The most common comment was that today's youth are happy if they have "a computer in hand."[74]

Even a successful club like the Cal-Rods showed signs of a gap between its aging founders and its newbies. Senior members whom I met noted with delight the music and good cheer of low riders at their shows, and recognized the necessity of passing their leadership on to a younger generation, noting that the youngest person on their board was fifty-five years old. Still, the "originals," who had been teens in the mid-1950s, lamented the passing of their friends and admitted to some discomfort with the large numbers of new members whom they don't know.[75]

The story is diverse. Parents still try to pass mechanical lore, skill, and ambition down to their children; and elders adapt to, as well as resent, how their children are different. But underlying both responses is recognition that the role of the car has changed: it may no longer be central to a young person's coming of age. The tuner imports have replaced earlier waves of youthful car enthusiasm, but clearly the newer wave is smaller. In the final chapter of this book, we ask: Has growing up with cars come to an end?

9

The End of Youth Car Culture?

In 2001 the historian and college president David Shi commented:

> There are now more than 200 million cars in the United States. Teens continue
> to fill high-school parking lots with automobiles. . . . America's love affair with
> the car has matured into a marriage—and an addiction. . . . . . The automobile
> retains its firm hold over our psyche because it continues to represent a meta-
> phor for what Americans have always prized: the seductive ideal of private
> freedom, personal mobility, and empowered spontaneity.[1]

Stacy Willis, a female reporter for the *Vegas Seven*, recalled growing up in the
1980s:

> I was restless by 13. So I routinely snuck out of my house in the middle of
> the night, pushed my parents' Datsun station wagon down the driveway so
> they wouldn't hear the engine start, got that sucker running, picked up my
> friends from various windows and backdoors, and we went rollin'. It was a
> gear-grinding madhouse of clumsy trips across town or into the tiny city core,
> just blaring the radio and laughing and seeing stuff. Thankfully, because I have
> hardworking angels, we always returned safely to our bedrooms before dawn.
> By the age of 15-and-a-half, nobody had to teach me how to work a stick shift.
> I got my license on my 16th birthday. At 8:05 a.m.[2]

Things certainly seem to have changed by the second decade of this century. Here are two comments by young people written in 2013: "My girlfriend
drives me everywhere. That sounds sad, and 20 years ago I'd be considered
pathetic, but it's almost normal now to be that way."[3]

And a male teen had this to say about his millennial generation:

Most people my age are incredibly lazy, so they want a car that can get them from point A to B without them putting in effort. . . . People my age aren't interested in the kind of tech that makes a car go faster, or handle better, they just want to be able to connect their iPhones to the car so they can blast their shitty music with the windows down.[4]

With 797 vehicles for every 1,000 Americans in 2014, the car has never been a greater part of American life. Despite the vast increase in automobility everywhere (with Western European countries with five to six hundred vehicles per thousand people), the American obsession with cars still stands out.[5] Yet, despite the multicar households, with vehicles aplenty available for teens, the lure of the automobile as a transition to adulthood seems to be in decline. By 2005, reports of delay in teen applications for driver's licenses were common. The recession of 2008, increased youth unemployment and education costs, and higher car prices provide an economic explanation. Public pressure, backed up by new legislation, made getting the once-coveted license at sixteen far more difficult; and law enforcement continued to block the old cruising culture.

But there was more: a change in attitude, from what Shi described in 2001 to the views of millennials in 2013. Perhaps there has been a generational revolution. Fathers have recently expressed frustration with the fact that their sons were no longer interested in carrying on dad's lifelong hobbies of repairing, restoring, and racing cars. I was a little surprised that no one in my undergraduate seminar on car culture, in fall 2016, had ever changed a tire or worked on a car. Only one quarter had operated a manual transmission.

The acquisition of mechanical skills, long a hallmark of the transition from boy to man, especially in the working class—has declined with the computerization of vehicles and other machines. Another obvious change is that teens today have substituted digital or "virtual" liberation from the constraints of family for the old mechanical and physical freedom provided by the car. A generation of youth has been immersed in digital devices since they were toddlers; the devices not only absorb their attention, diverting them from annoying siblings and demanding parents, but also connect them to friends both near and far. Sixteen is no longer that magical age. "Growing up," or at least liberation from elders, has recently become something that happens earlier with the smartphone, even if that freedom is confined to the digital screen rather than the "open road." As important is a shift in the social world of teens: public spaces like parking lots and streets, once available to them, have been closed off by the authorities. But youths have found other sites for self-expression and sexual exploration. Of course there is the Internet and social media, but the parental home also provides privacy, not only from the public but from adult controls, as both parents increasingly are away at work after school and even on weekends. All this suggests the decline of the car in sexual initiation and in peer culture.

Yet not all agree that growing up with cars is over. Millennials especially note the persistence of auto enthusiasm in their generation, and insist that their car culture is simply being ignored by self-absorbed elders, unable to look beyond their own youth of Deuce coupes and GTOs. It's a complex and interesting story.

New Roadblocks to Teen Automobility

Major cultural and attitudinal changes sometimes come quickly. This seems to be the case with an American shift away from marking maturity with cars. The Federal Highway Administration reported that the percentage of American sixteen-year-olds holding driver's licenses dropped from 43.8 percent in 1998 to just 29.8 percent in 2006 and only 24.5 in 2014. In the 1980s, about two-thirds of sixteen- to nineteen-year-olds had driver's licenses, but by 2012 only about half had them. And at the tail end of the teen years, 87.3 percent of nineteen-year-olds held licenses in 1983, but only 69 percent did so in 2014: a 21-percent decrease. Seven countries, including Canada, South Korea, Germany, and Japan, saw similar trends in the downward shift of teen drivers.[6] The millennials especially seem to be driving change. Young Americans between the ages of sixteen and thirty-four drove 23 percent fewer miles in 2009 than Americans in that that age group did in 2001. This generation may be in the vanguard of a less car-centric America in the twenty-first century.[7]

In my interviews of street-rodders, roughly between 2012 and 2016, I found that fathers were frustrated by the fact that their sons weren't interested in their rods, much less working on their own. Moreover, car dealers and manufacturers have become concerned that American youth has lost interest in their new and presumably ever more exciting offerings, despite the fact that Ford and Mercedes-Benz are focusing on their new digital gadgetry "that turns cars into moving smartphones." In 2012, GM offered Chevys in colors like "techno pink," "lemonade," and "denim," again presumably to lure the young back into their showrooms. The results were, predictably, disappointing.[8]

There are many explanations for the declining allure of the car. One, often advanced by industry, is that this is a temporary downswing caused by an economic recession that has had a greater impact on teens than on the adult population. Between 2006 and 2012, teen unemployment rose 11 percent, compared with only 5 percent among adults.[9] Given the estimated eight-thousand-dollar annual expense to operate a car for an average of fifteen thousand miles, many youths could no longer afford the luxury of wheels, especially of new or even relatively new rides.[10] The days of the amazingly cheap used car have long disappeared. A comment made in 2015 to a *Washington Post* article in 2015 catches the change: "My dad's '67 Chevelle cost him $400 in 1974, or about 200 hours' (half a summer) work at minimum wage. If a kid today wanted to buy a 2010 Camaro, it's going to cost him at least $15,000, or over 2000 hours minimum wage."[11]

Of course, not all youths were shut out of the auto market. Growing income disparity in the United States was reflected in the fact that cars increasingly have become a status symbol for children from affluent families, rather than the affirmation of working-class youth. In fact, the poor are overrepresented in the group of the carless. In 2012, only 25 percent of teens from poor families (earning less than twenty thousand dollars a year) had driver's licenses, in contrast to the 79 percent of sixteen- to eighteen-year-olds in households earning one hundred thousand dollars a year.[12] "We're not selling to everyone. We're selling to upper-middle-class and upper-class," notes the car industry's Center for Automotive Research.[13] So, to some degree, the decline of youthful drivers says less about the disappearance of teen car culture than it does about growing income inequality and, with it, the eclipse of a "greaser" culture based on the access of working-class youth to cars. The difference is even greater if we compare white with African-American and Latino teens: a 2010 survey of US high-school seniors showed that twice the percentage of blacks were unlicensed as that of whites (16 versus 39 percent).[14]

At least as important as these economic factors is the legal movement to restrict access of youth, especially those between the ages of sixteen and eighteen, to motorized wheels. There has been a long campaign to delegitimize that once cardinal date, the sixteenth birthday, as the marker of maturity and independence with the driver's license. In 2000 Daniel Mayhew, writing for the Insurance Institute for Highway Safety, offered a definitive critique, arguing that sixteen was an arbitrary age, essentially a compromise that began to emerge in the late 1920s. As noted in chapter 1, licensing had long been relatively lax in many states, especially in rural regions of the Midwest and West. Youths in their early and mid-teens were expected to work in the early twentieth century, especially on farms, and this often required them to drive motor vehicles, much as teens had driven teams of horses before the coming of the internal-combustion engine. While initially some accepted the age of fourteen for licensing, and others insisted on eighteen, by 1950 sixteen had become the standard.[15]

Yet there was much ambivalence about this decision, at least among the experts. Believing that the inexperience and immaturity of sixteen-year-old drivers posed a special danger, educators and the insurance industry promoted driver's education in high schools. By 1950, insurance companies were offering discounts to students trained in driver's education, and by 1960 a few states, like Michigan, even required drivers to pass such a course to obtain a license at sixteen. Federal highway funds in the 1960s and '70s were partially tied to state driver's education programs. By the 1980s, however, even though these courses appeared to lower teen accident rates, they also seemed also to encourage early licensing, and offered only basic skills. Partly for these reasons, in 1982 driver's education was dropped as a priority by the National Highway Traffic Safety Administration, eliminating the federal quid pro quo for funding. Even more important was the issue of costs for public schools, especially for on-the-road training. This led to the "privatization" of driver training, or a shift to the requirement of a certain number of hours of practice driving accompanied by an adult (usually a parent, not a driving instructor).[16]

All this made problematic the laws that allowed sixteen-year-olds to drive. From the 1970s on, psychologists, safety statisticians, legal scholars, and others promoted the idea that sixteen was simply too young to drive. Not only is this age standard rare in the world (most countries set it at eighteen), but, sixteen- and seventeen-year-olds were responsible for far more crashes than were eighteen- or nineteen-year-olds, especially at night and when other teens were in the car. As early as 1977, traffic safety organizations proposed a graduated driver license (GDL) to restrict the driving of sixteen- to eighteen-year-olds.[17]

Only in 1994, when the National Association of Independent Insurers, intent on lowering claim costs, wrote a model GDL bill, did the nation respond. Provisions included issuing learner's permits for teens to drive at fifteen years and nine months of age, under the supervision of a licensed driver aged twenty-one or older. A junior license could be issued at sixteen after the teen passed a driver's education test and had six hours of behind-the-wheel training. Holders of the junior license could not drive from midnight to 6 a.m., and were subject to special penalties for infractions. The proposal allowed a full license only after a year of safe driving or when the applicant was eighteen years old and a legal adult. Gradually, states adopted versions of the GDL.[18]

GDL laws were often complex and increasingly stringent. In 2007, for example. the GDL law in Massachusetts raised the requirement of formal instruction from six hours to twelve (even though most youths had to get this instruction from private driving schools), required forty hours of practice driving with a parent (who also had to take a two-hour class), and made other restrictions on night driving and teen passengers. New Jersey even required drivers under twenty-one to display a decal on their vehicles letting law enforcement know they were restricted.[19] However, these measures may not have had the expected results, because many waited until eighteen to apply for licenses (avoiding the bother but also the training required of sixteen to eighteen-year-old drivers). Accidents rose among unprepared eighteen-year olds.[20] In any case, these laws explain a lot of the recent decrease in teen driving.

Ultimately, these restrictions assume that sixteen-year-olds are psychologically unfit to drive without restrictions. And some, like Vincent Hamilton, argue for a ban on issuance of driver's licenses to sixteen-year-olds, citing research showing that they lack the emotional maturity to drive: they are less capable of focusing on driving, and tend to succumb to distractions like texting. Sixteen-year-olds, especially males, these experts argue, often presume themselves to be more skillful than they are. Many sixteen-year-olds treat driving as a form of liberation and, especially when in the company of teen peers, are susceptible to thrill-seeking.[21] Some academic writers have argued that this behavior is not merely social but biological, for competitive thrill-seeking is common in the adolescents of many mammals.[22] While advocating a ban on unsupervised driving before the age of eighteen, Hamilton stresses that, while younger Americans have rights, they should be granted "liberties of which they are capable," and which do not include unsupervised driving. The state must protect the young and the rest of the community from their "deficiencies."[23]

No matter how sound these arguments against sixteen-year-old driving may be, the new laws resulting from them have probably undermined the teen car culture. Their burdensome complexity, and the time often required to comply with them, especially in negotiating time with a parent for supervised driving practice, has led many a teen to shrug and say, "You know what? I don't need to get a license right now."[24] Also discouraging early licensing have been new costs: many public schools have ended free driver's education courses, and insurance costs for teens have increased. It's simply tougher and more expensive for a youth to drive today. No wonder many put off driving until later, when they have jobs and families.[25]

Is Driving Just Less Appealing These Days?

Beyond the economic and legal barriers to teen automobility, is there evidence that in recent years youths have just become less interested in cars, or have found substitutes for what the automobile once offered Americans on the cusp of adulthood? The reasons why teens aren't getting driver's licenses are revealing. In a 2012 AAA survey of sixteen-to eighteen-year-olds without cars,

39 percent claimed that they didn't need a vehicle, and another 35 percent said they just hadn't found time to obtain a driver's license. These responses suggest a new attitude, not just economic or legal constraint. The Public Interest Research Group reported that cities with the largest decreases in teen driving did not have higher levels of unemployment than the others, and concluded that a lifestyle change, rather than economics, might explain the trend. Getting access to a car was becoming less urgent, and alternatives were being found. Bike-sharing programs have sprouted in places like New York, Chicago, and San Francisco. There is some slight evidence of increased use of public transportation, especially in cities. With 88 percent of millennials in a 2009 survey wanting to live in urban environments, there may be finally a trend away from suburban living and from dependency on the car.[26]

There may also be another explanation for this trend. As the travel analyst Nick McGuckin notes, "The idea that the car means freedom . . . is over."[27] Car ownership is increasingly perceived as a burden, tying millennials down with the responsibilities of parking and maintaining a one-and-a-half- to two-ton machine, even if it is one that gets you somewhere you want to go. The shift may thus be less away from the prize of mobility than from the burdens of possession. Ownership itself may not be so desirable, and this change may run through a new and broader attitude about consumption. The young are increasingly content to stream music and movies and download books without needing physical possession in the form of DVDs or bound volumes. Renting, once a marker of penury or economic insecurity, has lost some of its stigma. Access when needed is more important that the boast of ownership. Thus, new car services like Uber, with ready smartphone access for the occasional special trip, attract some youths. Scott Griffith, the CEO of Zipcar, a short-term vehicle renting company, notes with self-interested exaggeration: "Millennials welcome the collaborative consumption movement with open arms, which we believe points to strong adoption of car sharing. . . ."[28]

Still, there may be a point here. According to Josh Allan Dykstra, the "death of ownership" results from the fact that so many desirable things are less scarce today, and (more persuasively to me) from the younger generation's increasing willingness to purchase a one-time utility or experience without the burden of permanent possession.[29] In this context, this means that some youth want access to mobility rather than possession of it with all the bother of the car's repairs, storage, and monthly payments.

Certainly the smartphone with continuous Internet access plays a crucial part in the declining desire for the car. In a sense, cruising the Internet has replaced cruising the streets. The aimless search for the chance encounter with hands on the wheel can be done more efficiently, safely, and cheaply with fingers on the touchscreen. Meetings, if "merely" virtual, still take place; and one can display or document oneself on Facebook, Twitter, and Instagram in ways that parallel or even improve upon casual encounters and conversations from a slow-moving or parked car. And these meetings can take place whenever one wants, not just on weekend nights. The "app generation" has experienced the new and the casual meeting in ways unknown to car-cruising predecessors. Digital encounters help still insecure and socially inexperienced teens reach out into a world of strangers, an essential part of the transition from dependence on the family circle to adulthood.[30] And of course the thrill of immersive video games has become a substitute for the emotional rush that once came with "putting the pedal to the metal" on the open road. Some may lament the sedentary ways of the app generation, but the virtual adventure is free of the physical danger of driving. Cars still have their utility for travel to some specific destination, like work, or for carrying bulky packages. Yet the car has lost some of its romance and become more of an appliance. Cars are just not that important any more.[31]

And there is a lot of anecdotal and survey evidence to confirm this: J. D. Power, a consumer rating service, admitted in a November 2010 report that "millennials don't talk about cars the way previous generations did. . . . Today young people care more about their cellphones than they do their cars."[32] And Sheryl Connelly, a global trends and futuring official at Ford Motor Company, said: "I don't think the car symbolizes freedom to Gen Y to the extent it did baby boomers, or to a lesser extent, Gen X-ers. Part of it is that there are a lot more toys out there competing for the hard-earned dollars of older teens and young adults."[33] A 2010 University of Michigan study found an inverse relationship between the percentage of teens and young adults with driver's licenses and their rates of Internet use, a trend evident throughout the developed world.[34] In effect, teens have virtual space and are no longer dependent upon the road. Peer relationships don't require public space, and adults discourage teen gatherings in any case. It is no surprise, then, that cars have lost their cruising function and have increasingly become modes of conveyance.[35]

For many teens the digital revolution has also led to the eclipse of the mechanical. From the days of steam engines, reapers, and even guns, knowledge of power trains, gears, cams, and levers marked the difference between the boy and the man, especially in and around the worlds of the artisan and farmer. In the twentieth century this meant learning about automobiles: engines, transmissions, differentials, radiators, breaks, and all the rest. These males learned how to fix cars, even if that meant little more than changing an oil filter or a flat tire. The coming of electric motors and even early electronics only expanded that world of machines, as boys again became men through making crystal radios, putting together amplifiers with Heathkits (following detailed instructions for soldering transistors), or installing phonograph cartridges on the tone arms of record players.

However, the arrival of the integrated circuit board and, even more, the computer chip and laser sensors drastically reduced the "workings" of electronic devices and the opportunity to construct, tinker, and repair. Early computers sometimes came as "bare bones" CPUs for the gadget-minded to upgrade with hard drives, memory cards, and DVD drives. But more recently, with the shift to notebook and tablet computers and smartphones, even this bit of tinkering has disappeared as the "works" have become inaccessible or nearly so. Computer-based engine technology and new auto body construction have also dramatically reduced the role of the teenage tinkerer and customizer. The "techie" impulse and the ability to display skill (now less masculine) have new outlets: software setup and repair, and even mastery of game controllers, but no grease from the elbow or the can. Computer diagnostics simplify repairs, but also require special equipment. Few dare to tinker with digitally regulated automobile engines.[36]

Another obvious change is the evident decline of the rites of cruising and "parking" for sexual encounter and exploration. The authorities have banned the cruise and closed off public spaces once available for teen romance, like parking lots and pulloffs on country roads. A recent study by Sarah Miller found that teens in a rural area in the Northeast had been banned from area shopping malls, forcing them to congregate at each other's homes and in the woods. Many still had sexual encounters in cars, but not at designated parking spots, which were more closely patrolled and deemed illicit.[37] Like so many other young people, these teens have found alternatives to public streets or the backseats of cars as places to meet others and explore sexuality. Thanks in part to the rise of the two-income family and the decline of parental supervision after school and on weekends, bedrooms and family-room couches now offer today's youth a more comfortable setting for sexual exploration. The hookup in group settings at parties provides them with new ways to meet and make out or engage in sex. As Sarah Miller notes, "It's rare for folks to go off on their own for a whole night. The idea that they would just pair off and drive away to go make out would seem odd, when you can just go into the next room, do what you're going to do, and then come back and continue socializing with the group." The male dominance of the old parking culture is less evident, as is the need to advertise a relationship to one's peers.[38]

Teens today seem to have less desire for the old parking rites. The practice of "going steady" that encouraged the ritual of necking and petting in high school has largely disappeared. And the pressure on girls to form romantic relationships with boys has diminished. The former imperative of having a "date" for the prom, at least in middle-class communities, has declined; and along with the date/dance culture, the expectation of "parking" afterwards seems to have gone too. Teen sex has also declined: from 1988 to 2010, experience of sexual intercourse has dropped from 51 to 43 percent for females between fifteen and nineteen years of age, and from 60 to 42 percent for males in the same age range.[39]

We should be wary of notions about major changes in attitudes and behavior today. While there is some evidence of American parents' greater toleration of the sexuality of their teen children, despite and in some measure because of their own experience in the "sexual revolution," those parents nonetheless attempt to control the sexuality of their adolescent offspring. Religious strictures, along with concern about unexpected pregnancies and its economic consequences, make American parents more guarded than their European counterparts, who are more secular and have stronger support networks. As it was in the past, teen sexuality in the United States is still often unacknowledged by adults, and is often furtive and secret.[40] The setting today, however, is less in the backseat of a car on Saturday night than perhaps on the rec room couch after school before mom and dad get home from work.

At the same time, new forms of "foreplay" have emerged that have partially replaced necking and petting in cars. "Sexting"—Internet texting with sexual images and messages—emerged along with smartphones in the first decade of the twenty-first century, though its popularity was exaggerated in the mass media. While it raises legal and moral questions when minors post pornographic images of themselves and others, this behavior is not so different from the sexual initiation rituals of teens in the car era: both behaviors toy with intimacy, arousal, and even romance, but are usually careful not to "go all the way."[41] Digital communication, like the car, has built-in constraints. And if "hooking up" at parties has partially replaced "parking" with a date after the high-school dance, neither ritual has usually meant unrestrained promiscuity. The double standard that makes a female with "too many partners" a "slut," and the male with many partners a "stud," has hardly changed from the 1950s and 1960s era of parking. Hooking up at teen parties, and later in bars and college dormitory rooms may be impersonal and lack commitment, in contrast to the necking and petting of dating couples in cars. Still, this difference may be due as much to delayed pair bonding as to greater promiscuity. Many young people engaging in hookups today, especially females, are exploring possibilities for more lasting relationships. Again, what has changed is the necessity of the car for these sexual initiation rites.[42]

In sum, the car has shaped the space and the material worlds of many

American teens across four generations. Adults today are decidedly less tolerant of teen autonomy, self-expression, and rebellion through automobility, but there are also new technologies that provide new "vehicles" of being, belonging, and becoming.

Teen Car Culture in the Twenty-First Century

But of course this story of decline isn't so simple. In the wake of the many postmortems of youth car culture, there has been a vitriolic reaction, especially from post–baby boomer car enthusiasts. According to one critic, 70 percent of millennials still drive most weekdays; and while they might find other conveyances cheaper, personal motorized travel remains their favorite option. Biking may be cool, but it is not safe. Public transportation has a "poor image" and often is inconvenient. Walking, while a healthy option, often isn't practical.[43] In modern towns and cities which are mostly designed for cars—and which are spread out across a large area, with few bikeways and reduced bus and train routes—it is no surprise that alternatives to the auto are not much more attractive to the young than they are to the old.

And if millennials are slow to purchase cars, it's not necessarily because they don't want them. Sean McAlinden, an economist with the Center for Automotive Research, argues that when the cost of owning a car drops to 10 percent of income, youths will stop saying that they aren't interested in automobiles, especially new ones. Thus, the current downswing in car ownership may be temporary.[44]

An even more common critique of the death of the car culture is simply that the auto obituary is simply wrong. Car culture is thriving, especially in import shows such as the Global RallyCross Race and Formula Drift, and on less visible online sites such as Jalopnik, Autoblog, Speedhunters, and Stanceworks. Especially prominent at these events and on these sites are the offspring of recent Asian and Latino immigrants who, according to a recently retired high-school teacher, are "obsessed with buying, repairing, decorating and upgrading their vehicles, for much the same reasons that white teens did forty and fifty years ago." What has diminished is the prevalence of the "greaser," and the historic dignity that car craft offered the white working-class male. At least in diminished form, the same dignity survives in new ethnic and cultural circles.[45]

Perhaps the most telling critique of the "death of youth car culture" thesis is that it is really only the lament of nostalgic old men who see the dying- off of their car world as the demise of all car culture. In a piece refuting a *Washington Post* story about young people's rejection of the car, Patrick George noticed that the author, Mark Fisher, had talked with few people under age of forty-five. "It's like saying music doesn't exist anymore because nobody does sock hops these days," George wrote. He went on to observe that *Hot Rod Magazine*'s list of the forty greatest car movies of all time included only two from the twenty-first century. The same critique could be, and often is, made of the selectees for the Rock and Roll Hall of Fame. In both cases, baby boomers insist that their youth culture alone counts, and that its decline is a measure of the decline in a distinct youth culture. The generational divide goes both ways. Another commentator on Fisher's article wrote: "I don't understand the fascination with American cars of the 1950s and 1960s and early 1970s. They were crap then and they are crap today. I watch these old fat Americans attending the auctions and paying up to $50,000 for a jazzed-up 50-year-old car. Good luck to those old fools. . . . If you're stupid enough to buy one of those clunkers just keep them in your garage and after a quart of Jack Daniel's they look beautiful. Just like the old hacks you used to screw."[46] The comment was pretty rough on old-guard greasers; but then, this clash of the young and the once-young is hardly surprising.

We've seen some of this clash of youth generations across the decades. The formerly young try in vain to preserve their teen memories through their old cars, and the currently young strive to define themselves through newer and different cars. Even if the conflict is abated by cross-generational bonding (especially in the Latino community) or in youth channeling of the youth of a past generation (as in the retro hot-rod crowd), these are exceptions to the rule.

The obvious nostalgia of the old car enthusiast, and the varied and even extreme ways in which the young deal with that tradition, only point to a decline of what cars once meant to people growing up. Cars are certainly not going out of style, but how the upcoming generation use them may be changing. While enthusiasm may survive, and may even be vibrant, the centrality of the car in defining how American youth define themselves ethnically, socially, and sexually no longer centers on the car.

By the close of the twentieth century, the automobile was no longer the transmission belt to maturity in America. The decline of cruising culture in the late 1980s anticipated a more important trend: the eclipse of the car culture itself among youth. This change appears to be quite sudden, and may be reversible. It may suggest a fading of the automobile's hold on the American psyche, as youthful lack of interest becomes adult habit. It may also mean that people enter car culture at a later age, thus causing it to be less shaped by adolescent preoccupations and less subject to romance and later nostalgia. Time will tell.

Notes

Chapter One

1. "Motorists Don't Make Socialists, They Say: Not Pictures of Arrogant Wealth, as Dr. Wilson Charged," *New York Times*, March 4, 1906, 12.

2. "The Spreading Automobile," *Harper's Weekly*, July 1, 1899, 655; Peter Marsh and Peter Collett, *Driving Passion: The Psychology of the Car* (Boston: Faber and Faber, 1986), 27, 29; James Flink, *America Adopts the Automobile, 1895–1910* (Cambridge, MA: MIT Press, 1970), 64–68; Clay McShane, *Down the Asphalt Path: The Automobile and the American City* (New York: Columbia University Press, 1996), 176–79.

3. Peter Ling, *America and the Automobile: Technology, Reform, and Social Change* (Manchester, UK: Manchester University Press, 1992), 7.

4. Wolfgang Sachs, *For Love of the Automobile: Looking Back into the History of Our Desires* (Berkeley: University of California Press, 1992 [1984]), 9, 10, 14, 45, 66.

5. Robert Casey, *The Model T: A Centennial History* (Baltimore: Johns Hopkins University Press, 2008), 60, 84.

6. John Rae, *The American Automobile: A Brief History* (Chicago: University of Chicago Press, 1965), 109; James Flink, *The Car Culture* (Cambridge, MA: MIT Press, 1976), 32–33; James Flink, *The Automobile Age* (Cambridge, MA: MIT Press, 1993), 47–51; James Rubenstein, *Making and Selling Cars: Innovation and Change in the U.S. Automotive Industry* (Baltimore: Johns Hopkins University Press, 2001), 18–31.

7. Flink, *America Adopts the Automobile*, 175, 177; Daniel Mayhew, "Why 16?" *Insurance Institute for Highway Safety* (August 2000), 4–5, wwwhjighwaysafety.org.

8. Michael Berger, *Devil Wagon in God's Country: The Automobile and Social Change in Rural America, 1893–1930* (New York: Shoe String Press, 1980), 31, 37.

9. *Facts and Figures of the Automobile Industry, 1928 Edition* (New York: National Automobile Chamber of Commerce, 1928), 53; Reynold Wik, *Ford and Grassroots America* (Ann Arbor: University of Michigan Press, 1972), 223; Flink, *Automobile Age*, 131–33.

10. Steven Gelber, *Horse Trading in the Age of Cars: Men in the Marketplace* (Baltimore: Johns Hopkins University Press, 2008), 3.

11. Gary Cross, *An All-Consuming Century: Why Commercialism Won in Modern America* (New York: Columbia University Press, 2000), ch. 2.

12. Gelber, *Horse Trading*, 3, 5, 151; Thorstein Veblen, *The Theory of the Leisure Class* (New

York: Dover, 1994 [1899]), 87. Paul Nystrom, *Automobile Selling: A Manual for Dealers* (New York: *Motor*, the National Magazine of Motoring, 1919), 77.

13. Gelber, *Horse Trading*, 20, 25, 30, 31, 32, 40, 63.

14. Flink, *Car Culture*, 38; Cotton Seiler, *A Republic of Drivers: A Cultural History of Automobility in America* (Chicago: University of Chicago Press, 2008), ch. 1.

15. Virginia Scharff, *Taking the Wheel: Women and the Coming of the Motor Age* (Santa Fe: University of New Mexico Press, 1992), 13, 161; Seiler, *Republic of Drivers*, 27, 41, 58–60; McShane, *Down the Asphalt Path*, 155, 157.

16. Seiler, *Republic of Drivers*, 43; Erik Leed, *The Mind of the Traveler* (New York: Basic, 1992), ch. 1.

17. The romance of the open road was featured endlessly in film and fiction. Katie Mills, *The Road Story and the Rebel: Moving Through Film, Fiction, and Television* (Carbondale: University of Southern Illinois Press, 2006); Kris Lackey, *Road Frame: The American Highway Narrative* (Omaha: University of Nebraska Press, 1997); David Laderman, *Driving Visions: Exploring the Road Movie* (Austin: University of Texas Press, 2002).

18. Seiler, *Republic of Drivers*, 13.

19. Seiler, *Republic of Drivers*, ch. 1.

20. Mayhew, "Why 16?"

21. Maureen Daly, *Profile of Youth by Members of the Staff of the Ladies' Home Journal* (Philadelphia: Lippincott, 1949), 46.

22. James Block, *The Crucible of Consent: American Child Rearing and the Forging of Liberal Society* (Cambridge, MA: Harvard University Press, 2012), ch. 3; Steven Mintz, *Huck's Raft: A History of American Childhood* (Cambridge: Harvard University Press, 2003).

23. Grace Palladino, *Teenagers: An American History* (New York: Basic, 1997), 165–67; James Lane, ed., *Steel Shavings: Rah Rahs and Rebel Rousers: Relationships between the Sexes in the Calumet Region during the Teen Years of the 1950s* (Valparaiso: Indiana University Northwest, 1994), 45–50.

24. Ellen Seiter, *Sold Separately: Children and Parents in Consumer Society* (New Brunswick, NJ: Rutgers University Press, 1993); Dan Cook, *The Commodification of Childhood: The Children's Clothing Industry and the Rise of the Child Consumer* (Durham, NC: Duke University Press, 2004).

25. Victor Appleton, *Tom Swift and His War Tank; or, Doing His Bit for Uncle Sam* (New York: Grosset & Dunlap, 1918); Carol Billman, *The Secret of the Stratemeyer Syndicate* (New York: Ungar, 1986), ch. 2.

26. Gary Cross, *Kids' Stuff: Toys and the Changing World of American Childhood* (Cambridge, MA: Harvard University Press), 54–55; Susan Douglas, *Inventing American Broadcasting, 1899–1922* (Baltimore: Johns Hopkins University Press, 1987).

27. "What a Car Means to a Boy," *Look*, (January 20, 1959, 84.

28. Jürgen Herbst, *The Once and Future School: Three Hundred and Fifty Years of American Secondary Education* (New York: Routledge, 1996), 7; William Reese, *The Origins of the American High School* (New Haven: Yale University Press, 1995).

29. Thomas D. Snyder, *120 Years of American Education: A Statistical Portrait* (Washington: US Department of Education, 1983), 16, 36.

30. David Angus and Jeffrey Mirel, *The Failed Promise of the American High School, 1890–1995* (New York: Teachers College Press, 1999), 70–71, 203.

31. Reed Ueda, *Avenues to Adulthood: The Origins of the High School and Social Mobility in an American Suburb* (New York: Cambridge University Press, 1987), 151.

32. For early introduction of auto shop into high schools, see Kevin Borg, *Auto Mechanics: Technology and Expertise in Twentieth-Century America* (Baltimore: Johns Hopkins University Press, 2007), ch. 4; Marvin Lazerson and W. Norton Grubb, *American Education and Vocationalism* (New York: Teachers' College Press, 1974).

33. A. B. Hollingshead, *Elmtown's Youth: The Impact of Social Classes on Adolescents* (New York: Wiley, 1949), 298; Wayne Gordon, *The Social System of the High School* (Glencoe, IL: Free Press, 1957); James Coleman, *The Adolescent Society: The Social Life of the Teenage and Its Impact on Education* (New York: Free Press, 1961), 142.

34. Palladino, *Teenagers*, ch. 1, 4, 10; Joseph Kett, *Rites of Passage: Adolescence in America, 1790 to the Present* (New York: Basic Books, 1977), 152–54,234–38; Ueda, *Avenues to Adulthood*, ch. 6. A more recent study of working-class male high schoolers is Michael Smith and Jeffrey Wilhelm, *"Reading Don't Fix No Chevys": Literacy in the Lives of Young Men* (Portsmouth, NH: Heinemann, 2003).

35. Beth Bailey, *From Front Porch to Back Seat: Courtship in Twentieth-Century America* (Baltimore: Johns Hopkins University Press, 1988), 3, 13, 19, 30, 32, 48–56; Robert Lynd and Helen Lynd, *Middletown: A Study in American Culture* (New York: Harcourt, 1959 [1929]), 34–35, 137–38; John Modell, *Into One's Own: From Youth to Adulthood in the United States, 1920–1975* (Berkeley: University of California Press, 1989), 85, 87, 89.

36. "The Spreading Automobile," *Harper's Weekly*, July 1, 1899, 655; Berger, *Devil Wagon*, ch. 1.

37. State of New York Crime Commission, Sub-Commission on Causes and Effects of Crime, *A Study of Delinquency in Two Rural Counties* (Albany: J.B. Lyon, 1927), 408–10; Lynd and Lynd, *Middletown*, 257; Jesse Steiner, "Recreation and Leisure Time Activities," in Report of the President's Research Committee on Social Trends, *Recent Social Trends in the United States* (New York: McGraw-Hill, 1933), 944; Berger, *Devil Wagon*, 6, 109.

38. My associate John Hoenig and I interviewed or gathered online responses to a survey from more than seventy individuals mostly between 2014 and 2017. Their contributions were invaluable. In addition, I want to thank members of the Cal-Rod Club (especially Vic Cunnyngham, Jeri Silva, and Sharon Davis), the author and collector Robert Genat, Don Stoner of *Autoculture*, and fellow academics Amy Best, Jack Dewitt, Sarah Miller, Cotton Seiler, and Amy Shalet.

Chapter Two

1. Virginia Scharff, *Taking the Wheel: Women and the Coming of the Motor Age* (Albuquerque: University of New Mexico Press, 1992).

2. Robert and Helen Lynd, *Middletown* (New York: Harcourt, 1929), 251–54; Charles Parlin and Fred Bremier, *The Passenger Car Industry* (Philadelphia: Curtis Publishing, 1932), 21.

3. Parlin and Bremier, *Passenger Car Industry*, 24.

4. Flink, *Automobile Age*, 293.

5. Parlin and Bremier, *Passenger Car Industry*, 20.

6. Automobile Manufacturers Association, *Automobile Facts and Figures, 1950*, 4, 21.

7. Lynd and Lynd, *Middletown*, 254–55; Franklin Reck, *A Car Traveling People* (Detroit: American Automobile Association, 1945), 42.

8. Reck, *Car Traveling People*, 43.

9. "The Rising Tide of Used Car Trades," *Motor Age*, May 21, 1925, 10–11; National Automobile Chamber of Commerce, *Facts and the Automobile Industry* (1924 edition), 10; Gelber, *Horse Trading*, 67.

10. "Depreciation of Used Cars," *Motor World*, April 27, 1925, 21; C.E. Packer, *How to Buy*

a Used Car (Chicago: Popular Mechanics, 1954), 49, 72, 105, 115; Alfred P. Sloan, *My Years with General Motors* (New York: Doubleday, 1963), 152–53. Robert Casey, *The Model T: A Centennial History* (Baltimore: Johns Hopkins University Press, 2008), 87, 93; Flink, *Car Culture*, 141, 151.

11. Parlin and Bremier, *Passenger Car Industry*, 77–78.

12. Jack DeWitt, "The American Hot Rod," *American Poetry Review* 38, no. 3 (May/June 2009): 16–17.

13. Albert Drake, *Hot Rodder! From Lakes to Street* (Osceola, WI: Classic Motorbooks, 1993), 9.

14. Drake, *Hot Rodder!*, 106; Thom Taylor, *Hot Rod and Custom Car Chronicle* (Morton Grove, IL: Publications International, 2006), 10–11.

15. Kathleen Franz, *Tinkering: Consumers Reinvent the Early Automobile* (Philadelphia: University of Pennsylvania Press, 2005), 5–23, 41, 45, 55, 108, 147.

16. Franz, *Tinkering*, ch. 3; John Rae, *The American Automobile: A Brief History* (Chicago: University of Chicago Press, 1965), 116. "United States Registrations," *Automotive Industries*, February 22, 1930, 227–29; Flink, *Car Culture*, 142.

17. Robert Lucsko, *The Business of Speed, The Hot Rod Industry in America, 1915–1990* (Baltimore: Johns Hopkins University Press, 2008), 16–18, 41–45, 64–68; Brock Yates, *The Hot Rod: Resurrection of a Legend* (St. Paul: Motorbooks, 2003), 47; Don Montgomery, *Authentic Hot Rods* (self-published), 13–14; William Carroll, *When the Hot Rods Ran: May 15, 1938* (San Marcos, CA: Auto Book Press, 1991), 4–5.

18. De Witt, "American Hot Rod," 16–17; Borg, *Auto Mechanics*, 122–28.

19. Drake, *Hot Rodder!*, 17, 29.

20. Tom Medley, *Tex Smith's Hot Rod History, Book One* (Driggs, IA: Tex Smith, 1990), 8–9, 18–19, 58–63, 122–23; Leroy Tex Smith, *Inside Hot Rodding: The Tex Smith Autobiography* (Castlemaine, Australia: Graffiti Publications, 2015).

21. Drake, *Hot Rodder!*, 112–13.

22. Sam quit the business and became a policeman in 1957. George Barris and David Fetherston, *Big Book of Barris* (St. Paul: MBI, 2002), 11–15, 18–25, 29; Michael Dregni, *All-American Hot Rod* (Stillwater, MN: Voyageur, 2004), 60–61. See also Tom Wolfe, *The Kandy-Kolored Tangerine-Flake Streamline Baby* (New York: Farrar, Straus, Giroux, 1963), 75–106; Matthew Ides, "Cruising for Community: Youth Culture and Politics in Los Angeles, 1910–1970," PhD dissertation, University of Michigan, 2009, 110.

23. Ed Roth and Tony Thacker, *Hot Rods* (Minneapolis: Motorbooks International, 1995), 8, 10–11.

24. Roth and Thacker, *Hot Rods*, 11, 22.

25. Kathy Waddill Ridley, *The Original Hot Rodder: The Biography of Bill Waddill* (self-published, 2009). See also *Hot Rod Magazine*, Winter 2004.

26. Drake, *Hot Rodder!*, 11.

27. "Night Racers Face Curbs," *Los Angeles Times*, April 13, 1940, A1; "Boy Speeders Face Jail Bars," *Los Angeles Times*, May 6, 1940, A3; "Ban on Auto Racers Urged," *Los Angeles Times*, June 23, 1940, A2; "Law Cracks Down on 100 Mile-an-Hour Club Suspects," *Los Angeles Times*, July 3, 1940, A2.

28. "Origins of a Speed Shop," *Hot Rod Magazine*, May 1948, 139; Wally Parks, "History of the Hot Rod Sport," *Hot Rods Trend Book* no. 102 (Los Angeles, 1951), 3; "How Come Hot Rods?" in *Hot Rod Handbook* (Greenwich, CT: Fawcett, 1951), 5–9; Dean Batchelor, *Dry Lakes and Drag Strips: The American Hot Rod* (Minneapolis: Motor Books, 2002), 12; Robert Genat, *The Birth of Hot Rodding* (Minneapolis: Motorbooks, 2003), 16.

29. Edward Radlauer, *Drag Racing: Quarter Mile Thunder* (New York: Abelard-Schuman,

1966),28; H.F. Moorhouse, *Driving Ambitions: An Analysis of the American Hot Rod Enthusiasm* (Manchester, UK: Manchester University Press, 1991), 27–32, 42–44; Michael K. Witzel and Kent Bash, *Cruisin': Car Culture in America* (Osceola, WI: MBI, 1997), 72–89; William Carroll, *Hot Rods on Muroc Dry Lake, May 15, 1938* (San Marcos, CA: Auto Press, 1991), 11; Drake, *Hot Rodder!*, 4; Batchelor, *Dry Lakes and Drag Strips*, 117–20.

30. Montgomery, *Authentic Hot Rods*, 12–13; Carroll, *Hot Rods on Muroc*, 6–7, 13–14.

31. Editors of *Hot Rod Magazine*, *50 Years of Hot Rods* (St. Paul: MBI, 1998), 9–10.

32. Taylor, *Hot Rod and Custom Car Chronicle*, 10–11, 28.

33. I am indebted to Dan Stoner of Autoculture.com for some of these and other details about hot-rodding.

34. Montgomery, *Authentic Hot Rods*, 11; Taylor, *Hot Rod and Custom Car Chronicle*, 13–14; *David Dregni and Mike Fetherston, All-American Hot Rod* (Stillwater, OK: Voyager Press, 2004), 55–57.

35. Carroll, *Hot Rods on Muroc*, 4–5; Genat, *The Birth of Hot Rodding*, 89.

36. Ruth Oldenziel, "Boys and their Toys: The Fischer Body Craftsman's Guild, 1930–1968, and the Making of a Male Technical Domain," *Technology and Culture* 38, no. 1 (January 1997): 63.

37. Don Montgomery, *Hot Rod Memories* (Fallbrook, CA: self published, 1991), 12–13; Taylor, *Hot Rod and Custom Car Chronicle*, 13.

Chapter Three

1. Don Montgomery, *Hot Rods in the 1940s* (Fallbrook, CA: self-published, 1987), 19–20; Taylor, *Hot Rod and Custom Chronicle* (Lincolnwood, IL: Publications International, 2006), 11, 35.

2. Bill Hayes, *The Original Wild Ones: Tales of the Boozefighters Motorcycle Club* (Osceola, WI: Motorbooks, 2005); David Luscko, *The Business of Speed: The Hot Rod Industry in America, 1915–1990* (Baltimore: Johns Hopkins University Press, 2008), 71.

3. Montgomery, *Hot Rods in the 1940s*, 19; Dean Batchelor, *American Hot Rod* (Osceola, WI: Motorbooks International, 1995), 78–97; "Teenage Drivers Speed at 100 MPH," *Life*, November 5, 1945, 56; "Hot Rods," *Time*, July 18, 1949, 54, 74.

4. Don Mansell and Joseph Hall, "Hot Rod Terms in the Pasadena Area," *American Speech* 29, no. 2 (May 1954): 93–102.

5. Batchelor, *American Hot Rod*, 36; Taylor, *Hot Rod and Custom Car Chronicle*, 40–41.

6. Batchelor, *American Hot Rod*, 38; Taylor, *Hot Rod and Custom Car Chronicle*, 38, 109; Robert Genat, *Hot Rod Nights; Boulevard Cruisin' in the USA* (Osceola, WI: Motorbooks International, 1998), 51–53, 55; Dain Gingerelli, *Hot Rod Milestones* (Osceola, WI: Motorbooks International, 1999), 12–13; Mark Foster, *A Nation on Wheels: Automobile Culture in America since 1945* (Belmont, CA: Thomson/Wadsworth, 2003), 75–76.

7. Batchelor, *American Hot Rod*, 207; Montgomery, *Hot Rods in the 1940s*, 143; quotation from Taylor, *Hot Rod and Custom Car Chronicle*, 2.

8. Drake, *Hot Rodder!*, 67–70.

9. "Are These Our Children?," *Look*, September 21, 1943, 20; Mark McGee and R.J. Robertson, *The J.D. Films* (McFarland: Jefferson, NC: 1982), 11–14.

10. "Delinquency Often Results from Truancy," *Los Angeles Times*, May 31, 1943, 5; Frank Manella, "Curfew Laws," *Florida Children's Commission Report*, no. 1(1956): 161–68.

11. Articles on drag racing: *Colliers*, July 26, 1941, 14, 56; *Time*, September 26, 1949, cited in H.F. Moorhouse, *Driving Ambitions: An Analysis of the American Hot Rod Enthusiasm* (Manchester, UK: Manchester University Press, 1991), 5, 33, 81; "Souped up Speed," *Colliers*, April 5, 1947, 34.

12. For the classic interpretation of the postwar moral panic, see James Gilbert, *A Cycle of Outrage: America's Reaction to the Juvenile Delinquent in the 1950s* (New York: Oxford University Press, 1986), especially ch. 6. For treatment of the comic book moral panic, see Amy Nyberg, *Seal of Approval: The History of the Comics Code* (Jackson: University Press of Mississippi, 1998), 5–6, 37–38; Bradford Wright, *Comic Book Nation* (Baltimore: Johns Hopkins University Press, 2001), 26–29.

13. "Hopped-Up Car Drivers Seized," *Los Angeles Times*, July 9, 1945, A1.

14. Ed Roth, *Ed "Big Daddy" Roth: A Retrospective* (San Francisco: New Langton Arts, 1990), 9–10.

15. "Action in a Prowl Car," *Saturday Evening Post*, September 14, 1946, 34; "Police Stage Mass Raid on Hot Rod Driver Meeting," *Los Angeles Times*, February 6, 1947, 2; "Judge Deals Out Jail Terms to 35 Hot Rodders," *Los Angeles Times*, March 12, 1948, A1.

16. "The Hot Rod Problem, *Life*, November 7, 1949, 122; "Highway Tag Tragedy," *Los Angeles Times*, September 21, 1947, 2; "Skidding Hot Rod Leaves Empty Hearst—Silent Toys," *San Antonio Express*, April 8, 1952, 1B.

17. Peter Stanfield, *The Cool and the Crazy: Pop Fifties Cinema* (New Brunswick, NJ: Rutgers University Press, 2015), 117–20.

18. "Police Stage Mass Raid," 2.

19. "War Starts on Hot Rods," *Los Angeles Times*, March 19, 1947, A1; "Hot Rodders Lose License," *Los Angeles Times*, July 17, 1947, A1.

20. "Teen-Agers in Hot Rods Cause Death, Injury," *Chicago Tribune*, December 11, 1949, 2, 6; "Teen-Age Traffic Fatalities," *Los Angeles Times*, April 7, 1950, A8.

21. "Sports Digest," *Council Bluffs Nonpareil*, August 3, 1949, 1; "A Few Beers, Two Fast Cars and the Kids Had a Race," *Delta Democrat-Times*, January 4, 1950, 1; "Police Use Hot Rods," *Cedar Rapids Gazette*, October 9, 1950, 1; "Police to Cool the Hotrods," *New York Times*, October 6, 1950, 21.

22. "Teen-Age Ego Held Road Peril," *New York Times*, June 19, 1949, 39; "Westchester Dawn Patrol is Set to Trap Teen-Age Auto Speeders," *New York Times*, September 9, 1950, 19.

23. "52 Miles of Terror," *Saturday Evening Post*, January 14, 1956, 17–21; Stanfield, *The Cool and the Crazy*, 114–15.

24. "Jalopy Jockeys Meet the Law," *Oakland Tribune*, May 20, 1047, 8C; *1949 California Statutes*, ch. 182, p. 492, section 3; "Our 14-Year-Old Automobile Drivers," *Los Angeles Times*, December 14, 1946, A4.

25. "Dewey Signs Bill Aimed at 'Hot Rod' Driver," *New York Times*, March 28, 1951, 31.

26. "Automotives: Hot Bads," *New York Times*, March 1, 1953.

27. "Hot Rod Can Get Young Fellow into Trouble," *Ada Evening News*, October 27, 1953, 4.

28. "Hot Rodders Lose License," *Los Angeles Times*, July 17, 1947, A1; Don Montgomery, *Authentic Hot Rods* (Fallbrook, CA: self-published, 1994), 21, 35.

29. "Police Capture 31 Youths with 'Souped Up' Jalopies," *Los Angeles Times*, June 18, 1947, A1; "Judge Fines 30 Hot Rod Drivers," *Los Angeles Times*, November 25, 1954, 2.

30. "21 in Hot Rod Tryouts Defy Police," *Chicago Tribune*, March 21, 1955, C6; "56 Drag Race Arrests," *Chicago Tribune*, September 1, 1960, E2; "Police Capture 31 Youths,"; "Justice Tells Parents about Racing Kids," *Gettysburg Times*, September 12, 1959, 2.

31. "Emotional Ills of the Child Linked to Hot Rodding," *Chicago Tribune*, April 28, 1956, D12.

32. "Teenage Drivers Speed at 100 MPH," *Life*, November 5, 1945; "I've Got a Thunderbolt in My Backyard," *Saturday Evening Post*, November 18, 1950, 108–14; "Random Thoughts, "*Amarillo*

Daily News, August 4, 1947, 1; "Hot Rodders Get Praise from Psychologist," *Indiana[PA]Evening Gazette*, August 28, 1952, 4.

33. "Hot Rod Auto Designs," *Los Angeles Times*, January 11, 1948, A5; "Original Hot Rod Group Pledges Safety Drive Aid," *Los Angeles Times*, September 23, 1948, 19; Genat, *The Birth of Hot Rodding*, 73; "Second Hot Rod Exposition," *Los Angeles Times*, January 22, 1949, A5.

34. "Oakland Roadster Show 1971," *Hot Rod Magazine*, July 1971, 104–8.

35. Moorhouse, *Driving Ambitions*, 50, 36–38,45, 63, 78; Wally Parks, *Drag Racing: Yesterday and Today* (New York: Trident Press, 1966), 2–3, 14, 22, 26–27; Editors of Hot Rod Magazine, *50 Years of Hot Rods* (Minneapolis: Motorbooks International, 1998), 10–13.

36. "Road to Riches: Hot Rod Craze Helps a Young Californian Build a Magazine Empire," *Wall Street Journal*, July 22, 1960, 1; "Motor Car Sports," *New York Times*, June 26, 1957, 54; "Prosperity on Wheels, *Time*, February 19, 1951, 52–54.

37. Moorhouse, *Driving Ambitions*, 50–53, 106, 119, 145, 151, 156, 201; Kevin Nelson, *Wheels of Change: From Zero to 600 M.P.H, The Amazing Story of California and the Automobile* (Berkeley: Heyday Books, 2009), ch. 23–24; Lucsko, *Business of Speed*, 2, 4, 76, 83–84; John De Witt, *Cool Cars, High Art* (Jackson: University of Mississippi Press, 2002); Robert Post, *High Performance: The Culture and Technology of Drag Racing, 1950–2000* (Baltimore: Johns Hopkins University Press, 2001).

38. "National Hot Rod Association," *Mansfield News Journal*, June 17, 1951, 12; Taylor, *Hot Rod and Custom Chronicle*, 6; Editors of Hot Rod Magazine, *50 Years of Hot Rodding*, 15–19; "Couple of Champs," *Rod and Custom*, March 1957, 33; "Now Hot Rods Are Organizing to Bring Safety," *Hutchison [Kansas]News Herald*, June 21, 1951, 13; Fred Thomas, *Hot Rod and Custom Car Clubs* (self-published, 2005),7–8.

39. "Hot Rod Truck Session Stirs Wide Protest," *Los Angeles Times*, April 8, 1947, 2; "Editorial," *Hot Rod Magazine*, November 1951, 4.

40. "Editorial," *Hot Rod Magazine*, October 1951, 5; "Editorial," *Hot Rod Magazine*, August 1950, 6.

41. "Editorial," *Hot Rod Magazine*, February 1950, 6; "Editorial," *Hot Rod Magazine*, September 1949, 4.

42. "Hot Rods," *New York Times*, June 19, 1949; cited in Gene Balsley, "Hot Rod Culture," *American Quarterly* 2, no. 4 (Winter 1950): 53.

43. Editorials, *Hot Rod Magazine*, November 1950, 4; May 1950, 7; June 1950, 7.

44. "Hot Rods," *Bakersfield Californian*, March 25, 1952, 4; William Parker, "Living at Peace with the Hot Rodder," *Transactions of the National Safety Congress* (1953): 103; "Dragnet: The Big Rod," https://thehannibal8.wordpress.com/2014/10/17/the-jack-webb-blogathon-dragnet-the-big-rod/.

45. Support for organized hot rodding included "Findlay Hot Rod Owners Say Cars Are No Menace," *Findlay Republican-Courier*, July 25, 1931, 16;"Hot Rodders Emphasizing Safe Driving," *El Paso Herald Post*, May 19, 1953, 11.

46. Editors of Hot Rod Magazine, *50 Years of Hot Rodding*, 31, 25; Taylor, *Hot Rod and Custom Chronicle*, 8–9.

47. "Westchester War on Hot Rods," *New York Times*, May 23, 1951, 37; "Teen Safety Show Seasoned with Fun," *New York Times*, June 2, 1951, 17.

48. "Cool Hot Rod," *Belvedere Citizen*, February 11, 1954, 3, cited in Matthew Ides, "Cruising for Community: Youth Culture and Politics in Los Angeles, 1910–1970," PhD dissertation, University of Michigan, 2009, 151; "Hartford Methodist Men to Entertain Hot Rod Clubs," *Al-*

toona Evening News, July 30, 1957, 9; "Cool Hot Rod," 1953, https://www.youtube.com/watch?v =cstlYdYJorQ.

49. "Cool Hot Rod."

50. Later in 1957, Richfield Oil produced a half-hour film, *Hot Rod Handicap*, to "educate the public in the value of organized hot rodding in promoting driver safety, personal initiative, and technical ingenuity among American youth." The story involved a dad who at first opposes his daughter's boyfriend because he is a hot rodder, only to be won over when he finds that the hobby can safe and sane. The film was made with the cooperation of the NHRA, California police forces, high school officials, and even drag strip operators. It was shown in movie houses and in meetings of hot rod clubs. "Hot Rod Handicap," *Rod and Custom*, January 1957, 51.

51. "Hot Rod Drivers," *Long Beach Independent*, July 27, 1947, 37; "Hot Rod Notes," *Daily Review* (Hayward, CA), November 30, 1951, 12.

52. "Hot Rod Racers Book Summer Heats in Winter," *Wisconsin State Journal*, February 9, 1950, S2, 1.

53. Taylor, *Hot Rod and Custom Chronicle*, 8–9.

54. "Teens Spook Reckless Drivers," *Chicago Tribune*, June 23, 1960, F13; "Court Steers Teen Drivers in Main High," *Chicago Tribune*, February 28, 1954, NW 8.

55. "Hot Rod Clubs," *Oakland Tribune*, December 9, 1949, D3.

56. "Youngsters' Auto Club," *Los Angeles Times*, December 14, 1952, A10; "Hot Rod Notes," *Daily Review* (Hayward, CA), Nov. 30, 1951, 12.

57. "Pasadena Club Presents 4th Annual Reliability Run," *Hot Rod Magazine*, February 1951, 7; "Hot Rodders Emphasize Safe Driving," *El Paso Herald Post*, May 19, 1953, 1; Taylor, *Hot Rod and Custom Chronicle*, 7–8; "Young Long Island Drivers Show their Skill," *New York Times*, April 29, 1957, 16.

58. Arnie and Bernie Shuman, *Cool Cars, Square Roll Bars* (Sharon, MA: Hammershop Press, 1998), 54–56, 66.

59. Genat, *Hot Rod Nights*, 25–30; Shuman, *Cool Cars*, 48; Taylor, *Hot Rod and Custom Chronicle*, 7–8; Mansell and Hall, "Hot Rod Terms," 89–102; "Young Car Demons Score Low with Hep Hot Rod Clubs," *Oxnard Press/Courier*, November 28, 1953, 1; "Dave Birchmeier Interview," Michigan Hot Rod Association, March 1998, mhraonline.orgt?daveb.html.

60. "The Juggers," *Rod and Custom*, March 1962, 48.

61. Shuman, *Cool Cars*, 74, 76, 78–82, 84, 90–96, 98, 104.

62. Interviews: Cal-Rod and Rodette members from 1954–56, June 17–19 and 30, 2016.

63. Cal-Rod website, http://cal-rods.org/About-Us.

64. Interviews: Sharon Davis and Jeri Silva of the Cal-Rodettes, June 18 and 30, 2016.

65. "Letter to Editor," *Oakland Tribune*, November 27, 1954, 4; "Drag Strips Wanted," *Chicago Tribune*, April 20, 1957, 8; "Hot Rod Enthusiasts Plan Track at Livermore Air Station," *Oakland Tribune*, March 24, 1949, 20D; "Tells of Need of a Drag Strip," *Blue Island Sun Standard* (South Chicago), October 1, 1953, 4.

66. "Hot Rodders Ask for Aid," *New York Times*, December 9, 1951, 12; "Hot Rodders Road Down the Road and Glen Cove Police are All for It," *New York Times*, July 13, 1953, 27.

67. "Lions Spearhead Drag Strip Drive," *Los Angeles Times*, January 23, 1955, H3; "Hot-Rod Idea Cuts Traffic Accidents," *Los Angeles Times*, February 24, 1955, 17; "Hot Rod Strips Reduce Accidents," *Los Angeles Times*, October 30, 1955, B3; "Young Long Island Drivers Show Their Skill," *New York Times*, April 29, 1957, 16; "County Plans Strip for Drag Racing," Los Angeles Times, May 25, 1955, A1.

68. "Drag Racing Gets Action," *San Mateo Times*, March 13, 1957, 28; "End Drag Racing," *New York Times*, September 24, 1956, 25.

69. California State Department of Education, *Guide for Driver Education and Driver Training* (Sacramento: State of California, 1948), iii.

70. Robbins Stoeckel, Mark May, and Richard Kirby, *Sense and Safety on the Road* (New York: D. Appleton-Century, 1936), 83–84, 90.

71. Stoeckel et al., *Sense and Safety*, 203, ch. 11. Similar points are made in Charles Dull (science teacher supervisor of Newark, NJ schools), *Safety First—and Last* (New York: Henry Holt, 1938), 144–45.

72. University of North Carolina, Institute of Government, *Driver Education in High School* (Chapel Hill: University of North Carolina Press, 1953), 1, 4–5; Herbert Stack, *History of Driver Education in the United States* (Washington: National Commission on Safety Education, 1966), 1–10, 15, 32.

73. Though the car simulators had some success in training students in the basic motor skills of driving, groups like the AAA and National Commission on Safety Education insisted on actual road experience. Auto manufacturers and local dealers loaned cars for driver education, often with dual controls. By 1965 there were more than ten thousand such cars on loan, an estimated 64 percent of the cars used in high school driver education. "Automobile Driving Enters School Curriculum," *American City*, November 1935, 81; Stack, *History of Driver Education*, 15–17, 33–37, 47; "A Review of *Man and His Motor Car*," *Phi Delta Kappan*, April 1936, 251; "Keeping Abreast," *Phi Delta Kappa International*, May 1936, 280. "Driver Education in Dallas," *Journal of Educational Sociology*, December 1951, 227–29; "Driver Education and Training," conference at the University of Kentucky led by Amos Neyhart and F. R. Noffsinger, 1938, 13.

74. Philip Attwood, "Healdsburg High School's Course on the Automobile," *Clearing House* (trade journal for teachers), September 1937, 480–50.

75. "Findings," *Clearing House*, May 1946, 550; Herbert Stack, "The Case for Driver Education in the High School," *High School Journal*, November-December 1947, 253–54; National Commission Safety Education, *High School Driver Education: Policies and Recommendations* (Washington: National Educational Association, 1950), 12; Stack, *History of Driver Education*, 19; "Our Youngsters Don't Have to Be Killers," *Saturday Evening Post*, December 17, 1949, 17.

76. Kentucky University (conference convened by Amos Neyhart and F. R. Noffsinger), *Drivers' Education and Training Course for Teachers* (Washington: American Automobile Association, 1938), 15–22, 47, 91, 109–12; Dull, *Safety First*, 146–55.

77. American Automobile Association, *Sportsmanlike Driving* (Washington: American Automobile Association, 1936), cited hereafter as *Sportsmanlike Driving* (1936); Driver Education Specialists, AAA, *Sportsmanlike Driving Teacher's Handbook*, Sixth Edition (New York: McGraw-Hill, 1970), cited hereafter as *Sportsmanlike Driving*(1970). Note also Albert Whitney (associate manager of the National Bureau of Casualty and Surety Underwriters), *Man and the Motor Car* (New York: National Bureau of Casualty and Surety Underwriters, 1936).

78. *Sportsmanlike Driving* (1936), 1–5, 65–69.

79. *Sportsmanlike Driving* (1936), 4, 12–14, 19, 23, 33, 38, 71, 75.

80. *Sportsmanlike Driving* (1970), 5, 12, 14.

81. Maxwell Halsey, *Let's Drive Right* (Chicago: Scott, Foresman, and Company, 1954), 40–50, 57, 431–34.

82. Harold Glenn, *Youth at the Wheel* (Peoria, IL: Charles A Bennett, 1958), 12–17, 35, 50–54.

83. Glenn, *Youth at the Wheel*, 50, 59, 70–71.

84. Henry Gregor Felsen, *Hot Rod: A Novel* (New York: Dutton, 1950), 147. Felsen made a career out of similar books, even writing *A Teen-ager's First Car* (New York: Dodd Mead, 1966), a practical advice book about the perils of buying one's first car.

85. William Gault, *Thunder Road* (New York: Dutton, 1952), 9.

86. Robert Bowen, *Hot Rod Rodeo* (New York: Criterion, 1964); Robert Bowen, *Hot Rod Patrol* (New York: Criterion, 1966). Note also Robert Bowen, *Hot Rod Showdown* (New York: Criterion, 1967).

87. A celebration of the outlaw behind the wheel became far more evident later, when the obligatory defeat of the lawbreaker disappeared in exploitation films like the *Fast and Furious* series (see chapter 8).

88. Other hot rod movies include *Dragstrip Girl* (1956), *Hot Rod Rumble* (1957), *Dragstrip Riot* (1958), and *Speed Crazy* (1959). Michael Dregni, *All-American Hot Rod* (Stillwater, MN: Voyageur, 2004), 87–88; Stanfield, *The Cool and the Crazy*, ch. 5.

Chapter Four

1. Interviews: "Old Fart Car Club," February 25, 2015; Historic Bellefonte Cruise, June 23, 2016; National Street Rod Show, York, Pennsylvania, June 11, 2016; Los Angeles Roadster Show, June 18–19, 2016.

2. Talcott Parsons, "Age and Sex in the Social Structure of the United States," in *Essays in Sociological Theory* (New York: Free Press, 1962), 89–103. For typical post–World War II approaches, note A. B. Hollingshead, *Elmtown's Youth and Elmtown Revisited* (New York: Wiley, 1975); James Colman, *The Adolescent Society* (Glencoe, IL: Free Press, 1961).

3. Jesse Bernard, "Teen-Age Culture," *Annals of the American Academy of Political and Social Science* 338 (November 1961), 1, 3, 7, 10; Jean Grambs, "The Community and Self-Governing Adolescent Groups," *Journal of Educational Sociology* 30, no. 2 (October 1956): 94–105; H. H. Remmers and D. H. Radler, *The American Teenager* (Indianapolis: Bobbs-Merrill, 1957), 80–85; Hilda Taba, *School Culture: Studies in Participation and Leadership* (Washington: American Council on Education, 1955).

4. H. H. Remmers, *The Purdue Opinion Panel: Youth Looks at Schools and Jobs* (Division of Educational Reference, Purdue University, April 1948), 8; H. H. Remmers, *The Purdue Opinion Panel: Teenagers' Attitudes toward Teenage Culture* (Division of Educational Reference, Purdue University, May 1959), 3–4, 11A, 13A; H. H. Remmers, *The Purdue Opinion Panel: Youth and Their Activities Outside of School*, March 1962 (Division of Educational Reference, Purdue University, March 1962), 11A.

5. Ross McFarland and Roland Moore, "Youth and the Automobile," in *Values and Ideals of American Youth*, ed. Eli Ginzberg (New York: Columbia University Press, 1961), 171–72.

6. H. H. Remmers, *The Purdue Opinion Panel: Youth Looks at the Parent Problem* (Division of Educational Reference, Purdue University, 1949), question 31; H. H. Remmers, *The Purdue Opinion Panel: Youth and Their Activities Outside of School* (Division of Educational Reference, Purdue University, March 1962), question 14.

7. Hollingshead, *Elmtown's Youth and Elmtown Revisited*, 297–98.

8. Robert Genat, *Hot Rod Nights: Boulevard Crusin' in the USA* (Minneapolis: Motorbooks International, 1998), 7, 12.

9. Interviews: Orange County Street Rod Show, February 26, 2015; Cal-Rod members, June 18, 2016.

10. Internet interviews: Growingupwithcars.com, June 21 and 22, 2015.

11. Internet interview: Growingupwithcars.com, May 15, 2015; interview, Vet Car Club, April 16, 2015.

12. Internet interview: Growingupwithcars.com, April 29, 2015.

13. Bonnie Morris, *The High School Scene in the 1950s: Voices from West Los Angeles* (Westport, CT: Bergin and Garvey, 1997), 23; "Hot-Rod," *Orange County Register*, August 5, 1984, J10; Internet interview, Growingupwithcars.com, May 13, 2015.

14. Internet interview, Growingupwithcars.com, May 14, 2015.

15. Interview, LA Roadster Show, June 18, 2016; "Teens Should Enjoy Cruising While They Can," *Wisconsin State Journal*, July 1, 1979, section 5, 2.

16. Matthew Ides, "Cruising for Community: Youth Culture and Politics in Los Angeles, 1910–1970," PhD dissertation, University of Michigan, 2009, 99.

17. "Gasoline Prices," *New Mexico Today*, October 16, 1980, 8B; "Teen CBers," *Daily Review*, April 9, 1977, 5; "Cruising Youths Seek Fun," *Ada Times*, November 13, 1977, 5B; Robert Genat, *Woodward Avenue: Cruising the Legendary Strip* (North Beach, MN: CarTec, 2013), 81; "Cruising Season Arrives," *Winchester Star*, May 9, 1984, 35; Anthony Ambrogio and Sharon Luckerman, *Cruising the Original Woodward Avenue* (Mt. Pleasant, SC: Arcadia Publishing, 2006).

18. Internet interview, Growingupwithcars.com, May 15, 2015.

19. Genat, *Woodward Avenue*, 81.

20. "On the Strip," *Oakland Tribune*, April 24, 1965, 7B; "All Nights, All Cruisers," *Tucson Daily Citizen*, September 13, 1969, 4–5; interview: LA Roadster Show, June 18, 2016.

21. Stacy Perman, *In-n-Out Burger: A Behind-the-Counter Look at the Fast-Food Chain That Breaks All the Rules* (New York: Collins Business, 2010), 50–51, 76; Interviews: Cal-Rod members, June 18, 19, 28, 2016; LA Roadster Show, June 18, 2015.

22. "The 'Strip,'" *Daily Review* (Hayward, CA), Jan 3, 1975, 14.

23. "Cruising Youth Seeks Fun," *Ada Sunday News*, November 13, 1977, 5B.

24. "Teens Flock to Cruise Streets of Goshen," *Goshen News*, September 15, 1982, 12. Similar is "Saturday Nights, Rock 'n' Roll and Cruising," *New Mexican*, April 9, 1979, B1.

25. "Cruising," *The Gazette* (Cedar Rapids, IA), September 15, 1983, 1.

26. "Youngsters Today," *Redlands Daily Facts*, March 12, 1969, 20; "All Night Cruising," 5; Genat, *Woodward Avenue*, 80–83.

27. James Lane, *Steel Shavings: Rah Rah and Rebel Rousers* (Gary: Indiana University Northwest, 1994), 48, 50, 52; Howard Meyerhoff and Barbara Meyerhoff, "Field Observations of Middle Class Gangs," in *Juvenile Delinquency*, ed. Rose Giallombardo (New York: John Wiley, 1966), 262.

28. Interviews: Cal-Rod members, June 18, 2016; LA Roadster Show, June 18, 2016; National Street Rod Show (York, PA), June 11, 2016; Old Farts Car Club Meeting, February 20, 2015.

29. Interviews: Old Farts Car Club Meeting, February 20, 2015; LA Roadster Show, June 18, 2016.

30. Internet interviews: Growingupwithcars.com, May 14, 2015, July 2, 2015.

31. Internet interviews: Growingupwithcars.com, April 29, 2015, June 4, 2016, May 15, 2015.

32. M. Licht, "Some Automotive Play Activities of Suburban Teenagers," *New York Folklore Quarterly* 30 (1974): 44–65.

33. Internet interview: Growingupwithcars.com, May 15, 2015.

34. Interview: LA Roadster Show, June 16, 2016.

35. Lane, *Steel Shavings*, 44.

36. Internet interviews: Growingupwithcars.com, April 29, 2015, July 26, 2015; interview: Santa Ana, CA, June 17, 2016.

37. Lane, *Steel Shavings*, 43, 46, 49–50.

38. Morris, *High School Scene*, 49, 62–63.

39. Lane, *Steel Shavings*, 51.

40. Interview: National Street Rod Show (York, PA), June 11, 2016.

41. Internet interview, Growingupwithcars.com, July 26, 2015.

42. A seventy-year old woman from the town of Berwick, Pennsylvania, whom I met in 2016 recalled that, despite her interest in building cars as a young teen, she had to borrow her parent's 1956 Chevrolet station wagon to cruise; but at least she'd received a license at sixteen, while her mother had had to wait until she was thirty-five. Interview: LA Roadster Show, June 18, 2016.

43. H. H. Remmers, *The Purdue Opinion Panel: Youth Attitudes Regarding Elections, Competition, Discipline, Status, Spare Time, Driving, Grandparents, and Health*, January 1960 (Division of Educational Reference, Purdue University, January 1960), 21A; H. H. Remmers, *The Purdue Opinion Panel: Youth and Their Activities Outside of School* (Division of Educational Reference, Purdue University, March 1962), 3a.

44. Lane, *Steel Shavings*, 44, 47.

45. Amy Best, *Fast Cars, Cool Rides: The Accelerating World of Youth and Their Cars* (New York: New York University Press, 2006), 64 for quotation, 63–79.

46. "Justice Tells Parents about Racing Kids," *Gettysburg Times*, September 12, 1959, 2; "Laws Put Penalty for Delinquency on Parents," *Independent* (Long Beach, CA), March 14, 1956, 7.

47. Charles McCormick, "Toward a Theory of Adolescent Cruising, Echoes from 1983," *Southern Folklore* 57, no. 1 (January 2000): 13; Ralph England, "A Theory of Middle Class Delinquency," *Journal of Criminal Law, Criminology, and Police Science* 50, no. 6 (March 1960): 535–40. Writing along similar lines is M. Eugene Gilliom, "The High School Culture and Academic Progress," *High School Journal* 47, no. 4 (January 1964): 153–58. He is critical of the expanded role of teen peer culture, and he argued for a reduced extracurriculum to improve academic performance.

48. McCormick, "Adolescent Cruising," 13–32; Charles McCormick, "There's Life beyond the Sonic: Adolescent Cruising as Sociocultural Perpetuation and Change," PhD dissertation, University of Pennsylvania, 1999, 7–8, 23.

49. Jerry Jacobs, *The Mall: An Attempted Escape from Everyday Life* (Prospect Heights, IL: Waveland Press, 1984); Susan Orlean, *Saturday Night* (New York: Simon & Schuster, 2014), 4–5; McCormick, "Life after Sonic," 9–12, 84, 88–91; McCormick, "Adolescent Culture," 20, 21, 26; Ronald Primeau, *Romance of the Road: The Literature of the American Highway* (Bowling Green, OH: Bowling Green State University Popular Press, 1996); Licht, "Automotive Play Activities," 45.

50. Erik Erikson, *Identity Youth and Crisis* (New York: Norton, 1968).

51. Among the many treatments of these themes, see Kenneth Roberts, *Youth, and Leisure* (Boston: Allen and Unwin, 1983), 56–57; Christopher Jenks, *Cultural Reproduction* (New York: Routledge, 1993), 1–16; Stuart Hall and T. Jefferson, *Resistance through Rituals* (London: Hutchinson, 1976); Chris Rojek, *Ways of Escape: Modern Transformations in Leisure and Travel* (Baltimore: Rowman and Littlefield, 1993), 109–10; Brian Sutton-Smith, *The Ambiguity of Play* (Cambridge, MA: Harvard University Press, 1997), 116; Paul Willis, *Common Culture* (Boulder, CO: Westview, 1990), ch. 1.

52. Classic studies of such mostly youthful "Saturnalian" practices include Robert Malcolmson, *Popular Recreations in English Society* (Cambridge: Cambridge University Press, 1973); William Addison, *English Fairs and Markets* (London: Batsford, 1953), 95–225; Jack Santino, *All around the Year: Holidays and Celebrations in American Life* (Urbana: University of Illinois Press, 1994), 90, 145–64; Peter Burke, *Popular Culture in Early Modern Europe* (New York: Harper, 1978), 178–204.

53. I owe much of this section to McCormick, "Beyond Sonic," 35–69.

54. Jason Reid, *Get Out of My Room: A History of Teen Bedrooms in America* (Chicago: University of Chicago Press, 2017).

55. McCormick, "Beyond Sonic," 1–2, 92–93, 128, 231, 268–69.

56. Robert Venturi, Denise Brown, and Steven Izenour, *Learning from Las Vegas: The Forgotten Symbolism of Architectural Form* (Cambridge: MIT Press, 1977); Rem Koolhaas, *Delirious New York: A Retroactive Manifesto for Manhattan* (New York: Monacelli Press, 1994; Gary Cross and John Walton, *The Playful Crowd: Pleasure Places in the Twentieth Century* (New York, Columbia University Press, 2005), ch. 3; McCormick, "Beyond Sonic," 116.

57. Marshal Berman, *All That Is Solid Melts into Air* (New York: Penguin, 1982).

58. McCormick, "Beyond Sonic," 243–560; James Kunstler, *Geography of Nowhere* (New York: Simon and Shuster, 1996), 86.

59. McCormick, "Beyond Sonic," 243–560; Sutton-Smith, *Ambiguity of Play*, 158–66.

60. McCormick, "Adolescent," 20, 23–24, 28.

61. Paul Landes, *Understanding Teen-Agers* (New York: Appleton-Century-Crofts, 1955), 138. See also Lester Kirkendall and Ruth Osborne, *Dating Days* (Chicago: Science Research Associates, 1949).

62. The authority on the history of dating is Beth Bailey, *From Front Porch to Back Seat: Courtship in Twentieth-Century America* (Baltimore: Johns Hopkins University Press, 1988), 19, 91; *Elmtown's Youth and Elmtown Revisited* (New York: Wiley, 1974), 314–16.

63. H. H. Remmers, *The Purdue Opinion Panel: Youth Looks at the Parent Problem* (Division of Educational Reference, Purdue University, 1949), question 14.

64. Remmers, *Youth Looks at the Parent Problem*, question 14; Remmers, *Teenagers' Attitudes toward Teenage Culture*, 13A, 21A; H. H. Remmers, *The Purdue Opinion Panel: Youth Looks at Schools and Jobs* (Division of Educational Reference, Purdue Univeristy, April 1948), question 17; H. H. Remmers, *The Purdue Opinion Panel: Youth's Attitudes toward Courtship and Marriage*, April 1961 (Division of Educational Reference, Purdue University, April 1961), 5a.

65. "Chicago Teens Look at Love," *Chicago Tribune*, June 24, 1956, G19.

66. Maureen Daly, *Profile of Youth* (Philadelphia: Lippincott, 1951); Robert Herman, "The Going Steady Complex," *Marriage and Family Living* 17 (February 1955): 36–40; Barbara Ehrenreich et al., *Re-making Love: The Feminization of Sex* (Garden City, NJ: Anchor, 1987), 25.

67. Ira Reiss, *Premarital Sexual Standards in America* (New York: Free Press, 1960), 56; Ira Reiss, "Sexual Codes of Teen-Age Culture," *Annals of the American Academy of Political and Social Sciences* (November 1961): 54–62.

68. Winifred Breines, *Young, White, and Miserable: Growing Up Female in the Fifties* (Boston: Beacon, 1992), 124; Dan Wakefield, *Going All the Way* (New York: Delacorte, 1970), 143–44; Albert Moe, "Make Out and Related Usages," *American Speech* 42, no. 2 (1966): 96–107, cited in Breines, *Growing Up*, 111.

69. Margaret Mead, *Male and Female: A Study of the Sexes in a Changing World* (New York: Penguin, 1950), 280.

70. Breines, *Young, White, and Miserable*, 111, 118–19; note also Winston Ehrmann, *Premarital Dating Behavior* (New York: Holt, 1959), 269–70.

71. Harrison Salisbury, *The Shook-Up Generation* (New York: Harper, 1958); Marynia Farnham, *The Adolescent* (New York: Harper, 1951). Note James Gilbert's classic, *Cycles of Outrage* (New York: Oxford University Press, 1986).

72. "Police Roundup 150 in Teen-Age Sex Orgy near Zion," *Chicago Tribune*, August 5, 1956, 3. The article mentions that the people arrested ranged from fourteen to twenty years of age, and that they gathered in parked cars, playing craps and having sex. Police claimed that they were

from the South, and that their families had come up after the war looking for jobs (presumably coded language to indicate that they were black). Yet another report ("Nab Teen-Agers in Sex Orgies, Auto Thefts," *Chicago Tribune*, August 3, 1954, 11) noted that the two teen children of "prominent citizens" were jailed as part of a car- and liquor-theft ring involved in gambling and sex. Similar was "Teen-Age 'Sex Circle' Cause Arrest of Four," *Chicago Tribune*, August 22, 1951, 3.

73. Frederick Allen, *Only Yesterday and since Yesterday* (New York: Bonanza Books, 1986; first published in 1931), 100, 115.

74. "Husband Sues Lovers' Lane Mystery Woman," *Chicago Tribune*, December 12, 1920, 17; "Lovers' Lane Slaying Solved," *Chicago Tribune*, September 11, 1923, 12.

75. "Refused Kiss Leads to Double Shooting," *New York Times*, April 12, 1928, 16; "Hold Suspect in Lovers' Lane," *Chicago Tribune*, August 10, 1947, 3; "Hunt of Mystery Pair in Lovers' Lane Murder," *Chicago Tribune*, June 28, 1948, 7; "Teen-age Lovers' Lane Gang Captured by Posse," *Los Angeles Times*, October 26, 1955, 4; "Chessman Fate Up to Governor Brown," *Evening Standard* (Uniontown, PA), October 10, 1959, 1.

76. "Texarkana Moonlight Murders by Nancy Hendricks," *Encyclopedia of Arkansas History & Culture*, http://www.encyclopediaofarkansas.net/encyclopedia/entry-detail.aspx?entryID=4478&type=Time+Period&item=World+War+II+through+the+Faubus+Era+%281941+-+1967 %29; Michael Newton, *The Texarkana Moonlight Murders: The Unsolved Case of the 1946 Phantom Killer* (Jefferson, NC: McFarland & Company, 2013); James Presley, *The Phantom Killer: Unlocking the Mystery of the Texarkana Serial Murders* (New York: Pegasus Books, 2014).

77. For example, "Man 76, Woman 45 (not Wife) Found Slain in a Lovers' Lane," *Chicago Tribune*, October 19, 1954, 12; "Nude Woman Murdered on Lonely 'Lovers' Lane,'" *Los Angeles Times*, May 27, 1943, 3.

78. *Profile of Youth*; Robert Herman, "The Going Steady Complex," *Marriage and Family Living*, 17 (February 1955): 36–40; Ehrenreich, *Re-making Love*, 25.

79. "Lovers' Lane Arrest," *Chicago Tribune*, January, 3, 1950, 4; "Nurse Kidnapped, Driver Slugged in 'Lovers' Lane,'" *Los Angeles Times*, April 22, 1950, 5; "Teen-Age Lovers' Lane Gang Captured by Posse," *Los Angeles Times*, October 26, 1955, 4.

80. "3 Lovers' Lane Couples Are Attacked by Man at Bowling Green," *Republic Courier* (Findlay, OH), June 2, 1951, 4.

81. "Lovers' Lane Murder," *Lima News*, June 9, 1950, 9; "Girl Strangled in Lovers' Lane," *Los Angeles Times*, June 30, 1949, 6; "Search Is On for Sadistic Killer," *Altoona Mirror*, July 23, 1957, 1.

82. Lovers' Lane Slaying," *Lima News*, February 12, 1952, 11.

83. Shailer Lawton and Jules Archer, *Sexual Conduct of the Teenager* (New York: Derby Press, 1951), 8, 71–77, 88–89.

84. Pat Boone, *Twixt Twelve and Twenty* (Englewood Cliffs, NJ: Prentice-Hall, 1967), 60; cited in Ehrenreich, *Remaking Love*, l19.

85. Ester Sweeney, *Dates and Dating* (Whiteside, NY: Woman's Press, 1948); Paul Landis, *Your Dating Days: Looking Forward to Successful Marriage* (New York: McGraw-Hill, 1954); Ann Landers, *Ann Landers Talks to Teen-Agers about Sex* (Englewood Cliffs, NJ: Prentice Hall, 1963); Evelyn Duvall, *Facts of Life and Love for Teen-Agers* (New York: Association Press, 1950); Evelyn Duvall, *Art of Dating* (New York: Association, 1967).

86. Duvall, *Facts of Life*, 237, 239, 251; Duvall, *Art of Dating*, 190.

87. Joan Beck, "Going Steady," *Chicago Tribune*, March 28, 1957, C1; Sheila Daly, "Petting Does Not Pay," *Chicago Tribune*, March 13, 1945, 14. Also by Sheila Daly, "Pointers for High Schoolers in Drive-In Movies," *Chicago Tribune*, May 16, 1953, 15; "Necking Is a Teen Age Problem," *Chicago Tribune*, September 2, 1953, B3.

88. Duvall, *Art*, 147, 190, 192; Duvall, *Facts*, 240.

89. Duvall, *Facts*, 242, 244, 255–57.

90. Duvall, *Facts*, 247–51; Duvall, *Art*, 265; Joan Beck, "Your Feelings Are Not Cheap," *Chicago Tribune*, June 6, 1960, B49; Sheila Daly "Necking Holds Little Merit as Date Act," *Chicago Tribune*, November 19, 1950, F7; Ellen Peck, *How to Get a Teen-Age Boy and What to Do with Him When You Get Him* (New York: Bernard Geis, 1962).

91. Sheila Daly, "Don't Wait to Say No until You're in a Lovers' Lane," *Chicago Tribune*, June 2, 1957, E2; Joan Beck, "What of Parking and Petting," May 23, 1957, D3.

92. "Teenagers' Attitudes toward Teenage Culture," 23a.

93. Ehrenreich, *Re-making Love*, 19, 23; Breines, *Growing Up Female*, 87. A sociological study of north Illinois high schools in the late 50s confirms this: James Coleman, *The Adolescent Society* (New York: Free Press, 1961), 119–23.

94. Virginia Scharff, *Taking the Wheel: Women and the Coming of the Motor Age* (Santa Fe: University of Mexico Press, 1991); Bailey, *From Front Porch to Back Seat*, 19, 91; Robert and Helen Lynd, *Middletown* (New York: Harcourt, 1929), 258; Carol Sanger, "Girls and the Getaway: Cars, Culture, and the Predicament of Gendered Space," *University of Pennsylvania Law Review* 144, no. 2 (December 1995): 705–56; 728, 744, 710 for quotations.

95. Lane, *Steel Shavings*, 31, 32, 34, 36–37; "Teenagers' Attitudes toward Teenage Culture," 21a.

96. H. H. Remmers, *The Purdue Opinion Panel: Teen-Age Personality in Our Culture* (Division of Educational Reference, Purdue University, May 1952), 6a; H. H. Remmers, *The Purdue Opinion Panel: Youth Looks at the Parent Problem* (Division of Educational Reference, Purdue University, 1949), question 22.

97. Lane, *Steel Shavings*, 42, 64; interview: Assembly of God of Covina Car Show, June 19, 2016.

98. Lane, *Steel Shavings*, 56–58.

99. Lane, *Steel Shavings*, 64–65, 75.

100. Phone interview to New Brunswick, NJ, August 15, 2015.

101. Phone interview to Spokane, January 6, 2016.

102. Internet interviews: Growingupwithcars.com, February 6, 2016; July 2, 2015; May 14, 2015.

103. Beth Bailey, *Sex in the Heartland* (Cambridge, MA: Harvard University Press, 1999).

104. Ralph Larkin, *Suburban Youth in Cultural Crisis* (New York: Oxford University Press, 1979), 104–7.

Chapter Five

1. Jack DeWitt, "Cars and Culture," *American Poetry Review*, September–October 2010, 47–50; *American Graffiti*, 1974; D. M. Considine, *The Cinema of Adolescence* (Jefferson, NC: McFarland, 1985), 112; Catherine Driscoll, *Teen Film: A Critical Introduction* (Oxford, UK: Berg, 2011), 66–68.

2. "The Muscle Car," *New York Times*, January 31, 1982, section 12, 6. For an account of cruising in Detroit, see http://info.detnews.com/history/story/index.cfm?id=216&category=life.

3. Jeffrey Zuehlke, *Muscle Cars: Motor Mania* (Minneapolis: Lerner Publications, 2006).

4. David Lucsko, *The Business of Speed: The Hot Rod Industry in America, 1915–1990* (Baltimore: Johns Hopkins University Press, 2008), ch. 5; "The Muscle Car," *New York Times*.

5. "Gasoline Prices Slow but Doesn't Stop California Cruising," *Northern New Mexico Today*, October 6, 1980, B13.

6. The "bibles" of this movement were John Muir, *How to Keep Your Volkswagen Alive: A Manual of Step by Step Procedures for the Compleat Idiot* (Santa Fe: J. Muir Publications, 1969), and Rick Greenspan, *Fixing Cars: A People's Primer* (San Francisco: San Francisco Institute of Automotive Ecology, 1974).

7. "Young Cruisers Travel in Footsteps of Parents," *Daily Intelligencer* (Goshen, IN), September 8, 1982, 16.

8. Ralph Larkin, *Suburban Youth in Cultural Crisis* (New York: Oxford University Press, 1979), 76–78, 82.

9. Driscoll, *Teen Film*, 30–31; Thomas Doherty, *Teenagers and Teenpics: The Juvenilization of American Movies in the 1950s* (Philadelphia: Temple University Press, 2002), 105; Considine, *Cinema of Adolescence*, ch. 9.

10. *Hot Rods to Hell* (MGM, 1967), https://www.youtube.com/watch?v=sLwRsdrfhyE.

11. Peter Stanfield, *The Cool and the Crazy: Pop Fifties Cinema* (New Brunswick, NJ: Rutgers University Press, 2015), 120; Mark McGee and R.J. Robertson, *The J.D. Films* (Jefferson, NC: McFarland, 1982), 54–58.

12. Jürgen Herbst, *The Once and Future School: Three Hundred and Fifty Years of American Secondary Education* (New York: Routledge, 1996), 7; William Reese, *The Origins of the American High School* (New Haven: Yale University Press, 1995).

13. Elmer Brown, *Making of Our Middle Schools* (New York: Longmans, 1902, 1970), 468–69; Herbst, *Future School*, 51, 65, 101, 136–37, 141.

14. John Modell, *Into One's Own: From Youth to Adulthood in the United States 1920–1975* (Berkeley: University of California Press, 1989), 77; Herbst, *Future School*, 152, 157;Claudia Goldin, "American Graduation from High School," *Journal of Education History* 56, no. 2 (June 1998): 351.

15. Joseph Kett, *Adolescence in America, 1790 to the Present* (New York: Basic Books, 1978).

16. For years, faculty and staff strived to control these groups and create extracurricular organizations linked to academics (science, literary, and music clubs). Greek organizations were banned, for example, in Chicago schools in 1904, though they survived long after in many parts of the country. Robert Pruter, *The Rise of American High School Sports and the Search for Control* (Syracuse, NY: Syracuse University Press, 2013), 13, 17, 65–83, 85; Reed Ueda, *Avenues to Adulthood: The Origins of the High School and Social Mobility in an American Suburb* (New York: Cambridge University Press, 1987), 151.

17. George Counts, *The Selective Character of American Secondary Education* (Chicago: University of Chicago Press, 1922), 33; William Smith, *Secondary Education in the United States* (New York: Macmillan, 1932), 343–45, 407. A later analysis of high-school peer culture is Philip Cusick, *Inside High School: The Student's World* (New York: Holt, Rinehart and Winston, 1973).

18. Kevin Borg, *Auto Mechanics: Technology and Expertise in Twentieth-Century America* (Baltimore: Johns Hopkins University Press, 2007), ch. 4; 92 for quotation.

19. Robert Lynd and Helen Lynd, *Middletown in Transition: A Study in Cultural Conflicts* (New York: Harcourt, 1937), 452; David Angus and Jeffrey Mirel, *The Failed Promise of the American High School, 1890–1995* (New York: Teachers College Press, 1999), 70–71, 203; Edward Krug, *The Shaping of the American High School, 1920–1941*, vol. 2 (Madison: University of Wisconsin Press, 1972).

20. Charles Prosser, *Secondary Education and Life* (Cambridge, MA: Harvard University Press, 1939), 86–87; Angus and Mirel, *Failed Promise*, 73; Howard Bell, *Matching Youth and Jobs* (Washington: American Council on Education, 1940), 56; Jon Savage, *Teenager* (New York: Penguin, 2007), 95.

21. A. B. Hollingshead, *Elmstown's Youth: The Impact of Social Classes on Adolescents* (New

York, Wiley, 1949), 168; W. Lloyd Warner, Robert Havighurst, and Martin Loeb, *Who Shall Be Educated?* (New York: Harper and Brothers, 1944), 49–50; Herbst, *Future High School*, ch. 2, 14.

22. Hollingshead, *Elmstown's Youth*, 112, 298; James Coleman, *The Adolescent Society: The Social Life of the Teenage and its Impact on Education* (New York: Free Press, 1961), 142.

23. These ethnographies of high-school peer culture focused on the issue of social prestige (with many "sociographs" identifying informal relationships) rather than on subcultures (like the hot-rod greaser) that were formed away from school and were outside the prestige networks. C. Wayne Gordon, *The Social System of the High School* (Glencoe, IL: Free Press, 1957), 61; Note also William Graebner's *Coming of Age in Buffalo: Youth and Authority in the Postwar Era* (Philadelphia: Temple University Press, 1990) reveals minimal interest in cars, much less in hot rods, even in this study of the 1950s. But then, the Buffalo high schools studied were in the inner city, though mostly white.

24. H. H. Remmers, *The Purdue Opinion Panel: Youth Attitudes Regarding Elections, Competition, Discipline, Status, Spare Time, Driving, Grandparents, and Health* (Division of Educational Reference, Purdue University, January 1960), 15a, 21a; H. H. Remmers, *The Purdue Opinion Panel: Teenagers' Attitudes toward Teenage Culture* (Division of Educational Reference, Purdue University, May 1959), 11a.

25. Coleman, *The Adolescent Society*, 23, 129, 142.

26. Hollingshead, *Elmstown's Youth*, 121.

27. Grace Palladino, *Teenagers: An American History* (New York: Basic Books, 1996), chs. 1, 4, 10; Kett, *Rites of Passage*, 152–54, 234–38; Ueda, *Avenues to Adulthood*, ch. 6.

28. Licht, "Automotive Play Activities," 44–65.

29. Richard Sennett and Jonathan Cobb, *The Hidden Injuries of Class* (New York: Vintage, 1972), 7, 84; Arthur Stinchcombe, *Rebellion in a High School* (Chicago: Quadrangle Books, 1964), 9, 103, 107; Robert Havighurst et al., *Growing Up in River City* (New York: Wiley, 1962), 66–67, 88.

30. Internet interviews: Growingupwithcars.com, May 14, 2015; February 7, 2016; June 22, 2015.

31. Interviews: George Chopit, Stanton, California, May 1, 2015; Over the Hill Car Club, April 28, 2015; LA Roadster Show, June 19, 2016; Riverside Car Show, May 2, 2015.

32. Internet interviews: Growingupswithcars.com, October 11, 2015; May 15, 2015.

33. Internet interviews: Growingupwithcars.com, May 13, 2015.

34. Internet interviews: Growingupswithcars.com, February 6, 2016; May 13, 2015; June 5, 2015.

35. Interviews: LA Roadster Show, June 18, 2016; Old Fart Car Club, February 20, 2015.

36. Interview: Over the Hill Car Club, April 28, 2015.

37. Internet interview: Growingupswithcars.com, June 21, 2015.

38. Interviews: Orange County Car Show, February 26, 2015; Jack Little, Elmwood, Texas, May 21, 2015; Historical Bellefonte Cruise, June 23, 2015.

39. Internet interview: Growingupwithcars.com, February 6, 2016; May 14, 2015.

40. Interviews: Los Angeles Police Department Valley Traffic Division Car Show, May 30, 2015; LA Roadster Show, June 19, 2016.

41. Internet interview: Growingupwithcars.com, April 29, 2015.

42. Interviews: So Cal Speed Shop Car Show, June 17, 2016; LA Roadster Show, June 18, 2016.

43. Internet interviews: Growingupwithcars.com, June 22, 2015, May 8, 2016, June 15, 2015, May 14, 2015.

44. Interview: John Cesareo, Los Angeles, June 30, 2015.

45. Internet interviews: Growingupwithcars.com, May 14, 2015, May 16, 2015.

46. Interviews: Los Angeles Police Department Valley Traffic Division Car Show, May 30, 2015; LA Roadster Show, June 18, 2016.

47. Interview: George Chopit, Stanton, California, May 1, 2015.

48. Interview: National Street Rod Association Show, York, Pennsylvania, June 11, 2016.

49. "Letters," *Rod and Custom*, September 1961, 7.

50. Various features on go-carts and Revelle models, 1957–61, *Rod and Custom*.

51. For example, "Life Can Be a Beautiful Find," *Rod and Custom*, April 1960, 64–65; hip graphic stories by Kohler include "Arin Cee," *Rod and Custom*, January 1960, 52–56; and "Mc-Model and the Missing Miniature," March 1960, 46–49.

52. "Letters," *Rod and Custom*, September 1959, 8; September 1960, 8.

53. "Letters," *Rod and Custom*, April 1959, 7.

54. The magazine recalled that the use of a "pin-up" photo of a young woman in shorts and a sweater in the opening issue had resulted in a "great controversy," and that the feature was soon discontinued. Editorial, *Rod and Custom*, April 1954, 28.

55. I develop this theme in my *All-Consuming Century: How Commercialism Won in Modern America* (New York: Columbia University Press, 2000), chs. 1, 2.

56. Robert Genat, *Hot Rod Nights: Boulevard Cruisin' in the USA* (Osceola, WI: Motorbooks International, 1998), 34–35; "Editorial," *Rod and Custom*, April 1954, 4; "Restyling with Resin," *Rod and Custom*, January 1957, 57.

57. "Channeled for a Change," *Rod and Custom*, April 1967, 34–35.

58. "How to Own a Custom Car," *Rod and Custom*, May 1959, 32–34; "Magnificent Custom of Kuttup McGoody," *Rod and Custom*, December. 1960, 41,

59. "Live '25," *Rod and Custom*, December 1957, 39–41.

60. Arnie and Bernie Shuman, *Cool Cars, Square Roll Bars* (Sharon, MA: Hammershop Press, 1998), 184.

61. Among the many examples are "T for Two," *Rod and Custom*, July 1954, 34–35; "Wisconsin's Red Wagon," February 1958, 13; "Peanuts," *Rod and Custom*, December 1966, 38; "Glamour Grilles," *Hot Rod Magazine*, May 1953, 94–97; "It's the Family Custom," *Hot Rod Magazine*, November 1959, 304–7.

62. Editorial, *Rod and Custom*, Jan. 1959, 6.

63. James Lane, *Steel Shavings: Rah Rah and Rebel Rousers* (Gary: Indiana University Northwest, 1994), 48; "Stripped Down," *Rod and Custom*, July 1954, 46–50.

64. "Build a Fuel Block," *Rod and Custom*, April 1967, 19.

65. "The Odd Rod," *Rod and Custom*, October 1959, 33, 72; Robert Post, "Hot Rod and Customs," *Technology and Culture*, 39, no. 1 (January 1998): 116.

66. "Presenting the 1949 Ford," *Hot Rod Magazine*, July 1948, 175.

67. "Non-Conformity Spoken," *Rod and Custom*, August 1958, 22–24; "Attention Detroit," *Rod and Custom*, April 1954, 19; Editorial, *Rod and Custom*, January 1959, 6.

68. Georg Simmel, "Fashion," *International Quarterly* (1904), reprinted in *American Journal of Sociology* 62 (1957): 541–58; Bill Osgerby, *Playboys in Paradise: Masculinity, Youth and Leisure-Style in Modern America* (Oxford, UK: Berg, 2001), ch. 1.

69. Lydia Simmons, "Not from the Back Seat," *Michigan Quarterly Review* 29, no. 4 (Fall 1980), in Jean Lindamood Jenkins, ed., *Road Trips, Head Trips and Other Car-Crazed Writings* (New York: Atlantic Monthly Press, 1996), 187.

70. "Parts with Appeal," *Hot Rod Magazine*, November 1948 to 1954; "Cheesecake Derby," *Hot Rod Magazine*, June 1951, 24–25; cartoon, *Hot Rod Magazine*, February 1948, 41.

71. Amy Best, *Fast Cars, Cool Rides: The Accelerating World of Youth and their Cars* (New York: New York University Press, 2006), 105.

72. Internet interview: Growingupwithcars.com, May 15, 2015.

73. Internet interviews: Growingupwithcars.com, August 12, 2015; May 14, 2015.

74. Internet interviews: Growingupwithcars.com, February 4, 2016; August 12, 2015; February 7, 2016.

75. Interviews: AACA Museum, Hershey, Pennsylvania, with Warren Earl and William Smith, September 15, 2015.

76. ACCA interviews: September 15, 2015.

77. Matthew Ides, "Cruising for Community: Youth Culture and Politics in Los Angeles, 1910–1970," PhD dissertation, University of Michigan, 2009,113, 119, 140, 152–53, 154, 166; Lane, *Steel Shavings*, 45, 50; Gene Balsey, "The Hot-Rod Culture," *American Quarterly* 2, no. 4, (1950): 353–58.

78. "Lots of Pickup," *Rod and Custom*, September 1957, 16–18; "T vs. A," *Rod and Custom*, July 1957, 18; "Deuce Today," *Rod and Custom*, November 1957, 34; "Customizing the 41-48 Ford," *Rod and Custom*, April 1957, 45–46.

79. "Seattle Sizzler," *Rod and Custom*, March 1957, 36–37.

80. Editorial, *Rod and Custom*, January 1958, 33.

81. "The Grasp of Roth," *Rod and Custom*, June 1960, 24; "Roth Restyles Revelle's HOs," *Rod and Custom*, October 1961, 37; Tom Wolfe, *The Kandy-Kolored Tangerine-Flake Streamline Baby* (New York: Noonday, 1963), 87–98; Ed Roth, *Confessions of a Rat Fink: The Life and Times of Ed "Big Daddy" Roth* (New York: Pharos Books, 1992).

82. "Everyday Deuces," *Rod and Custom*, August 1961, 16; letter to the editor, *Rod and Custom*, August 1961, 10.

83. Editorial, *Rod and Custom*, February 1967, 7.

84. "Tricks for Trucks," *Rod and Custom*, January 1959, 15; *Hot Rod Magazine: 50 Years of the Hot Rod* (Minneapolis: Motorbooks, 1998), 90, 105.

Chapter Six

1. For clarity, I'll use the spelling "lowrider" for the car and "low rider" for the person owning or driving the car.

2. Interview cited in Denise M. Sandoval, "Bajito y Suavecito/Low and Slow: Cruising through Lowrider Culture," PhD thesis, Claremont Graduate University, 2003, 82.

3. Brenda Bright, "Heart Like a Car: Hispano/Chicano Culture in Northern New Mexico, *American Ethnologist* 25, no. 4 (November 1998): 583–609; Sandoval, "Bajito y Suavecito," 25–26, 42–43, 80–86, 88.

4. "Julio Ochoa Ruelas, 62; One of the 'Godfathers of Lowriding,'" *Los Angeles Times*, February 11, 2007, 11; "Fernando Ruelas Dies at 60; Co-founder of Lowrider Car Club Duke's So. Cal," *Los Angeles Times*, October 27, 2010, 27; "Fernando Ruelas, Duke Car Club President," *Lowrider Magazine*, January 28, 2011, http://www.lowrider.com/news/1103-lrmp-duke-president-fernando -ruelas/.

5. Interview: Jorge Schement of Texas, August 15, 2015.

6. Interview: Car show, Assembly of God, Covina, California, June 18, 2016.

7. Internet interview: Growingupwithcars.com, May 25, 2015.

8. Paige Penland, *Lowrider: History, Pride, Culture* (St. Paul: MBI Publ., 2003), 10–14, 29. Penland was long associated with *Lowrider Magazine* in Anaheim. Sandoval, "Bajito y Suavecito,"

ch. 2; LR network, "Chapter 1: Lowrider History Book," 2002, http://www.lowrider.com/features
/0000lrm-history1/.

9. The 1958 regulation can be found at http://codes.findlaw.com/ca/vehicle-code/veh-sect
-24008.html; Frank Hamilton, *How to Build a Lowrider* (North Branch, MN: Cartech, 1999), 2–5;
Penland, *Lowrider*, 16; "Del Norte Club Rides Low and Slow," *New Mexican*, August 19, 1979, B1;
Sandoval, "Bajito y Suavecito," 42–45.

10. Penland, *Lowrider*, 9–10, 29; Luis Plascencia, "Low Riding in the Southwest: Cultural
Symbols in the Mexican Community," in *History, Culture and Society: Chicano Studies in the
1980s*, National Association of Chicano Studies, ed. (Tempe, AR: Bilingual Press, 1983), 155–56;
Ben Chappell, *Lowrider Space: Aesthetics and Politics of Mexican American Custom Cars* (Austin:
University of Texas Press. 2012), ch. 2.

11. Plascencia, "Low Riding in the Southwest," 149–54; "Zoot Suits and Service Stripes: Race
Tensions behind the Riots," *Newsweek*, June 21, 1943, 39–40; Stuart Cosgrove, "The Zoot Suit and
Style Warfare," *History Workshop Journal* (Autumn 1984): 77–83; Brenda Jo Bright, "Remappings:
Los Angeles Low Riders," in *Looking High and Low*, Brenda Bright and Liza Bakewell, eds. (Tuc-
son: University of Arizona Press, 1995), 102–3; "Cholos Cultivate Belle Image with Style," *Los
Angeles Times*, September 9, 1984, SD A1; Amy Best, *Fast Cars, Cool Rides: The Accelerating World
of Youth and Their Cars* (New York: New York University Press, 2006), 33–37.

12. Penland, *Lowrider*, 11; William Stone, "Bajito y Suavecito [Low and Slow]: Low Riding and
the 'Class of Class,'" *Studies in Latin American Popular Culture* 9 (1990): 86–126.

13. Allen Taylor, "Low, Slow, and Soulful," *Utne Reader*, May 2012, 76–77; Carmella Padilla,
Low 'n Slow: Lowriding in New Mexico (Santa Fe: Museum of New Mexico Press, 1999), 16–17;
Charles Tatum, *Lowriders in Chicano Culture: From Low to Slow to Show* (Santa Barbara: ABC-
Clio, 2011).

14. Bright, "Remappings," 98–99; quotation cited, 99 from R. Rodriguez, *Assault with a
Deadly Weapon: About an Incident in ELA and the Closing of Whittier Boulevard* (Los Angeles:
Rainbow Press, 1984), 23; interview: So Cal Speed Shop Car Show, June 17, 2016.

15. Matthew Ides, "Cruising for Community: Youth Culture and Politics in Los Angeles,
1910–1970," PhD dissertation, University of Michigan, 2009, 161–63; Penland, *Lowrider*, 22–26,
34–35, 88; Padilla, *Low 'n Slow*, 19–20; Sandoval, "Bajito y Suavecito," 57–62; Bright, "Remappings," 105–6; James Vigil, "Car Charros: Cruising and Lowriding in the Barrios of East Los
Angeles," *Latino Studies Journal* 2, no. 2, (1991): 71–79.

16. Ides, "Cruising for Community," 161–63; Padilla, *Low 'n Slow*, 19; Bright, "Remappings,"104–8; Penland, *Lowrider*, 60; Sandoval, "Bajito y Suavecito," 59–60.

17. "Low Riders: Low and Slow is the Way to Go," *Ukiah Daily Journal*, January 6, 1980, 3;
Plascencia, "Low Riding in the Southwest," 141; Ted West, "Low and Slow," *Car and Driver*, 22,
(1976): 47–51; "Chicanos Riding Close to the Ground but Going in Style," *New York Times*, May
9, 1981, 34.

18. Penland, *Lowrider*, 33.

19. Penland, *Lowrider*, 33, 40–43, 46; Ignacio Garcia, *Chicanismo: The Forging of a Militant
Ethos among Mexican Americans* (Tucson: University of Arizona Press, 1997); Marguerite Morin,
Social Protest in an Urban Barrio: A Study of the Chicano Movement, 1966-1974 (Lanham, MD:
University Press of America, 1991); Best, *Fast Cars, Cool Rider*, 200–201.

20. "Whittier Cruising: A Tradition Gone Sour," *Los Angeles Times*, August 8, 1979, E1.

21. Barrio Boychik, "The Cruising Culture of East Los Angeles," https://barrioboychik
.wordpress.com/2015/12/29/the-cruising-culture-of-east-los-angeles/; "Low Rider Times,"
https://barrioboychik.files.wordpress.com/2016/03/tumblr_m7t0nk1ljd1rwyjy001_1280.jpg.

22. Bright, "Remappings," 99–100; quotation cited, 99 from R. Rodriguez, *Assault with a Deadly Weapon: About an Incident in ELA and the Closing of Whittier Boulevard* (Los Angeles: Rainbow Press, 1984); "Boulevard Nights: Filming a Cultural Turmoil," *Los Angeles Times*, January 3, 1979, F1; "A Tradition Gone Sour;" "Whittier Cruising," *Los Angeles Times*, October 21, 1979, B11; "Chicano Group to Fill Suit over Arrests," *Los Angeles Times*, September. 15, 1979, 5D.

23. Penland, *Lowrider*, 65; "Friday Night Live with Hollywood Lowriders," *Los Angeles Times*, July 14, 1981, F1; Sandoval, "Bajito y Suavecito," 145–46; *Lowrider Magazine*, October 1979, 3.

24. "San Fernando Road Becomes New Mecca for Cruisers," *Los Angeles Times*, Nov. 18, 1979, V1.

25. "Police Bring a Stop to Boulevard Nights," *Los Angeles Times*, September 10, 1979, SD A1.

26. Penland, *Lowrider*, 100.

27. "Low Riders Set to Exhibit on the Santa Fe Plaza Today," *New Mexican*, Oct. 19, 1980, B3; "Low Riders in Espanola," *New Mexican*, May 23, 1984, A1; Penland, *Lowrider*, 48–49, 70–71, 89; Best, *Fast Cars, Cool Rides*, 31–55.

28. "Lowrider Magazine Riding Higher Than Ever," *Los Angeles Times*, April 19, 2000, G2; Plascencia, "Low Riding in the Southwest," 147–48; Penland, *Lowrider*, 74–75; "Consumer Magazines," *Alliance for Audited Media*, http://abcas3.auditedmedia.com/ecirc/magtitlesearch.asp; Sandoval, "Bajito y Suavecito," 120–26, 130, 156.

29. Photos, *Lowrider Magazine*, March 1979, 50; Stone, "Low Riding," 4; interview: car show Assembly of God, Covina, CA, June 19, 2016.

30. "Letter to the Editor," *Lowrider Magazine*, October 1978, 2; Sandoval, "Bajito y Suavecito," 142–45.

31. Sandoval, "Bajito y Suavecito, 198–207; *Lowrider Magazine*, 5; (September 1984), 5, for example.

32. *Lowrider Magazine*, May 1993, June 1993, July 1993, and January 1994.

33. Cover, *Lowrider Magazine*, Dec. 1988

34. Plascencia, "Low Riding in the Southwest," 168; Budweiser ad, *Lowrider Magazine*, December 1988, 20; "El Pachuco" ad, *Lowrider Magazine*, May 1993, 7.

35. Sandoval, "Bajito y Suavecito, 128–30; "Car Culture Becomes Mainstream," *DSN Retailing Toda* 12, no. 16 (August 22, 2005):10.

36. Sandoval, "Bajito y Suavecito," ch. 5; Chappell, *Lowrider Space*, 108–14.

37. "Low Slow, and Soulful," 76–77, 79; Ruben Molina, *The Old Barrio Guide to Low Rider Music, 1950–1975* (La Puente, CA: Mictlan Pub., 2005).

38. "Del Norte Club;" Padilla, *Low 'n Slow*, 9–10.

39. Padilla, *Low 'n Slow*, 9–10; Martin Høyem, "'I Want My Car to Look Like a Whore': Lowriding and Poetics of Outlaw Aesthetics," PhD dissertation, University of Oslo, 2007, 50, 85–101. Penland, *Lowrider*, 44; James Vigil, *Barrio Gangs: Street Life and Identity in California* (Austin: University of Texas Press, 1988), 3–5.

40. Octavio Paz, *The Labyrinth of Solitude and Other Writings* (New York: Grove Press, 1985, 1950 original), 12; Høyem, "Lowriding," 39–40, 62–73; Thorstein Veblen, *Theory of the Leisure Class* (1899), 65–67; Pierre Bourdieu, *Distinction* (Cambridge, MA: Harvard University Press, 1979).

41. Ides, "Cruising for Community," 166. See also Michael Chavez, "Performance of Chicano Masculinity in Lowrider Car Culture," PhD thesis, University of California, Riverside, 2012, 2–8.

42. "La Raza Report," *Lowrider Magazine*, May 1993, 14. Penland, *Lowrider*, 127.

43. "Lowriders: They've Shifted from Old Cars to Customized Trucks," Los Angeles Times, October 30, 1986, A1; Padilla, *Low 'n Slow*, 17.

Chapter Seven

1. Though there is anecdotal evidence of more intense policing of lovers' lanes since the 1980s (see chapter 9), I found little documentation of it in the press or elsewhere. Probably the decline of cruising and drive-in theaters, along with changing courtship customs (see chapter 9), contributed to the decline of these sites of teen romance.

2. Gary Cross, *The Cute and the Cool: Wondrous Innocence and Modern American Children's Culture* (New York: Oxford University Press, 2003), chs. 5, 6; James Gilbert, *A Cycle of Outrage: America's Reaction to the Juvenile Delinquent in the 1950s* (New York: Oxford University Press, 1986); Thomas Doghery, *Teenagers and Teenpics: Juvenilization of American Movies* (Philadelphia: Temple University Press, 2002).

3. Grace Palladino, *Teenagers: An American History* (New York: Basic, 1996), chs. 8, 9.

4. Michael Witzel and Kent Bash, *Crusin': Car Culture in America* (Osceola, WI: Motorbooks, 1997), 56–67.

5. "Teen-Age Ritual Fades," *Washington Post*, February 11, 1980, C1.

6. "Teen-Age Ritual Fades"; "Cruising: Gas Costs Hurt but Youth Find It Hard to Abandon Cars," *Daily Intelligencer* (Allentown, PA), June 2, 1980, 5. Similar are "Time Is Running Out on a Way of Life," *Winchester Star*, September 3, 1980; "Teens Should Enjoy Cruising While They Can," *Wisconsin State Journal*, July 1, 1979, 2, section 5, 1.

7. "Royal Oak Sets Crackdown," *Holland Sentinel*, September 18, 1963, 3.

8. By 1967, *Drive In Restaurant Magazine* carried "Ordinance Roundup," informing tradespeople of laws passed around the country to restrict cruising. Robert Genat, *Woodward Avenue, Cruisin' the Legendary Strip* (Forest Lake, MN: Cartech, 2013), 57–61, 77.

9. "Youth Violence on Woodward," *Detroit News*, August 27, 1968, 1; "Royal Oak Is Placed under Curfew," *Holland Sentinel*, August 26, 1970, 26.

10. "Cruising 'Summit,'" *Oakland Tribune*, June 30, 1977, 1; "It's No Crime if You Choose to Cruise," *Oakland Tribune*, October 14, 1975, 1; "The Strip," *Daily Review* (Hayward, CA), January 3, 1975, 14.

11. Recall from chapter 4 how in 1968, fenderless cars driven by "outsiders" were ticketed in Downey, but not the stripped-down vehicles of local boys. Interview: LA Roadster Show, with a male born in 1951 from Downey, California, June 18, 2016.

12. "Teen-Age Gangs," *Los Angeles Times*, July 5, 1961, B1; "Cruising Bands of Teen-Agers Harass Shopping Center Merchants," *Los Angeles Times*, July 3, 1966, B1.

13. "Car Clubs Irate: 'Cruise Night' Ban Called 'Runaround,'" *Los Angeles Times*, March 17, 1974, B2; "Bellflower Puts Skids on Boulevard Cruising," July 28, 1974, SE 3; "One-Way Traffic Plan Curbs Cruiser Crush in Bellflower," *Los Angeles Times*, August 29, 1974, SE1.

14. "Police 'Cruise Night' Crackdown to Continue," *Los Angeles Times*, July 6, 1975, B1.

15. "Cruisers Parade Nightly: Whittier Blvd. Phenomena More Than Passing Fancy," *Los Angeles Times*, August 5, 1976, SE1.

16. "Cruising, A Tradition Gone Sour," *Los Angeles Times*, August 8, 1979, E1; "Police Bring a Stop to Boulevard Nights," *Los Angeles Times*, September 10, 1979, A1.

17. "San Fernando Road Becomes New Mecca for Cruisers," *Los Angeles Times*, November 18, 1979, V1; "As Long as There Are Cruisers Some People Will Object," *Orange County Register*, August 5, 1984, J10.

18. "Merchants Praise, Resent Cruise Night Shutdown," *Los Angeles Times*, July 13, 1980, V2; "An Old Tradition Dies Hard," *Los Angeles Times*, July 23, 1980, G1.

19. "Merchants Praise Recent Cruise Night Shutdown"; "The 'Solution' to Cruising on Van Nuys: Cars Shift as Street Closed," *Los Angeles Times*, July 23, 1980, G1.

20. "Cruisers Shift to Hollywood Boulevard," *Los Angeles Times*, February 26, 1981, LB2; "City to Proceed with Barricade," *Los Angeles Times*, February 12, 1981, LB1; "Boulevard Blocked," *Los Angeles Times*, June 14, 1981, SE2.

21. "Friday Night Live with Hollywood Lowriders," *Los Angeles Times*, July 24, 1981, F1; "Police Closures of Hollywood Blvd. Approved," *Los Angeles Times*, August 5, 1981, D1.

22. "Rules of the Road," California Legal Code, sec. 1 of statutes, 1982, C710, p. 2869.

23. "Cruising a Ritual—So Is Roadblock," *Los Angeles Times*, July 18, 1982, GB8; "Cruising Results in 120 Arrests," *Los Angeles Times*, September 11, 1984, A4; "Cruising Van Nuys," *Los Angeles Times*, May 11, 1986, R44.

24. "Cruisers Move their Cars to Elysian Park," *Los Angeles Times*, March 5, 1985, C1.

25. "Crackdown on Cruising Studied," *Los Angeles Times*, January 16, 1986, LB1; "Cruisers Cool It after Feeling Heat," *Los Angeles Times*, August 3, 1986, OC A1; "L.A. Approves Anti-Cruising Ordinance." October 16, 1986, OC 2.

26. "Los Angeles Council Passes Measure to Put Breaks on Cruising," *Los Angeles Times*, July 27, 1988, D3; "Computer Helps Curb Hollywood Boulevard Cruisers," *Los Angeles Times*, July 24, 1988, ASB1.

27. Some examples: "Curbing Cruisers," *Los Angeles Times*, June 3, 1990, OCB1; "Cities Move to Lower the Boom on Boxes," *Los Angeles Times*, August. 19, 1989, OC1; "Whittier Boulevard, in East Los Angeles on the Mend," *Los Angeles Times*, May 15, 1989, OC12.

28. "Cruise Control: Hawthorne Seeks to Drive Youths out of Town," *Los Angeles Times*, October 17, 1990, VYB9.

29. "American Graffiti City Puts Breaks on Cruising," *Orange County Register*, March 28, 1990, A3–4; "Modesto's Cruisers Vow to Defy New Ban," *Los Angeles Times*, March 29, 1990, A2; "Pure Hysteria as Cruisers Hit Modesto Streets." *Los Angeles Times*, June 11, 1990, A1; "Cruising Is Still Alive, but Not Well," *New York Times*, March 13, 1990, A20.

30. "Strip's Quiet Year after Cruise Ban," *Press-Courier* (Oxnard, CA), April 27, 1991, 1.

31. "Still Cruising after All these Years," *Los Angeles Times*, August 12, 1990, VC B1; "Cruiser Task Force," *Los Angeles Times*, July 31, 1991, B1; "Huntington Beach Ok'd Curfew Fee," *Los Angeles Times*, May 3, 1995, 1; "Teen-Age Rites," *Daily News* (Los Angeles), January 14, 1997, N4; "Anti-Cruising Law Cuts Traffic," *Los Angeles Times*, December. 15, 1999, 6; "Barricade to Keep Lid on Cruising," *Los Angeles Times*, June 27, 1999, 1.

32. "Still Cruising after All These Years;" "Knowing How to Bend a Little," *Press-Courier* (Oxnard), January 13, 1991, 4; "Oxnard Council Bans Youth's Sunday Night Cruising," *Los Angeles Times*, September 10, 1992, 10.

33. "Pleasant Memories of Teenhood Cruising," *Laurel Leader* (Mississippi), October 17, 1988, 4; "Cruisers Hit Mercer Street," *Bluefield Daily Telegraph*, August 30, 1989, 1.

34. "Teens Say Cruising Plan Is Admirable but Doomed," *Cedar Rapids Gazette*, May 20, 1991, 6A.

35. "Support for Center," *Hutchinson News*, June 13, 1989, 3.

36. "Report Addresses Cruising Problems," *Wisconsin State Journal*, September 10, 1999, C1.

37. "Still Cruising in '93," *New Castle News*, July 15, 1993, 4.

38. "Cruising," *Anderson Herald Bulletin*, July 31, 1993, A12.

39. "Curfew Ends Tradition of Car Cruising," *Walla Walla Union Bulletin*, April 4, 1994, 9.

40. "Teenage Cruising Takes a Bruising," *Newsweek*, August 2, 1990, 44–45; "Cruising,"

Capital Times, July 23, 1984, 1; "Alderman Proposes Zone for Cruising," *Milwaukee Journal Sentinel*, June 19, 2004, 1A; "Anti-Cruising Tools Tested," *Milwaukee Tribune Business News*, April 24, 2007, 1.

41. "Cruising Teens," *Galveston Daily News*, September 2, 1985, 11A.

42. "Fast Cars, Young Riders," *New York Times*, June 10, 1987, B1.

43. "Crackdown Begins," *Joplin Globe*, May 9, 1992, 16A.

44. "Mixed Results in Stopping Cruising," *San Antonio Express News*, August 1. 2000, 1A; Police Tweaking Curbs on Cruising," *Portland Oregonian*, May 5, 1999, B2.

45. "Call it Tradition; Call it a Nuisance; It's Cruising Season," *Santa Fe New Mexican*, April 20, 1994, A1; "Cruising Beeping; It's Stronger than Ever," *Greensburo News Record*, August 9, 1998, D1.

46. Internet interview, Growingupwithcars.com, June 22, 2015.

47. "Summer Crackdown on Crime," *Washington Post*, August 4, 1985, C1.

48. "Cruising Clamor is Back on Main Street, USA," *New York Times*, October 5, 1986, 55; "Cracking Down on Cruising," *Gettysburg Times*, August 22, 1986, 1; "Cruising in Hopkins," *Minnesota Star and Tribune*, February 19, 1987, 14; "Cruising Memories," *Dispatch* (Lexington, NC), August 30, 2013, 1.

49. "Police to Close Beach Roads," *St. Petersburg Times*, March 6, 1988, 8B; "Clearwater Cruising," *St. Petersburg Times*, July 25, 1990, 11; "Cruising Won't Fly with Jacksonville Beach Cops," *Florida Times Union*, March 27, 2002, L1.

50. "Cruising Cruises into History," *Gazette Telegraph* (Fargo, ND), March 6, 1996, D8; "Cruising," *Milwaukee Journal*, November 15, 1994, A8; "The Night Shift," *Yakima Herald-Republic*, July 19, 1998, C1.

51. "Police Chief Calls for Stop to Cruising along River Front Streets," *St. Louis Post Dispatch*, March 11, 1999, B3; Tracking Taillights on State Street," *Salt Lake Tribune*, May 23, 1999, C1; "City Council to Discourage Cruising," *Arizona Star*, May 9, 2000, B2.

52. "Curfew," *Tuscaloosa News*, March 19, 2009, 1.

53. "Cruising Memories," *Dispatch* (Lexington, NC), August 30, 2013, 1.

Chapter Eight

1. Clay McShane, *The Automobile: A Chronology of its Antecedents, Development, and Impact* (Santa Barbara: Greenwood, 1997), 128.

2. Tex Smith, "Street Rods," *Rod and Custom*, July 1971, 102–3; Jerry Wessner, "The Bob McGee /Dick Scritchfield /Bruce Meyer Roadster," *Hot Rod Network*, July 7, 2005, http://www .hotrod.com/features/history/articles/0203sr-milestone-bob-mcgee-deuce-roadster/; "Long Beach's Early Times Hot Rod Club Turning 50 this Year," *Orange County Register*, May 28, 2014, http://www.ocregister.com/articles/times-616170-early-club.html.

3. "Rod Running Frisco," *Rod and Custom*, December 1969, 12–13; editorial, *Rod and Custom*, August 1969, 5; letter to the editor, *Rod and Custom*, August 1969, 9; "Roadster Roundup," *Rod and Custom*, December 1969, 12–13; "Rusty Gold in Them Thar Hills," *Rod and Custom*, December 1969, 35.

4. Richard Goldstein, "Sha Na Na, 'The Unreal Fifties,'" *Vogue*, November 1969, 126; Daniel Marcus, *Happy Days and Wonder Years: The Fifties and the Sixties in Contemporary Cultural Politics* (New Brunswick, NJ: Rutgers University Press, 2004), 12; Simon Reynolds, *Retromania: Pop Culture's Addiction to Its Own Past* (London: Faber and Faber, 2011), 283–85; Gary Cross,

Consumed Nostalgia: Memory in the Age of Fast Capitalism (New York: Columbia University Press, 2015), ch. 6.

5. Tex Smith, "Car Clubs," *Rod and Custom*, September 1970, 20–22; Smith, "Street Rods," *Rod and Custom*, October 1970, 39.

6. Interview: LA Roadster Show, June 19, 2016; "Fastest Wheels in Town Back on Detroit Streets," *New York Times*, September 17, 1984, A16; Albert Drake, *Hot Rodder! From Lakes to Street* (Classic Motorbooks, 1993), 166.

7. "Fastest Wheels in Town: Back on a Detroit Street," *New York Times*, September 17, 1984, A16; "Sounds of Money Mingle with Rumbles of Street Rods," *Syracuse Herald American*, June 30, 1995, A4; Taylor, *Hot Rods*, 154–55, 184–85, 214, 260–61; Drake, *Hot Rodder!*, 144.

8. "At 30, Goodguys Rod & Custom Association Still Strives to Be Relevant," *Dallas Daily News*, May 24, 2016, B1; Interviews: Old Farts Car Club, February 25, 2015; LA Roadster Show, June 19, 2016; Orange County Rod and Custom Show, February 26, 2015. For a large list of car show events throughout the United States, see carshowlinks.com.

9. By 1952 there were eighteen categories to accommodate newer and more diverse cars at the AACA meet. After 1975, separate classes were created for Ford V8s, Chevrolet Corvettes, Ford Thunderbirds, Ford Mustangs, and even 1955–57 Chevrolets, all reflecting the popularity of these models by that time. Antique Automobile Club of America, http://www.aaca.org/about /default.aspx. For a large list of the full range of old car clubs organized by state, see http://www .classiccarcommunity.com/. Interview: Antique Automobile Club of America, September 15, 2015.

10. Interview: George Barris Car Show, May 9, 2015.

11. Michael Pickering and Emily Keightley, "The Modalities of Nostalgia," *Current Sociology* 54, no. 6 (November 2006): 919–41. Nostalgia is defined as a longing for a lost time, for something that is no longer attainable.

12. "Nostalgia in Vintage Cars," *Los Angeles Times*, October 8, 1981, H1.

13. Later, the rules of cruise-ins were codified by Rod Reprogle, *The Mother of All Car Books: How to Get More Fun & Profit Buying, Showing & Selling Vintage & Classic Cars* (Los Alamitos, CA: Duncliff's International, 1995), 158–59. Arguing that young and old car enthusiasts did not mix, Reprogle went on to insist that cruise-ins should ban SUVs and minitrucks.

14. "Cruisin' Party at Fairgrounds," *Orange County Register*, September 9, 1991, B7; I develop this theme in *Consumed Nostalgia*, ch. 3.

15. "Saturday on Balboa Avenue Parking Lot," *Los Angeles Times*, September 11, 1984, JI.

16. "Nostalgia to Take Another Cruise Down the Boulevard," *Los Angeles Times*, May 14, 1986, A6.

17. "As Long as There Are Cruisers, Some People Will Object," *Orange County Register*, August 5, 1984, J10; "Cruisin' Party at Fairgrounds," *Orange County Register*, September 9, 1991, B7.

18. "Sattler Brothers Route 66 Rendezvous," http://www.route-66.org/media.htm. In 2013 the event was canceled because of the town's financial crisis; it was moved to nearby Ontario, California.

19. "Hot August Nights," http://www.hotaugustnights.net.

20. Detroit Free Press, *Joy Ride: 10 Years of the Woodward Dream Cruise* (Detroit: Detroit Free Press, 2004), 57–61; "Cruising Woodward," *Auto Week* 57, no. 31 (July 30, 2007), 23; "Woodward Dreams," *Auto Week* 58, no. 30 (July 28, 2008), 20; Anthony Ambrogio and Sharon Luckerman, *Cruising the Original Woodward Avenue* (Mt. Pleasant, SC: Arcadia Publishing, 2006); Michigan Street Rod Association, "Back to the 50s," *Old Car Weekly*, June 30, 2011, 9; in www.msra.com ;backtothe50s.htm.

21. "Blue Suede Cruise," http://www.bluesc.com/.

22. Typical in the 1990s was radio station 96.1 in central New York state, which sponsored a summer round of biweekly cruise-ins at the parking lots of a retro soda fountain and pizza parlor; http://www.oldiez96.com.

23. Michael Witzel and Kent Bash, *Crusin': Car Culture in America* (Osceola, WI: Motorbooks, 1997), 141; Robert Genat, *Hot Rod Nights* (Minneapolis: Motorbooks International, 1998), 15–17; "An Engine's Low Purr," *Washington Post*, June 22, 1993, B1; "Petaluma's Salute to American Graffiti," http://www.sonomacounty.com/sonoma-events/petalumas-salute-american-graffiti. "About 30,000 Turn Out to Celebrate American Graffiti in Petaluma," *Press Democrat*, May 18, 2013, 1.

24. "Car Shows in the Northeast in May 2016," carshowlinks.com/May.html.

25. "Classic Crusin,'" *Milwaukee Journal Sentinel*, July 28, 2003, 1E.

26. Genat, *Hot Rod Nights*, 9.

27. Online interview: Growingupwithcars.com, July 2, 2015.

28. Online Interviews: Growingupwithcars.com, May 14, 2015; February 9, 1916; Assembly of God car show, Covina, California, June 19, 2016.

29. Interview: LA Roadster Show, June 18–19, 2015.

30. Robert Post, "Exhibition Review: Hot Rods and Customs: The Men and Machines of California's Car Culture," *Technology and Culture* 39, no. 1 (January 1998): 16.

31. Chris Lezotte, "Contemporary Women and the Classic Muscle Car," *Frontiers: A Journal of Women Studies* 34, no. 2 (2013): 83–113. For the theme of women and cars, note Virginia Scarf, *Taking the Wheel: Women and the Coming of the Motor Age* (Albuquerque: University of New Mexico Press, 1991); Deborah Clarke, *Driving Women: Fiction and Automobile Culture in Twentieth-Century America* (Baltimore: Johns Hopkins University Press, 2007).

32. "Lost in the Fifties," *Boston Globe*, August 14, 1999, C1.

33. Interviews: Old Farts Car Club, February 25, 2015; Orange County Rod and Custom Show, February 26, 2015.

34. Interviews: LA Roadster Show, June 19, 2016; Old Farts Car Club, February 20, 2015

35. Interview: Penny Pichette, West Coast Kustoms, April 16, 2015.

36. Interviews: Cal Rod "originals," June 17, 18, 19, and 30. Also, Cal-Rod website: http://cal-rods.org/About-Us.

37. Denise M. Sandoval, "Bajito y Suavecito / Low and Slow: Cruising through Lowrider Culture," PhD thesis, Claremont Graduate University (2003), 84–85, 92–110.

38. Interview: Assembly of God of Covina, California car show, June 19, 2016.

39. Amy Best, *Fast Cars, Cool Rides: The Accelerating World of Youth and Their Cars* (New York: New York University Press, 2006), 5, 12–13, 119; "In the Lot of Luxury," *San Diego Union Tribune*, June 23, 2004, A1.

40. Best, *Fast Cars, Cool Rides*, 45–53.

41. Gary Cross, *Men to Boys: The Making of Modern Immaturity* (New York: Columbia University Press, 2005), 199.

42. "Hot to Trot," *Advertising Age*, November 20, 2000, S12; "Too Fast, Too Furious, Too Old," *New York Times*, October 31, 2003, F1; "Rice Rockets," *Asian Week*, June 27, 2001, 18; "Teen Dream Machines," *Los Angeles Times*, September 21, 1991, DL1; Best, *Fast Cars, Cool Rides*, 81–82.

43. Soo Ah Kwon, "Autoexoticizing Asian-American Youth and the Import Car Scene," *Journal of Asian American Studies* 7, no. 1 (April 2005): 1–26; "Rice Rockets," *Asian Week*, June 27, 2001, 18; Victor Namkung, "Reinventing the Wheel: Import Car Racing in Southern California," in *Asian American Youth: Culture, Identity, and Ethnicity*, ed. Jennifer Lee and Min Zhou (New York: Routledge, 2004), 160.

44. Cross, *Men to Boys*; Michael Kimmel, *Guyland: The Perilous World Where Boys Become Men* (New York: Harper, 2008).

45. "Tuning In: Trick Out Trends Turns on Carmakers," *Advertising Age*, November 3, 2003, 4, 59; "Hot to Trot," *Advertising Age*, November 20, 2000, S12.

46. "Modified for Maximum Impact," *Los Angeles Times*, June 3, 2001, C 4; "Hot Rodding Shifts Gears," *USA Today*, June 25, 2001, 1D; "Youth Seek Deadly Rush," *Los Angeles Times*, April 14, 2002, A1.

47. "Cops Are behind Fast Teens," *Los Angeles Times*, June 6, 2003, A1; "Hot Rodding Shifts Gears."

48. *The Fast and the Furious*, 2001; Ken Hollings, "*The Fast and The Furious*," *Sight and Sound* 11 (November 2001), 46–47; Charles Whitehouse, "Hot Rod Rumble (Fast and Furious)," *Sight and Sound* 13, no. 6 (June 2003), 1–23.

49. "Furious 2 Gets a New Driver," *Chicago Tribune*, February 25, 2003, 3. There is even a guidebook to the cars in the *Fast and Furious* movies. Kris Palmer, *The Fast and the Furious: The Official Car Guide* (St. Paul: Motorbooks, 2006).

50. "Hollywood Revs Up its Love Affair with Fast Cars," *Los Angeles Times*, June 26, 2001, F3; "*The Fast and Furious* Is Lame yet Lively," *Los Angeles Times*, June 27, 2001, G1; Whitehouse, "Hot Rod Rumble," 23.

51. "Street Racing Movie Alarms Police," *USA Today*, June 21, 2001, 6D.

52. "Hot Rod Hondas Sure to Get Hearts Racing," *Los Angeles Times*, June 25, 1999, 8D; "'Rice Rockets' Find Appeal in Mainstream," *Los Angeles Times*, September 24, 2002, B2; "Honda Civic Si," *Motor Trend*, January 2002, 67.

53. "The Civic Loses its Cool," *Wall Street Journal*, March 25, 2004, B1; "Toyota's Generation of Gamble," *Wall Street Journal*, July 30, 2003, B1; "Look Who's Driving Design," *Christian Science Monitor*, June 30, 2003, 13.

54. "SVT Focus Priced to Move," *Automotive News*, February 9, 2001, 3; "When Men Were Men and Cars Were Cars," *Forbes*, December 18, 1995, 37; Best, *Fast Cars, Cool Rides*, 12; "Today's Image-Conscious Youth Embraces Car Culture: Kids Head Back to School in Customized Rides," *PR Newswire* [New York], August 26, 2004, 1. Thanks also to Dan Stoner of Autoculture.com for information.

55. "Scion, Toyota's Oddball Youth Brand, Never Had a Chance," *Washington Post* Blogs, February 3, 2016.

56. "Hey Kid, Wanna Buy a Honda?" *Rolling Stone*, November 13, 2003, 12; "Toyota to Test New Youth-Oriented Scion," *Knight Ritter Tribune Business News*, June 9, 2003, 1; "Toyota Unveils New Concept 'Echo' Designed for Youth Appeal," Autochannel, January 4, 1999; http://www.theautochannel.com/news/press/date/19990104/press002018.html.

57. "LA's Automakers Target Youth at LA Show," *Los Angeles Times*, May 3, 2003, B3; "Hey Kid, Wanna Buy a Honda?"; "Toyota Aims at Youth Subculture," *Adweek*, April 4, 2005, 12.

58. According to the Entertainment Software Association, representing the video industry, in 1997 more than half of all video game players were younger than eighteen. By 2016 the average age had risen to thirty-five, roughly charting the aging of the Gen-Xers who were introduced to video games as children. Sixty-three percent of American households have one player who devotes at least three hours a week to video games. http://www.theesa.com/archives/files/Essential%20Facts%202006.pdf; http://essentialfacts.theesa.com/.

59. "Automakers Play to Strengths of Video Games," *Automotive News*, April 17, 2006, 66; "Ford Lures Young Buyers with Video Games," *Automotive News*, April 25, 2005, 20D; "Video Games Whet Drivers' Appetites," *USA Today*, May 2, 2005, 2B.

60. See, for example, "The Cutting Edge: Making a Killing; Violence Sells in Video Games," *Los Angeles Times*, January 26, 1998, 1.

61. "Hey Kid, Wanna Buy a Honda?"; "LA Automakers Target Youth."

62. Stanceworks.com.

63. An interesting commentary on this is in Stanley Lim, "Muscle Car versus Rice Burner," *Korea Times*, June 30, 1999, 5.

64. "Restomod vs. Restore;" Retromodstore.com.

65. "Rat Rod: A Statement Made of Rust," *New York Times*, March 30, 2014, AU1; "Rat Rod Magazine Hits the Road," *McClatchy Tribune Business News*, January 31, 2011, 1; "Hot Rod Pinstrippers Keep Old Art Form Alive," *Los Angeles Times*, March 22, 2012, B7.

66. "1999 Billet Proof Car Show: Billet Proof 99," *Hot Rod Network*, June 1, 2001, http://www .hotrod.com/events/coverage/hrdp-0006-1999-billet-proof-car-show/; "Billetproof Sold: New Owner Plans Expansion," *Hemmings Daily*, April 26, 2007, http://blog.hemmings.com/index.php /2007/04/26/billetproof-sold-new-owner-plans-expansion/.

67. Jack DeWitt, "Cars and Culture: Rat Rods," *American Poetry Review* 40, no. 6 (November–December 2011): 15–17.

68. DeWitt, "Rat Rods," 16; "Rat Rod: A Statement in Rust." Interviews: NSRA Show (York, Pennsylvania), June 4, 2016; LA Roadster Show, June 18, 2016.

69. Cross, *Consumed Nostalgia*.

70. Quotations in DeWitt, "Rat Rods," 17.

71. Interviews: NSRA Show (York), June 4, 2016; Over the Hill Club, April 16, 2015; Old Farts Car Club, February 25, 2015.

72. Interviews: LA Roadster Show, June 19, 2016; Assembly of God, Covina, California car show, June 19, 2016; Over the Hill Club, April 16, 2015.

73. Interview: LA Roadster Show, June 18, 2016.

74. Interviews: Old Farts Car Club, February 20, 2015; National Street Rod Association Show (York), June 11, 2016.

75. Interviews: Cal-Rod Club members, June 17–19 and 28, 2016.

Chapter Nine

1. David Shi, "Well, America: Is the Car Culture Working?" *Philadelphia Inquirer*, July 9, 2000, 1.

2. Stacy Willis, "Teens without Wheels, A World Gone Mad: Why Do Millennials Seem Less Excited about Driving?" *Vegas Seven*, September 19, 2013, http://vegasseven.com/2013/09 /19/teens-without-wheels-a-world-gone-mad/#sthash.Hdq1YKWk.dpuf.

3. "Cars in America: Is the Love Story Over?" *Idea Stream*, August 18, 2013, http://www .ideastream.org/news/npr/213263841.

4. "Why Teenagers My Age Are Not Interested in Cars," *Jalopnik*, http://oppositelock.jalopnik .com/why-teenagers-my-age-are-not-interested-in-cars-485191515.

5. "Motor Vehicles per 1000 People," 2014, *Nation Master*, http://www.nationmaster.com /country-info/stats/Transport/Road/Motor-vehicles-per-1000-people.

6. "Do Kids Hate Cars? America's Youth Is Falling Out of Love with the Automobile," *Edmunds.com*, February 6, 2012, http://www.edmunds.com/car-reviews/features/do-kids-hate -cars.html; AAA Foundation for Traffic Safety, "Timing of Driver's License Acquisition and Reasons for Delay among Young People in the United States," 2012, https://www.aaafoundation .org/timing-driver%E2%80%99s-license-acquisition-and-reasons-delay-among-young-people

-united-states-2012; Michael Sivak and Brandon Schoettle, "Recent Changes in the Age Composition of Drivers in 15 Countries," University of Michigan Transportation Research Institute Ann Arbor, Michigan 48109–2150 U.S.A. Report No. UMTRI-2011-43, October 2011, http://www.verkeersnet.nl/downloads/sivak.pdf; "Percentage of Teen Drivers Continues to Drop," *Michigan News*, http://ns.umich.edu/new/releases/20646-percentage-of-teen-drivers-continues-to-drop; "No Hurry: Fewer Teens with Driver's Licenses," *Telegram & Gazette* (Worcester, MA), July 14, 2014, A.1; Julian Beck, "The Decline of the Driver's License," *Atlantic*, January 22, 2016, http://www.theatlantic.com/technology/archive/2016/01/the-decline-of-the-drivers-license/425169/; Michael Sivak and Brandon Schoettle, "Recent Decreases in the Proportion of Persons with a Driver's License across All Age Groups," *Performing Organization Report No. UMTRI-2016-49*, University of Michigan Transportation Research Institute, January 2016, http://www.umich.edu/~umtriswt/PDF/UMTRI-2016-4.pdf.

7. "Kids These Days Just Don't Care about Cars," *Gristmill*, May 14, 2013, http://grist.org/news/youngs-kill-car-culture/.

8. "Do Kids Hate Cars?" "Why Don't Young Americans Buy Cars?" *Atlantic*, March 25, 2012, http://www.theatlantic.com/business/archive/2012/03/why-dont-young-americans-buy-cars/255001/.

9. "Why Don't US Teenagers Care about Driving Anymore?" *Denver Post*, October 13, 2013, http://www.denverpost.com/ci_24418033/why-dont-us-teenagers-care-about-driving-anymore.

10. "Teenagers Are Driving Less, But Why?" October 23, 2013, WSJ Blogs, http://blogs.wsj.com/corporate-intelligence/2013/10/24/teenagers-are-driving-less-but-why/; "What Less Teen Driving Means for Brands," *Media Post*, November 7, 2013, http://www.mediapost.com/publications/article/212835/what-less-teen-driving-means-for-brands.html; "Economy Puts the Brakes on Parent's Spending for Teen Cars, Driving Expenses," *Investment Weekly News*, October 8, 2011, 369.

11. Marc Fisher, "Cruising toward Oblivion: America's Once Magical, Now Mundane Love Affair with Cars," *Washington Post*, September 2, 2015, 12, comments, fttp://www.washingtonpost.com/sf/style/2015/09/02/americas-fading-car-culture/.

12. AAA, "Timing of Driver's License Acquisition."

13. AAA, "Timing of Driver's License Acquisition"; "Americans Driving Less as Car Culture Wanes," *Evening Sun*, August 29, 2013, http://www.eveningsun.com/ci_23976624/americans-driving-less-car-culture-wanes.

14. Centers for Disease Control and Prevention, "Driving among High School Students: United States, 2013," *Morbidity and Mortality Weekly Report*, April 3, 2015, 313–17, https://www.cdc.gov/mmwr/preview/mmwrhtml/mm6412a1.htm.

15. Daniel Mayhew, "Why 16?" *Insurance Institute for Highway Safety* (Aug 2000), 4–5, 11, 14, 16, wwwhighwaysafety.org.

16. Mayhew, "Why 16?," 16–20; Allan Williams, "Young Drivers' Risk Factors," *Injury Prevention* 14, supp. I (2006): 14–15.

17. Vincent Hamilton, "Liberty without Capacity: Why States Should Ban Adolescent Driving," *Georgia Law Review* 48 (Summer 2014): 1019–83.

18. While California introduced a provisional driver's license in 1983, it was only in 1996, when Florida adopted the GDL, that it became common. James Hedlund et al., "What We Know, What We Don't Know, and What We Need to Know about Graduated Driver Licensing," *Journal of Safety Research* 34 (2003): 107; Joseph Allen and B. Bradford, "Adolescents, Peers, and Motor Vehicles: The Perfect Storm?" *American Journal of Preventive Medicine* 35, no. 3 (September 2008): S289–93.

19. Lloyd Sandbulte, "Graduated Driver Licensing," *Society of Chartered Property and Casualty Underwriters Journal* 52, no. 5 (Winter 1999): 248–55; Amy Best, *Fast Cars, Cool Rides: The Accelerating World of Youth and Their Cars* (New York: New York University Press, 2006), 195.

20. Allan Williams, however, documents a decline in fatal crashes of sixteen- and seventeen-year-olds from 2,267 in 1995 to 1,150 in 2010. Allan Williams, "Graduated Driver's Licensing Research," *Journal of Safety Research* 43, no. 3 (July 2012): 195–203; Hamilton, "Liberty without Capacity," 1082; "Safer Drivers?" *Telegram and Gazette*, August 19, 2012, A1; Scott Masten and Robert Hagge, "Evaluation of California's Graduated Driver Licensing Program, *Journal of Safety Research* 35, no. 5 (2004): 523–35.

21. Bridie Scott-Parker, "Understanding the Psychological Factors Influencing the Risky Behavior of Young Drivers," *Transportation Research, Part F: Traffic Psychology and Behavior* 12 (2009): 470–73; Allen and Bradford, "Adolescents, Peers," S289–90, 292; Hamilton, "Liberty without Capacity," 1045–63; Allan Williams, "Young Drivers' Risk Factors," *Injury Prevention* 12, supp. I (2006): 14.

22. Ronald Dahl, "Biological Developmental and Neurobehavioral Factors Relevant to Adolescent Driving Risks," *American Journal of Preventive Medicine* 35, no. 3 (2008): S278.

23. Hamilton, "Liberty without Capacity," 1064.

24. "Cars In America: Is the Love Story Over?"

25. In Massachusetts, for example, sixteen-year-old license holders dropped from 10,418 in 2000 to 7,608 in 2011, probably because of costly driver's education courses and hours of supervised driving required for those under eighteen years of age, as well other restrictions. "No Hurry."

26. AAA, "Timing of Driver's License Acquisition," "The End of America's Car Culture?" "Why Don't Young Americans Buy Cars?"

27. "Americans Driving Less as Car Culture Wanes."

28. "Do Kids Hate Cars?"

29. "Generation Y and Consumerism: Waning Interest in Car Ownership a Sign of a Deeper Shift," *Huffington Post*, January 18, 2013, http://www.huffingtonpost.ca/2013/01/18/generation-y-consumerism-ownership_n_2500697.html; "Why Millennials Don't Want to Buy Stuff," *Fast Company*, July 13, 2012, https://www.fastcompany.com/1842581/why-millennials-dont-want-buy-stuff.

30. Howard Gardner and Katie Davis, *The App Generation: How Today's Youth Navigate Identity, Intimacy, and Imagination in a Digital World* (New Haven: Yale University Press, 2014), ch. 5; danah boyd, *It's Complicated: The Social Lives of Networked Teens* (New Haven: Yale University Press, 2014), ch. 1; Henry Jenkins, Mizuko Ito, and danah boyd, *Participatory Culture in a Networked Era: A Conversation on Youth, Learning, Commerce, and Politics* (Malden, MA: Polity, 2016), ch. 2.

31. National Public Radio, "The Changing Story of Teens and Cars, Millennials and the Changing Car Culture," http://www.npr.org/2013/08/09/210253451/the-changing-story-of-teens-and-car.

32. "Young People are Putting the Brakes on Car Culture," *Toronto Star*, June 8, 2010, B2.

33. "Is the Digital Revolution Driving a Decline in America's Car Culture?" *Advertising Age* 81, no. 22 (May 31, 2010): 1, 22, http://adage.com/article/digital/digital-revolution-driving-decline-u-s-car-culture/144155/.

34. Marianne Lavelle, "U.S. Teenagers Are Driving Much Less: 4 Theories About Why," *National Geographic*, December 17, 2013; http://news.nationalgeographic.com/news/energy/2013/12/131217-four-theories-why-teens-drive-less-today/; "Americans Driving Less as Car Culture

Wanes;" "Is the Digital Revolution Driving a Decline?"; Jordan Weissmann, "Young People Aren't Buying Cars because They're Buying Smart Phones Instead," *Atlantic*, August. 8, 2012, http://www.citylab.com/tech/2012/08/young-people-arent-buying-cars-because-theyre-buying-smart-phones-instead/2873/.

35. The personal role of the teacher and community leader in shaping youth in the extracurriculum, schools, and even car clubs has been supplanted by impersonal institutional authorities (like police in the schools), especially in those institutions where the students are minorities and the poor. These adult intermediaries have also been partially replaced by ever-vigilant parents—especially in affluent families, who limit their offspring's public social interactions. Interview with Amy Best, professor of sociology, George Mason University, November 14, 2016.

36. "American Driving Less as Car Culture Wanes."

37. Sarah Miller, e-mail correspondence, February 7, 2017: "Teens know that having a centralized location where everyone goes to 'park' would only attract unwanted attention. My hunch is that because they are more regulated, they are also considered shadier. There was a parking lot at the top of a hill with a beautiful view very close to the high school I studied, a perfect, remote, potentially romantic site for a tryst, yet the lot was highly patrolled, and also locked up at night—not a site where teens would or could go. (I'll bet this was the spot Township teens went to park in the '50s, though)."

38. Sarah Miller, e-mail correspondence, February 7, 2017.

39. Amy Best, *Prom Night: Youth, Schools and Popular Culture* (New York: Routledge, 2000).

40. Amy Schalet, *Not under My Roof: Parents, Teens, and the Culture of Sex* (Chicago: University of Chicago Press, 2011), chs. 1, 3, 5; Joel Best and Kathleen Bogle, *Kids Gone Wild: From Rainbow Parties to Sexting, Understanding the Hype over Teen Sex* (New York: New York University Press, 2014), 126–27.

41. Best and Bogle, *Kids Gone Wild*, ch.5.

42. Though it is a study of hooking up in college (rather than in high school), the best source on this topic is Kathleen Bogle, *Hooking Up: Sex, Dating, and Relationships on Campus* (New York: New York University Press, 2008).

43. "Millennials and Car Culture: They Care about Driving, But Not about Driving New Cars," *Business Community*, March 29, 2012, http://www.business2community.com/automotive/millennials-and-car-culture-they-care-about-driving-but-not-about-driving-new-cars-0155715.

44. Fisher, "Cruising toward Oblivion," comments.

45. Patrick George, "Youth Car Culture Isn't Dead, This *Washington Post* Story Just Sucks," http://jalopnik.com/youth-car-culture-isnt-dead-this-washington-post-story-1728346138, Fisher, "Cruising toward Oblivion," comments.

46. George, "Youth Car Culture Isn't Dead"; Fisher, "Cruising toward Oblivion," comments.

Index

The letter *f* following a page number denotes a figure.